Joseph Lemuel Saywell

The Parochial History of Ackworth, Yorks

Joseph Lemuel Saywell

The Parochial History of Ackworth, Yorks

ISBN/EAN: 9783337029043

Printed in Europe, USA, Canada, Australia, Japan

Cover: Foto ©ninafisch / pixelio.de

More available books at **www.hansebooks.com**

THE
PAROCHIAL HISTORY

OF

ACKWORTH,

YORKS.,

WITH ARCHÆOLOGICAL, ANTIQUARIAN, AND BIOGRAPHICAL NOTES & RECORDS,

BY THE

REV. J. L. SAYWELL,

FELLOW OF THE ROYAL HISTORICAL SOCIETY, AND AUTHOR OF THE
"HISTORY AND ANNALS OF NORTHALLERTON, YORKS.," &c.,

WITH AN

INTRODUCTION

BY THE

REV. R. V. TAYLOR, B.A.,

AUTHOR OF "YORKSHIRE ANECDOTES," "WORTHIES AND CHURCHES OF LEEDS," &c.

"Rem omnem a principio audies."—*Ter.*
"Res fortasse vērae, certe grāves."—*Cic.*

PONTEFRACT:
JAMES ATKINSON & SON, PRINTERS & PUBLISHERS, 5, MARKET PLACE.

LONDON:
SIMPKIN, MARSHALL, HAMILTON, KENT & CO., PATERNOSTER ROW.
1894.

TO

ROWLAND, BARON ST. OSWALD,

OF

NOSTEL PRIORY,

WITH WHOSE FAMILY MUCH OF THE EARLY HISTORY OF
ACKWORTH IS INTERWOVEN,

AND TO THE

LORDS OF THE MANOR OF ACKWORTH,

THIS VOLUME IS, BY KIND PERMISSION,

DEDICATED

BY THE COMPILER.

AUTHOR'S PREFACE.

EVERY parish in England ought to have upon the shelves of its village library an attractive, reliable, and inexpensive volume of its own history. Until now Ackworth has not; but here it is. Let those who like it, read it, and those who don't, produce a better. It is not by any means complete, but it will form a good foundation upon which someone else can, if they think fit, rear an ornate superstructure. What has been built, however, cannot be pulled down. J. L. S.

INTRODUCTION.

HAVING been requested by my friend, the Rev. J. L. Saywell, to write an introduction to his "Parochial History of Ackworth," I do so with peculiar pleasure, because it will afford me an opportunity of saying a few words on Parochial Histories in general, and on the "History of Ackworth" in particular. It is pleasing to observe that much greater attention is now paid to Parochial Histories and subjects of research than formerly. Parochial Histories seem to be very much wanted at the present time, as there is a growing demand for them; several having been recently published, including those of Askrigg, Hemingboro', Northallerton, Ingleton, Morley, Pudsey, etc. It is not an easy thing to write the history of a parish, from the earliest times to the present, with the Roman remains, Saxon earthworks, Danish antiquities, Norman architecture, Domesday extracts, ancient wills and fines, or transfers of land, etc. In order to make a Parochial History as complete as possible, it is very desirable that it should be well indexed, not only as regards persons and places, but also the principal subjects. It should also contain as many engravings as possible of the principal persons, places, and subjects, with pedigrees of the most important families. It is also desirable that biographical sketches of the principal people in each parish should be included. The clergy, as a rule, from their position and education, are best qualified for preparing these Parochial Histories, as each one ought to be as familiar as possible with his own parish, having the registers, with lists of clergy and patrons, etc., in his own possession, with a certain amount of the requisite leisure. It is almost the work of a lifetime to become fully conversant even with the principal events in our Parochial Histories, and then one ought to have a general knowledge of those in the immediate neighbourhood.. Many clergymen are now issuing Parish Magazines, with a page or two of local history each month, but, unfortunately, there are comparatively few people in our country parishes who care sufficiently about the ancient history of their native places even to spend a penny in purchasing a parish magazine, much less subscribe 2/6 or 5/- for a history of their parish. Very often the outsiders, and those who have gone away, care more for it than those living in the place. These local histories seem to be much more appreciated in America than they are in this country. Even a small, or poor history is better than none at all; being not so difficult to compile, less expensive, and much easier to enlarge. Now that the Bishop of Carlisle has followed the example of the Archbishop of Canterbury, and the late Bishop of Durham, in recommending the clergy to write the history of their parishes, it is most desirable that the Archbishop of York and the Bishop of Ripon should do the same with respect to the numerous parishes in Yorkshire, and then a complete and comprehensive "History of Yorkshire" would be speedily accomplished, an undertaking which would be of great service to the Church generally and especially agreeable to the principal people in each of the respective parishes. Many of the clergy have already published a considerable amount of local history in their parish magazines, which might be utilised, and reference might also be made to the various Directories, Diocesan Calendars, Lawton's "Ecclesiastical Collections," to the different histories already published, to Bawdwen's "Domesday Book," to Kirkby's "Inquest," the "Nonæ Rolls," the "Liber Regis," the Surtees Society's Publications, Langdale's "Topographical Dictionary," the Yorkshire Archæological Journals, and the Record Series; Allen's, Baines's, Bigland's, Black's and Murray's "Yorkshire," and also to Torre's and Archbishop Sharp's MSS. at York, and the Diocesan Registers, etc. In order to prove that Parochial Histories are very much wanted, I might quote the following extracts from a letter by the

Rev. Charles A. Wells, Organising Secretary of the Church Defence Institution. "At the recent Church Congress at Wakefield, the question of the best means of instructing the classes, as well as the masses, in the origin, history, revenues, and work of the Church was proposed, but does not seem to have received any very definite reply. You will perhaps, therefore, allow me to make one or two practical suggestions, as to the best way of attaining the object in hand: 1. A history of the Parish Church, its architecture, registers, and endowments, written by one of the clergy, or some other well qualified person, should be circulated in pamphlet form throughout every parish. This is the first step towards arousing interest in Church history and Church work. 2. A list of rectors or vicars, from the foundation of the Church and formation of the parish, should be placed within or without every Church; and, where possible, the names of patrons, curates, and churchwardens should be added. If the parochial chest will not furnish requisite information, a visit to the diocesan registry generally will. 3. Local biographies are also most interesting, of which each parish might easily furnish one or more. 4. Interest should also be secured in the local press, mis-statements should be at once corrected, and sound information given; short articles and notes on Church questions, with local sketches, should be offered to the different editors. 5. Historical and instructive leaflets should be widely circulated, and lectures on Church history, illustrated by the magic lantern, should be arranged for in every parish during the winter months. Both illustrated lectures and leaflets can be obtained on application to the offices of the Church Defence Institution." It is, therefore, most desirable that the clergy should be encouraged to do what they can towards writing a history of their own parishes. The Rev. J. L. Saywell, who has written the "History of Northallerton," and who was formerly curate of Ackworth, is well qualified to write the "Parochial History of Ackworth," and it is hoped that the book will have an extensive sale, so as not only to pay the expenses of the press, but also to leave the compiler a margin of profit for his trouble; otherwise there is no encouragement for others to copy his example, in writing and publishing the histories of their parishes, etc. Ackworth is a place well known for its Foundling Hospital, and Quakers' School; the benevolent John Fothergill, M.D., F.R.S., and John Gully, the sporting M.P., etc. Mr. Saywell has set a praiseworthy example to his brother clergymen, who, having exceptional opportunities for becoming acquainted with the history, past and present, and the local traditions and customs of the parishes under their charge, can render immense service to antiquaries, archæologists, and county historians, by preserving, for the information of future generations, matter of much general interest, which would otherwise lie hidden, or be forgotten.

R. V. TAYLOR, B.A.

Melbecks Vicarage,
Nr. Richmond, Yorks.

INDEX.

☞ *Personal names are necessarily omitted.*

A.

Ackworth, Foundling Hospital, viii., 8, 32.
,, Quakers' School, viii.
,, Church Tower, 1.
,, High, 2.
,, Low, 2.
,, Middle, 2.
,, Parish of, 2.
,, derivation of, 3.
,, William, 4.
,, Church, 8—18, 252.
,, Manor of, 17, 44, 139—144.
,, Charities, 16, 17, 108, 163-203.
,, Reversion of, 44.
,, battle at, 47.
,, Rev. George, 52.
,, mortgaged, 54.
,, military rendezvous, 57.
,, Park, 77, 87, 88, 144.
,, *Gazette*, 84.
,, *Review*, 89.
,, *Telegraph*, 91.
,, Spa, 89.
,, Feast, 89.
,, morality of, 99.
,, Railway Station, 112.
,, College, 145-147.
Accidents, 89, 94, 104.
Acworthe, John de, 46.
Akeworth, Henry de, 43.
Alban, St., 29.
Alfred, King, sonnet by, 17.
Anne, Queen, 54.
Arson and Sacrilege, 107.
Augustine, St., 28, 29, 30, 52.

B.

Badsworth, 1, 41.
Badsworth Hunt, Past Masters of, 246.
Banns, forbidden, 68, 72, 73, 74.
Bargain, a curious, 68.
Bath, old Chalybeate, 162.
Bedstead, antique, 61.
Belfry rules, 11, 12.
Bells, Church, 10, 11, 12, 119.
Benefactions to Poor, 16, 17.
Birth, a quadruple, 72.

Boisil, Monk of Melrose, 29.
Boot and Shoe, Hostelry, 2, 61.
Boroughbridge, Battle of, 44.
Boundary bridge, 69.
Brackenhill, 2, 59.
Bradley's Almshouses, 203.
Bright, John, 91.
British School, 94.
Burial ground, Friends', 63.

C.

Calcutta, Bishop of, 92.
Calf, a wonderful, 89.
Calverley's Dole, 187.
Carr Bridge, 4.
Castle Syke, 1, 155.
Cawood's old Chapel, 57.
Celebrities, 203-239.
Centenary celebrations, 114-119.
Charities, 16, 17, 108, 163-203.
Charter, free warren, 43.
Chantry of St. Mary, 38.
,, Priests, 38.
,, Close, 38.
Cholera, 96.
Church Porch, 12.
,, Plate, 18, 19, 20.
,, ,, confiscated, 18.
Church Schools, 151.
Church rates, 96.
Churchyard, new, 113.
Civil Wars, 56.
Clergy, loyal, 56.
Clock, Church, 119.
Coincidence, singular, 60.
Conscription, 79.
Constitution Hill, 3.
Coronation Festivities, 91.
Court Leet, 81.
Cowpasture, 128-132.
Cromwell, 60.
Cross, Village, 158.
Curious Nomenclature, 37.
Cuthbert, St., 12, 28.

D.

Dame's School, 87.
Danish Antiquities, v.

INDEX.

Dearth, 76.
Derby, the, 90, 94 97.
Destitution, Spiritual, 82.
Dictionary, Topographical, Langdale's, vi.
Diocesan Calendars, vi.
Diocesan Registers, vi.
Document, curious, 62.
Domesday Book, Bawden's, vi.
Domesday Book, 3, 41.
Domesday Extracts, v.
Don, River, 4.

E.

Ebba, St., 29.
Ecclesiastical Collection, Lawton's, vi.
Ecclesiastical Discipline, 35, 66, 67.
Edmund, St., 28.
Edulph, 8.
Elm, Village, 98, 120, 156.
Encroachments, 101.
Enthusiast, a religious, 90.
Epitaphs, 75, 92, 250.
Ethelfrid, King, 29.
"Eulogium Historiarum," 1.
Execution, 77.
Explosion, Colliery, 97.

F.

Farmer, a model, 109.
Featherstone, 53.
Ferrar, Robert, Prior of Nostel, 49, 51.
Fires, 59, 107.
Fines, Yorkshire, 44, 48, 51, 52, 53, 54.
Flood, a great, 105.
Folk-lore, 120.
Font, 14.
Formulas, Latin, 68.
Fossils, 7, 123.
Foundling Hospital, 69, 72, 73.
Fountain, village, 108.
Friends' Burial Ground, 63.
Friends' School, 73, 113, 147-151, 245.
Funeral, a unique, 70, 71.

G.

Gas, introduction of, 92.
Gas meeting, 122.
Geological Characteristics, 5, 6, 7.
Gift, deed of, 47.
Gloucester, Duke of, 26.
Goldsmith's Hall, 20.
Grace, Pilgrimage of, 48.
Grammar School, Abp. Holgate's, 49.
Grange, the, 2.
Great Rebellion, 8.
Grotto, the, 159.

Gully, Robert, shipwrecked and murdered, 23.
Gwethin street, 2.

H.

Hailstone storm, 97.
Hall, the old, 159.
Hardwick, East, 1, 54, 57, 59, 108, 109.
Hardwick, West, 2.
Harriers, Dr. Lee's, 70.
Harsley East, Church, 18.
Hearse, Parish, 79.
Hessle, 38, 47, 55, 239, 240.
Hemsworth, 1.
Herbert's "Church Porch," 13, 14.
Hilda, St., 29.
Hook's, Dean, memorable sermon, 102.
Hopton Monumental Slab, 22.
Horticultural Show, 93.
Hospital, Watkinson's, 73, 199.
House, old, 61.
Howard, Luke, works of, 247, 248.
Hundfridus, 42.
Hundhill, 2, 85.

I.

Ikeneld street, 1.
"Inquest," Kirkby's, vi.
Interments, in Friends' Burial Ground, 64-66.
Interments in Low Ackworth Burial Ground, 94-95.
Irvingism, 91.

J.

Jubilee Celebrations, 124-126.

K.

Killingbeck, paintings by, 39

L.

Lacy, family of, 38, 43, 44.
Lacy, Ilbert de, 1-42.
Lady-well, 156.
Lambe's Charity, 185.
Lectern, 15.
Leger, St, the, 90.
"Leline," i
Leprosy, 75.
"Liber Regis," vi.
Lindsay's Legacy, 197.
Link, a missing, 66.
Literature, 112.
Livingstone's, Dr., visit, 102.
Local Meteorology, 7.
Longevity, interesting record of, 70-71.

Long Lane, 6.
Lowther's Charity, 198.
Lowther's Hospital, 17.
Loyalty, 102.
Lych-gate, 9.

M.

Manifesto, a Rector's, 110
Manor, Lords of, 38, 41, 42, 83, 100, 243.
Marriage festivities. 102, 103.
Marriage, frustrated, 72.
Marriages before Justices, 33.
Mechanic's Library, 91.
Melton's Register, 45
Methodists. Primitive, 155.
Midland Railway, 3.
Military rendezvous, 57.
Military service, 54.
Militia, Local, 79.
Monumental Inscriptions, 20-8.
Moor Top, 2.
Monica, St., 30
Murders, 73, 77.

N.

Nevison, the highwayman, 160
Nomenclature, curious, 37.
"Nonœ Rolls," vi.
Norman, Architecture, v.
Norman Chapel, 8.
Northallerton, History of, vii
North Eastern Railway, 3.
Nostel, 38, 59, 67.
„ Priory, 39, 49, 67.
„ Arms, 40.
Nostel pool, 4, 67.

O.

Obelisks, 162.
Organ, Church, 109, 110.
Osalf, 8, 43.
Osgoldcross, Wapentake of, 1, 3.
Oswald's Cross, 1.
Oswald, St., 28, 29.

P.

Palsy, 75.
Parliament, Rump, 57.
Parochial Histories, v.
Parish Magazines, vi.
Parish Register, 31-37.
Paulinus, St., 28, 30.
Petyt family, 87.
Pilgrimage of Grace, 48.
Plague, The, 34, 57.
Plague stone, 57, 161.
Plymouth Brethren, 94.

Poll, a parish, 106.
Poll-tax, returns, 45.
Pontefract, 41.
Pontefract, Boothroyd's History of, 1.
Pontefract, Castle, 1, 43.
Pontefract, Deanery of, 2.
„ Fox's History of, 2.
Pontefract, St. Clement's Chapel, 42.
Poor's Estate, Ackworth, 168.
Population, 84, 94.
Prints and engravings, local, 249.
Publications, Surtees Society's, vi.
Pudding Bush, 17.
Puritan intolerance, 57.
Purston, 1.

R.

Rectors and Curates, List of, 241, 242.
Rectory, the, 38, 39.
Reform Bill, the, 88.
"Regina v. Johnson," 101.
Register, Skelton's, 45.
Restoration Services, 97.
Returns, Poll-tax, 45.
Richmond, Yorks., viii.
Rikeneld street, 1.
Rishworth's Charity, 192.
Roman Road, 1, 67.
Royal visit, 85.

S.

Sacrilege, 93.
Savile Arms, 20.
Saxon Earthworks, v.
School, Mrs. Howard's, 152.
Seaton's Bequest, 197.
Sharlston Car, 4.
Skelton Castle, 16.
Slavery Emancipation commemoration, 91
Sporting Curate, a, 84.
Stage Coaches, 83.
Stained Glass, 28-31.
Stamford Bridge, 1, 41.
Standing Flat Bridge, 1.
Statistics, interesting, 81.
Stead Lane, 17.
Stocks, the Village, 104.
Stone, Style Acre, 38.
Storm, great, 121.
Streethouse Bar, 4.
Suffocation, 76.
Survey, the great, 42.
Sykehouse, 4.
Sykes, the family of, 76.

T.

Taxes, curious, 251.
Tempest family, 2, 48.

Terriers, Ecclesiastical, 133-139.
Thomas, a foundling, 32.
Tongues in trees. 93.
Topham's Grant, 197.
Torres' M.S.S., vi.
Townsman, a worthy, 123.
Townsley's Estate, the, 197.
Trees, commemoration, 103.

V.

Veronica, St., 30.
"Vessels of pewter," 18
Vestments, 53.
Vestry screen, 15.

W.

"Walks about Yorkshire," Banks', 2, 4.
Wand, the official, 95.
Warren, free, 44.
Watchmen, last of, 121.
Watling street, 2.
Water, analysis of, 5.
Water, boring for, 97.
Weather, phenomenal, 89.
Went, river, 3.

Wentbridge, 1.
Wesleyan Chapel, 100, 153.
Wesley's Visits, 73, 74.
West Riding, garden of, 1.
Whitby Abbey, 29.
Windfall, a, 80.
Windmill, 16.
Workhouse, the old, 111.
Wormald's Charity, 163.
Wragby, 1.

Y.

Yorkshire, Archæological Journal, vi.
    ,,   Allen's, vi.
    ,,   Baines,' vi.
    ,,   Bigland's vi.
    ,,   Black's, vi.
    ,,   History of, vi.
    ,,   Murray's, vi.
    ,,   records, 48,
    ,,   Record, series, vi.
    ,,   fines, 44, 48, 51, 52, 53, 54.

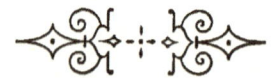

ACKWORTH,
YORKSHIRE:
ITS HISTORY AND ANNALS.

---o---

Situation.

" Sweet Auburn! loveliest village of the plain." *

PLEASANT for situation, the ancient † and charming village of Ackworth, which has sometimes been called the "garden of the West Riding," is not seen by the traveller until almost within a stone's-throw of the Church tower, which is the first object to attract notice on reaching the summit of Castle Syke Hill, from the north. It is bounded on the north by Pontefract, of historic renown, Standing Flat Bridge, the scene of the battle of Stamford Bridge, being the boundary mark between the parishes of Ackworth, Badsworth, and Pontefract,‡ on the south by Hemsworth, on the east by East Hardwick and Wentbridge, and on the west by Purston and Wragby. Its present position is in the upper division of the hundred (*hundredum centuria*) or wapentake (*wæpontac*)§ of Osgoldcross (Oswald's Cross). The Roman road from Doncaster to Castleford called Ikeneld or Rikeneld street, which the author of the "Eulogium Historiarum" styles the "Leline,"

---

* " Seen from a distance, as from the top of 'Robinson Close,' Ackworth is always a picture, especially towards sunset on a summer's evening."

† In 1080, Ilbert de Lacy built Pontefract Castle. At that time Ackworth had only just passed out of Saxon proprietorship.

‡ Vide " Boothroyd's Hist. Pont." The statement, however, that Standing Flat Bridge is the scene of the Battle of Stamford Bridge is sufficiently hypothetical and unauthenticated to be untrustworthy. J. L. S.

§ *Wæpon*, arms; and *tac*, take or touch.

crossed the Gwethin (Watling) street at Pontefract near the park, and thence through Ackworth on the ridge called Castle Syke to Hemsworth and Worcester.* Ackworth is a large village, and one of the best in the district.† It was originally a Saxon hamlet, which is proved by the derivation of its name, and by the names of its first proprietors. As to ecclesiastical jurisdiction, Ackworth is situated in the Deanery of Pontefract and Archdeaconry of the West Riding and Diocese of York. The parish consists of three parts, High,‡ Low, and Middle Ackworth, with the newly sprung up and increasing settlement of Moor Top, and the little hamlet of Brackenhill. Brackenhill is almost entirely inhabited by stoneworkers. Less than a century ago it was a sweetly pretty dell, the abode of a reputed witch, whose tenement is still pointed out. Moor Top consists of several good houses, the rest are the cottages of miners and quarryworkers. Its most interesting feature is unquestionably the old "Boot and Shoe" hostelry, where the last of the old coaches of the district stopped to convey passengers the first stages of their journey home. Middle Ackworth is chiefly inhabited by members of the Society of Friends, who possess a large school and college in the vicinity. Hundill, or Hundhill, which gives its name to a mansion and a few servants' cottages around it, formed a part of the parish of Ackworth prior to 1876, as also did the Grange, the seat of the Tempest family, but both hamlets are now in the parish of East Hardwick.§ The Tempests are an old Roman Catholic family of County standing, and maintain a domestic chaplain, chapel and school for the use of the household and retainers. The school is under government inspection, and invariably secures an excellent report. The parish of Ackworth is within the magisterial division of Pontefract, the Poor Law Union of Hemsworth, and

---

* Vide "Fox's Hist. Pont.," p. 83.
† Bauks' "Walks about Yorkshire," p. 287.
‡ So called because it stands upon a higher level.
§ It is more than probable that both East and West Hardwick were at one time incorporated with Pontefract.

the newly formed Parliamentary division of Osgoldcross. The new branch of the Midland and North Eastern Railway from Sheffield to York is the boundary between the parishes of Ackworth and East Hardwick. The ecclesiastical jurisdiction of the parish of Ackworth formerly included High, Low,* and Middle Ackworth, Moor Top, Brackenhill, Hundill, Constitution Hill, and East Hardwick, but in 1876 East Hardwick was separated from the mother parish, and constituted a distinct benefice, the gift being vested in trustees. Moor Top has of late years become so populous that at no distant period a division must of necessity take place. The new parish would include Brackenhill and Constitution Hill, and the gift would be vested in the Rector of Ackworth for the time being.† The acreage of the parish is said to be 2,270.

Name.

The etymology of the name Ackworth is interesting. It is generally supposed to be derived from A.S., *Ake* or *Aken*, oak; and *Uurt*, worth, which is more than probable, for very often places took their names from the kind of wood or timber which flourished in the neighbourhood. In Domesday Book, the parish is called *Aceuurde*, which seems to strengthen the conjecture, for the prefix *ac* in *acorn* is plainly equivalent to *ace* in *Aceuurde*. Oaks certainly flourish at Ackworth now, but they may have been more plentiful when forest hunting was the chief pastime of the nobility. The affix "*worth*" is generally supposed to mean a hamlet or village, a term which seems almost entirely confined to the West Riding of Yorkshire, just as *thorpe* (farm) and *ton* (town) abound in the east and north ridings respectively. The name Ackworth is therefore Anglo-Saxon or Scandinavian from its root upwards. The Rev. N. Greenwell says Ackworth properly means, *the estate of the oak*, from Æc., O.E., an oak, and worth, (from *wyrth* or *weorthig*,

* Formerly noted for its "sumptuous growth of roses and sheaves of white lilies."

† The river Went would be the division line between the two parishes.

O.E., an estate or manor,) a close or farm, usually one well watered. It denotes a place *warded* or protected, and is derived from the old English word *warian*, to ward or defend.* Brackenhill takes its name from the large quantity of bracken or eagle fern (*eupteris aquilina*) which flourishes on the adjoining common. The prefix *Hund* in Hundill comes from *Hund*, O.E., a hound, hence Hound-hill or Hundhill. Ackworth like many other ancient places, gave its name to families resident therein. The Rector of Plumstead in 1853 was a William Ackworth, whose ancestors, there can be no doubt, sprung from Ackworth, and bore the then common appellation of *de Ackworth*. Families of this name are still numerous, but its etymology is various. Ackworth is the only place-name in England, although there are three others with the prefix *Ack*, and several which enjoy the uncorrupted prefix *Ac*.

Waters.

The river Went flows through Ackworth, indeed the village may be said to stand upon it. Camden gives the Nostel pool as the source of the river; but the ordnance survey appropriates the name Went beck to the stream which rises on Sharlston Car, near Streethouse Bar, flows across Went lane, parallel to Ackworth, and thence under Ackworth Car Bridge.† There are other smaller streams, by which the lands are well irrigated, and rendered wood productive. The pretty little hamlet of Wentbridge takes its name from the river Went, and the bridge which there crosses it. From this point the Went deepens and widens, until it empties itself into the river Don, about three miles below Sykehouse, and six or seven below Goole.

The quality of the spring water at Ackworth is uniformly excellent, that of the lower springs being a little softer than that of the upper. The following is an analysis of spring

---

* Vide "Old Yorkshire," vol. 1, p. 170.

† Banks' "Walks about Yorkshire," p. 273.

water, taken at a depth of 100 feet, by Joseph Spence, of York. "50 grains of solid matter to the gallon, 44 of which could be dissolved in distilled water, the remainder being clay, with a trace of organic matter. Of the 44 grains nearly 10 were common salt, and 34 carbonate of soda, with a little sulphate and oxide of iron. The water proved perfectly sweet at every stage of the process of evaporation. It is obviously suitable for domestic use, and particularly so for washing. On account of the absence of the sulphate of iron, lead would be acted upon by it, and therefore pipes and cisterns of that metal should be avoided." The above analysis will be found a generally accurate description of Ackworth water, but the following analysis, taken at a depth of 140 feet, is, perhaps, nearer the mark. "51 grains of solid matter to the gallon, viz.: carbonate of soda, 47 ; potash, traces; lime, 1·5 ; magnesia, 0·2 ; iron, traces ; common salt, 2 ; silica, alumina, and iron (clay), 0·3. Slight traces of nitrates appeared, but no iodides or bromides."* It will be seen, therefore, that Ackworth water is "of very uncommon occurrence, since carbonate of soda is very rarely found in well water, and, in the few cases known, in much smaller quantities." Such, too, is the opinion of Richard Reynolds, F.C.S., of Leeds.

Geological Characteristics.

The soil of Ackworth may be described as a rich clay. Reference to a geological map of the district will shew that there is a substratum of stone underlying nearly the whole area of the parish, but, unfortunately, not thick enough for quarrying, except towards the south and south-west, where extensive quarrying operations are carried on. In many places it runs very near the surface. The Ackworth stone, as a rule, is good, but in places it is exceptionally soft, and unfit for building purposes, which accounts for so many "faults."

* Vide "Hist. Ackworth School," pp. 258-9.

Coal abounds in the vicinity, and, it is thought, might be found at greater depths within the boundaries of the parish. An experimental bore of 153 feet was made in a field in Long lane, in 1860, but coal was not reached, although there were indications of its existence at a still lower level. Rich veins of iron ore are known to exist at certain points, especially in Low Ackworth, inasmuch as many of the natural water springs are strongly oxidised. It will therefore be seen that there is much hidden wealth lying beneath Ackworth, and it is not a too great stretch of imagination to predict that in fifty years' time, or even less, the picturesque village of Ackworth will have become one of the busiest mining centres of the West Riding of Yorkshire. Some account of the upper strata will be interesting to the reader. A boring made in 1851 revealed the following layers:—

Clay	12 ft. 6 in.
Sandstone	14 ft. 0 in.
Shale	2 ft. 0 in.
Sandstone	5 ft. 0 in.
Clay	7 ft. 0 in.
Sandstone	3 ft. 0 in.
Clay	14 ft. 0 in.
Sandstone	18 ft. 0 in.
Shale	6 ft. 0 in.
Sandstone	46 ft. 0 in.
Clay	7 ft. 0 in.
Shale	2 ft. 0 in.
Sandstone	

Total depth, 136 feet. In 1861 another bore was made at some distance from the first, with the following result:—

Clay and Sandstone	14 ft. 0 in.
Light Shale	1 ft. 4 in.
Sandstone	14 ft. 8 in.
Black boss	9 ft. 0 in.
Pottery Clay	18 ft. 0 in.
Ironstone	8 ft. 0 in.
Light Shale	0 ft. 6 in.
Sandstone	9 ft. 0 in.
Light Shale	9 ft. 6 in.
Sandstone	32 ft. 0 in.

Total depth, 116 feet. Coal probably, indeed doubtless, lies still deeper.* Fossils of different periods and species have been found in the strata of the stone beds, the most common being that of the *Equiseta*, or gigantic horsetail of the secondary period, scaled like the cones of the fir.

Local Meteorology.

The climate and temperature of Ackworth are such as to make the village and its neighbourhood a most desirable place of residence, and accordingly we find a goodly number of country houses and neat villas adorning the landscape in all directions. In 1842, Luke Howard, Esq., F.R.S., published a brochure, entitled, " A cycle of eighteen years in the seasons of Great Britain; deduced from meteorological observations made at Ackworth, in the West Riding of Yorkshire, from 1824 to 1841; compared with others before made for a like period (ending with 1823) in the vicinity of London." The work is embellished with five diagramic plates, together with elaborate and exhaustive tables, shewing the mean heights of the barometer, yearly mean temperatures, cycle of rain, total depths of rain for each month of the year, supplemented by many useful notes on the seasons. The book is dedicated to the Right Hon. the Earl Fitzwilliam, and published in London. From it the following facts are deduced. Both the climate and temperature of Ackworth are singularly even, both in cold and warm periods; if, however, an exceedingly dry season should intervene (which is of rare occurrence), it is quickly compensated for by an exceedingly wet one; and an exceedingly cold winter by an exceedingly hot summer. At Ackworth, Mr. Howard has observed, that upon the whole October is the wettest month in the year, the rain, however, falling mostly by night, verifying a remark which has nearly become proverbial, that " there are always twenty fine *days* in October." As a rule, April is (un-

* The stone strata at Ackworth is undoubtedly a large " throw " extending east and west, the Hemsworth coal seam dipping at Ackworth, and appearing again at Pontefract. J. L. S.

fortunately for the farmers) a comparitively dry month, but, as Mr. Howard observes, "it is the arrangement of the All-Wise Creator, and ordered, no doubt, for the best on the great scale of things." In other respects it is shown that the climate of Ackworth is especially suitable for invalids, a fact no doubt discovered by the promoters of the Foundling Hospital, a little too relaxing, but, on the whole, helpful to weak constitutions, and Mr. Howard advises his readers to make a trial of it, before resorting to other skies more favoured by natural position. Agriculturists may also derive considerable comfort and useful information from Mr. Howard's little book. The death-rate at Ackworth is very low, the mean average for the last twenty years being 20·7. The per centage for 1884-5 was 1·1, with a population of nearly 2,300.

The Church.

The original Church of Ackworth, like the village itself, was undoubtedly Saxon, founded, probably, either by the first Saxon proprietors of the parish—Edulph and Osalf—or their immediate predecessors.* This is conclusively proved by the words "*Iba Ecclesia et Presbyter*" in the Domesday Survey; and the Church itself would of course share the fortunes and experience the same vicissitudes as the village. Of these demolitions, rebuildings, additions, and alterations, there is, unfortunately, no record, but an impression generally prevails that the nave of the Church was desecrated during the Great Rebellion (*bellum fanaticorum*), by being transformed into a vast stable and military inn, at which time the edifice sustained very severe damage, both internally and externally, notably the font, which was pulled down and buried in the churchyard. When the Church was completely renovated and restored (?) by public subscription, in the year 1852, the remains of an ancient Norman Chapel, occupying the site of the present nave, were distinctly traceable, especially on the south side, where one of

---

* Vide "Hist. Pont.," pp. 58-104. The living has remained in the patronage of the Crown, as Dukes of Lancaster, from the time of the Lacys.

the arches was nearly entire, but whatever relics of the past remained, or were brought to light during the operations, were either destroyed by the workmen, or confiscated to the private use of the contractor, or other persons of a scientific turn of mind who happened to visit the scene. It is said that barrow loads of old carving, both in stone and wood, were removed wholesale by private persons, wherewith to ornament their gardens and to give the rooms of their houses an antique appearance! And this was done without one word of expostulation from the architect, contractor, or building committee! The Society for the Preservation of Ancient Buildings and Monuments was, unfortunately, not in existence at that time, but it is marvellous how persons with any idea of propriety could tolerate such vandalism and spoliation. Be that as it may, there is abundance of evidence to confirm the statement, for wherever the eye is turned, ecclesiastical relics abound, and that not on sacred ground.

Interesting Features.

Situated near the centre of the village, the Church and Rectory, although standing back from the road in rural seclusion, occupy a somewhat elevated position. The first object, on approaching the Church, to attract the visitor's notice is the

Lych-gate,

which presents a rustic and pretty appearance. It is built of Norwegian Oak, and is now nearly black, although quite modern. It bears the following inscription, engraved upon a brass plate.

This Lych-Gate Erected 1878.

In Memory of
The Rev. Joseph Kenworthy.
He was 31 years Rector of this Parish, and carried out the Restoration of this Church.
DIED A.D. 1875.

Passing through the lych-gate, the tower and south porch of

the Church are the principal external features which strike the eye. The

Tower

is the oldest part of the Church, indeed, it is the only portion of it which remains in its entirety after the restoration of 1852. It is solid and well built, and dates from about the fourteenth century. It contains a peal of six bells, each bearing a legend or inscription. Height: 68 feet, 9 inches.

The Bells.

An authority on Campanology says: "the bells at Ackworth appear to be of three dates, two of pre-reformation times, one of the seventeenth century, and one of the eighteenth century, with all the self-glorification and self-assertion thereto belonging."†

No. 1 is in the key of C sharp, and bears the following inscription:
TIMOTHY : LEE : D.D. : RECTOR : 1760.

No. 2. The note of this bell is B, and the inscription:
W : WAGNER : I : GARLICK : CHURCHWARDENS : 1760.

No. 3. Key of A. This bell bears the common legend of
* IESVS * BE * OVR * SPEED * A.S. * W.C. FECIT. * 1662. *

Where the asterisks are placed there is a coat of arms, repeated eight times, very difficult to decipher, except this much: *party per pale, 1, a chevron between three bells, two and one; 2, three bougets, also two and one.*

---

† This enumeration is incorrect; there are three eighteenth century bells; the two oldest are not dated.

No. 4. This bell is probably older than No. 3. It bears no date, and its note is G sharp. "The inscription upon it," says Mr. Holmes, "is probably a rhyming couplet."

✠ Laudamus [Fleur de lis] ✠ a-tis ✠ campana ✠ fit ✠ hæc ✠ Trinitatis. ✠

The initial coat of arms has the following bearings: *party per pale 1 and 2, a bend, with a cross crosslet for difference*.

No. 5. Key of F sharp, No date, and no legend, only
✠ [Fleur de lis] I. H. S. ✠
Armorial bearings same as No. 4.

No. 6. The note of this tenor bell is E. It was founded in 1760, and recast in 1880. Inscription:

: CAST : BY : IOHN : WARNER : AND : SONS :
: LONDON : 1880 :
: ALL : MEN : WHO : HEAR : MY : MOVRNFVL : SOVND :
: REPENT : BEFORE : YOV : LIE : IN : GROVND :
: W : WAGNER : I : GARLICK :
: CHVRCHWARDENS :
: I : LVDLVM : ROTHERHAM : FOVNDER : 1760 :

This is the bell upon which the clock strikes the hours, and upon which the passing and funeral dirges are tolled. The original bell was very imperfectly founded, and had a piece cut out, as if in partial remedy.* Its weight is nearly 6 cwts., and the key of the peal is C sharp, minor.

The following excellent rules are supposed to be observed by the ringers.

ACKWORTH PARISH CHURCH. BELFRY RULES.

—o—

(1) It is to be understood that the Church Tower and Bells are altogether under the control of the Rector and Churchwardens; and that no one can ring the bells without their permission; or be entered upon the list of Ringers, without their appointment.

(2) That the Ringers be members of the Church of England and of known good character: that they be appointed by the Rector: that they shall be regular in their attendance at Church, and conduct themselves reverently and quietly in their duties.

---

* Vide "Old Yorkshire," vol. 1, p. 80.

(3) That one of their number be appointed Leader, who will be responsible for good order in the Belfry; who will give directions to the Ringers and keep a Belfry book. That the Leader be appointed by the Rector annually.

(4) That no one, except the Ringers and those of the Parish who are learning to ring, shall be in the Belfry at ringing or practising time. The introduction of a Friend to the Belfry at a practice, by any Ringer, need not be regarded as a breach of this rule.

(5) That no drinking or smoking be allowed in the Belfry at any time: that if any Ringer break this rule or be quarrelsome or use bad language, the Leader shall at once stop the ringing for that occasion and shall report the same to the Rector.

(6) That the duty of the Ringers be to ring on Sundays for both Services: also on Christmas Day, New Year's Day, and on the Queen's Birthday: also on any other occasion, with the distinct consent of the Rector and one of the Churchwardens, but not without it.

(7) That the Ringers assemble for regular practice on one evening, at least, in the week, as may be arranged; or more frequently, if they desire it: that the ringing on such occasions shall cease, at the latest, at 9 o'clock p.m. Any Ringer absent from the Belfry for four weeks in succession, without giving due notice to the Leader, and satisfactory reasons for his absence, shall be considered to have resigned and his name shall be at once removed from the List of Ringers.

(8) That, in case of ringing the Bells by request, and with the Rector's express permission, on the occasion of weddings or any other joyous occasion, money only shall be taken as payment, which shall be divided at once amongst the Ringers, in equal portions by the Leader.

(9) That any subject of dispute or misunderstanding arising amongst the Ringers shall be immediately referred to the Rector and Churchwardens, and their decision shall be considered final.

(10) That no one be appointed Ringer without consenting first to these rules, and signing them: and all Ringers are to understand that these rules are only intended for the comfort and good ordering of all concerned; and it is hoped that they will all cordially assist in observing and maintaining them.

"Let all things be done decently and in order."

W. M. FALLOON, Rector.
JOSEPH NELSTROP, }
J. HEATON CADMAN, } Churchwardens.

In a niche over the outside of the

Porch .

is an effigy of St. Cuthbert, the patron saint, holding in his dexter hand a crozier. Inside the porch on both sides of the wall are inscribed appropriate stanzas, selected from Herbert's *Church Porch*, as follows:—

On the right hand side above the *foramen* is the first verse of the "*Superliminare*," thus—

> "Thou, whom the former precepts have
> Sprinkled, and taught how to behave
> Thyself in Church; approach, and taste
> The Church's mystical repast."

On the right beneath are two verses from the "*Perirhanterium*"—

> "Sum up, at night, what thou hast done by day;
> And, in the morning, what thou hast to do.
> Dress and undress thy soul, mark the decay
> And growth of it. If, with thy watch, *that* too
>   Be down, then wind up both. Since we shall be
>   Most surely judged, make thy accounts agree.
>
> In brief, acquit thee bravely: play the man.
> Look not on pleasures as they come, but go.
> Defer not the least virtue. Life's poor span
> Make not an ell, by trifling in thy woe.
>   If thou do ill, the joy fades, not the pains:
>   If well, the pain doth fade, the joy remains."

On the left—

> "Judge not the preacher; for he is *thy* judge.
> If thou mislike him, thou conceiv'st him not.
> God calleth preaching, folly. Do not grudge
> To pick out treasures from an earthen pot.
>   The worst speak something good. If *all* want sense,
>   God takes a text, and preacheth patience.
>
> He that gets patience, and the blessing which
> Preachers conclude with, hath not lost his pains.
> He that by being at Church, escapes the ditch
> Which he might fall in by companions, gains.
>   He that loves God's abode, and to combine
>   With saints on earth, shall one day with them shine."

Above the *foramen* on the left hand side is the remaining verse of the "*Superliminare.*"—

> "Avoid profaneness; come not near.
> Nothing but holy, pure, and clear,
> Or that which groaneth to be so,
> May, at his peril, further go."

On the left below, a continuation of the *Perirhanterium.*"

> "Sundays observe. Think, when the bells do chime,
> 'Tis angels' music; therefore come not late.
> God then deals blessings: if a king did so,
> Who would not haste, nay, give, to see the show?
>   Resort to sermons, but to prayers most:
>   Praying's the *end* of preaching.
>
> When once thy foot enters the church, be bare.
> God is more there than thou: for thou art there
> Only by His permission. Then beware;
> And make thyself all reverence and fear.
>   Kneeling ne'er spoil'd silk stocking. Quit thy state.
>   All equal are within the church's gate."

And on the right—

"In time of service seal up both thine eyes,
And send them to thy heart; that, spying sin,
They may weep out the stains by them did rise.
Those doors being shut, all by the ear comes in.
   Who marks in church-time others' symmetry,
   Makes all their beauty his deformity.

Let vain or busy thoughts have there no part,
Bring not thy plough, thy plots, thy pleasures thither.
Christ purged His Temple; so must thou, thy heart.
All worldly thoughts are but thieves met together
   To cozen thee. Look to thy actions well;
   For churches either are our heaven, or hell."

Over the inner door upon a scroll are the Latin words—

Domus Dei
Porta Cœli.*

Unfortunately, the restoration was carried out almost entirely with Ackworth stone, which is, as a rule, of a soft and perishable nature, consequently portions of the exterior of the church are much weather-worn and decayed, although not forty years old.

The next object of interest is the

Font,

which is well worth the notice of the Archæologist and Antiquarian. It is octagonal in shape, and running around it is the following inscription: "*Thomas Bradley, D.D., Rectore, H.A., T.C. Gardianis, Baptisterium Bello Phanaticorum Dirutum Deuno Erectum, 1663.*" That is: "Thomas Bradley, Doctor in Divinity, being Rector, H.A. and T.C., Churchwardens. This font thrown down in the war of the Fanatics, was set up again in the year 1663." It is probable that Ackworth Church suffered greatly during the civil wars, not only from its proximity to Pontefract, but also from the circumstance of one of the King's chaplains being its rector. We know for certain that the ancient font was broken down. The first baptism, in the font newly set up, was 24th November, 1663. When the Church was restored in 1852, the basin of an ancient Norman font was discovered under one of the north aisle pillars, of which, indeed, it formed the foundation. The erection of this

---

* The House of God, the gate of Heaven.

aisle having been subsequent to the civil wars, it is exceedingly probable that this was the bowl of the ancient church font, which had been placed there, on the erection of the aisle in question, to prevent its being desecrated. During the progress of the works, and whilst the Rector was absent from home, it disappeared, and was supposed by the workmen to have been broken up, and used in the building of the new chancel wall. In the course of a year or two, however, this ancient relic re-appeared as a flower-vase in a garden, which was then the property of one of the sub-contractors. Unfortunately, by the builder's contract, it was provided that all refuse materials which could not be used in the re-erection of the church were to be the property of the contractor. But, surely, the removal of so sacred an object as the bowl of the ancient church font was never contemplated by that clause, and its present sacrilegious exhibition in the centre of the village can be regarded by no right-minded person in any other light than as an offence against public decorum. Dr. Bradley (during whose incumbency the present font was set up) had been Chaplain to Charles I., and Prebendary of York, and had married Lady Frances, daughter of John Baron Saville,* of Pontefract, and he seems to have been proud of his relationship and antecedents. His grand-child, Charles, son of Mr. Danyell Godfrey, was the first to be baptized in the new font. This is recorded at full length in the parish register, as having occurred 24th November, 1663.

The *Brass Lectern* is a handsome one, and was presented to the Church by J. Heaton Cadman, Esq., Recorder of Pontefract.

The *Vestry Screen*, consisting of two parts, and enclosing the north-east corner of the Church, is a fine specimen of carved oak, the work of A. Hayball, Sheffield, Sc., and bears the following inscription. "*These two screens are the gift of Joseph and Caroline Nelstrop, of Ackworth Lodge. Erected A.D. 1874.* The organ case is intended to be *en suite*, and the inscription upon it is as follows: "*Organ Case. Donor: C. M. Kenworthy,*

---

* Vide Monumental Epitaphs, and Biography of Dr. Bradley.

Ackworth Rectory, A.D. 1874." The choir stall finials are also worthy of notice.* On the west wall of the north aisle is painted the following:—

Benefactions to the Poor of the Parish of Ackworth.

Year	Donor	£	s	d
1692.	Elizabeth, relict of Sir John Lowther, Bart. gave	20	0	0
1717.	Robert Lowther, of Ackworth, Esq.	50	0	0
1718.	Margaret, wife of William Norton, of Sawley, Esq.	20	0	0
1722.	Ralph Lowther, of Ackworth Park, Esq.	20	0	0
1724.	Ann, daughter of Ralph Lowther, Esq.	50	0	0
1724.	Elizabeth, daughter of Lawson Trotter, of Skelton Castle, Esq.	10	0	0
1729.	John Lowther, of Ackworth Park, Esq.	50	0	0
1739.	Thomas Bright, of Badsworth, Esq.	20	0	0
1744.	The Rev. William Key	20	0	0
1703.	Robert Mason, Gent.	10	0	0
	Ann, Relict of the Rev. J. Bolton	10	0	0
	By Cash from a Stock of Cows	20	0	0

A. R. P.
13 3 4
See the award.

N.B.—The above Benefactions are laid out in House and Land upon Lease to Anthony Surtees, Esq., for £12 0s. 0d. per year, which Lease expires in the year of our Lord 1862.†

Yearly Payments.

Year	Donor	£	s	d
1701.	Ann, Relict of Robert Calverley	10	0	0‡
	Matthew Lambe, Yeoman	10	0	0
	For the Land on which the Windmill is erected	0	5	0
	Jervas Seaton, of East Hardwick, for one acre in Thorpleys	0	6	8
	John Wormald, to the poor	0	8	0
	And for putting out poor children	1	0	0

* These stalls were inserted in 1852.

† Ackworth House was subsequently sold to J. M. Hepworth, Esq., for £2,316, which sum is now invested in the 3 per cent. Annuities.

‡ This is an error on the board. The payment is only ten shillings a year.

Stephen Cawood, to the poor	1	0	0
And for repairing house, Stead lane ...	0	10	0
John Rushforth, to the poor	1	0	0
John Topham, for one acre of land on the Common	0	4	8

1803. Sarah and Francis Townsley, died intestate, and in possession of a house, malt-kiln, etc., and 7 acres of land adjoining the Rectory on the East, and 4 acres of land called Pudding Bush, which Estate for want of heirs went to the Trustees of the Manor of Ackworth, for the benefit of the Freeholders.

1810. Henry Mitton, of Ackworth, left £20 (Duty deducted), the interest to be paid to 20 poor widows, yearly, on New-Year's Day, by the Churchwardens and Overseers.

1873. David Lindsay,[*] of Leeds, invested for inmates of Lowther's Hospital [†] ... 150 0 0

Inside the Church, near the South door, on the right-hand side going in, painted on a sheet of zinc may be seen the sublime prayer of King Alfred, as follows :—

"Forgive now, ever Good! and give to us
That in our minds we soar up to Thee,
Maker of all things! Through these troublous ways;
And from amongst these busy things of life,
O tender Father! wielder of the world!
Come unto Thee, and through Thy good speed
With the mind's eyes well opened we may see
The welling spring of Good. that Good Thyself,
O Lord, the King of Glory! Then make whole
The eyes of our understandings, so that we
Father of angels, fasten them on Thee!
Drive away this thick mist, which long while now
Hath hung before our mind's eyes heavy and dark;
Enlighten now the mind's eyes with Thy light.
Master of Life! for Thou, O tender Father,
Art very brightness of the True Light Thyself;

---

[*] Buried at the east side of the Church. Died Oct. 7, 1874, aged 77.
[†] Vide Charities.

B

> Thyself Almighty Father! the sure rest
> Of all Thy fast and true ones; winningly
> Thou orderest it, that we may see Thyself;
> Thou art of all things origin and end,
> O Lord of all men! Father of angels! Thou
> Easily bearest all things without toil;
> Thou art Thyself the way and leader too
> Of everyone that lives, and the pure place
> That the way leads to; all men from this soil
> Throughout the breadth of being, yearn to Thee."
>
> KING ALFRED THE GREAT AND GOOD.

The seats in the Church are partly free, and partly appropriated. In 1852, the Incorporated Society for the building of Churches, granted £120 towards the re-building of Ackworth Church, upon condition that 173 seats* numbered 1 to 34 be reserved therein for the use of the poorer inhabitants of the parish. This fact is recorded upon a small board hung up in the vestry. Accommodation is provided for five hundred and six people, which, compared with the population, is certainly insufficient.

The nave is three bays in length, the arches of which rest upon piers of three-quarter cylindrical shafts, with circular moulded capitals. The corbels are all carved with symbolical figures. The tower and chancel arches are lofty and elegant, with lightly foliaged capitals, the whole effect of which would undoubtedly be improved by the additional height and light imparted by a clerestorie. The entire length of the Church is 70 feet, and the entire width 50 feet.

CHURCH PLATE.

There can be no doubt that the original Church plate of Ackworth was confiscated by the Duke of Northumberland, in common with nearly all the plate of the Yorkshire Churches, to the personal use of the "Royal Harry," in May, 1553. How long the Holy Communion was consecrated and administered at Ackworth in "vessels of pewter" we do not know, but the oldest silver chalice is dated 1631,† and bears the following

---

* A clerical error. The word "seats" ought to be "sittings."

† There is a silver paten at East Harlsey Church, near Northallerton, which bears date 1571.

inscription: "*This cup belongeth to Ackwith prih.*" It is plainly chased, and the cover, which is tightly fitting, is thus inscribed: "wt. 16 lcs. 2 dt. Ao: Dni: 1631." The hall marks are the same, both on cup and lid. On a shield the letters

in a circle a combination of three ostrich feathers, crown, rose, and thistle; and in a third shield a device too obliterated to be intelligible. The second chalice is more elaborately chased, and is, perhaps, older than the first, the chasing being less distinct, and the inscription indicative of an earlier existence than that of the date which appears upon it. "*This old cup was given by the Rector to Ackworth parish, A.D. 1829.*" The cover evidently dates from the period of the gift, and seems to have been made and fitted to the old chalice to supply the place of the original lid, which had been probably lost. This conjecture is strengthened by the dissimilarity of the hall marks which appear on the lid and cup, and the freshness of the chasing on the lid compared with that upon the chalice. The following is engraved upon the knop of the lid: "Ao: Dni: 1829;" and the hall mark, which is quite distinct, is

|J.H.|

on a square, a bust in a circle, a lion passant guardant, and the letter "n," both on squares. The hall mark on the cup is much less distinct, but appears to be the letter "g" on a shield, a lion statant (?), a device resembling a stag's head with antlers or coronet, and the letters RD (R D) combined. The two flagons are alike in every particular, and are therefore contemporary. On the breast of each there is a floriated circle, in the centre of which are six lozenges arranged in the form of a triangle, graduating in size downwards, with a star for difference. The hall marks are the letters "G.A." coronetted, two devices resembling griffins, followed by the letter C on a shield. In other respects they are plain and tasteless. The larger paten is also very plain, the hall marks, which are nearly obliterated, being the only marks to attract attention. The first mark is

the next is unintelligible, then comes a lion passant guardant, and the letter ℭ. The pedestal, which is probably older than the paten, looks as if it had been fixed on at a comparatively recent period. The smaller paten is much more ancient, the chasing being nearly invisible, and the coat of arms much defaced. The field of the shield is uncertain, but it is emblazoned with two bars fesse, and chief indented. The supporters are feathers, but that is all that can be made out. The hall marks are H, with a star below, a lion's head ensigned with an imperial crown, a lion passant guardant, and the letter ℭ. The above description, although crude and imperfect, will nevertheless be interesting to archæologists, antiquarians, and students of heraldry. It is, however, quite certain that the Ackworth Church plate was not manufactured in London, nor assayed at Goldsmiths' Hall, but that it is of provincial manufacture, and assayed at one of the provincial assay offices.

Monumental Inscriptions.

The monuments in Ackworth Church are few, and of simple construction, but in one or two instances the inscriptions thereon are extremely interesting. In the vestry, against the east wall, there are two stone slabs, one broader than the other. The left-hand slab bears the following inscription :—

A cherub partially veiled, holding a wreath of immortelles, inside which is an heraldic shield. *Arms*—Per pale argent and gules—*Bradley*. Gules, a fess or, charged with three buckles or, and a crescent for difference. *Savile.*—Argent on a bent sable three owls of the field.

FRANCIS . THE . DAUGHTER . OF . THE . RIGHT . HONBLE. . JOHN SAVILE . BARON . OF . PONTEFRACT . AND . WIFE . TO . THOMAS BRADLEY . DOCTOR . IN . DIVINITY . PRÆBEND . OF . YORKE . RECTOR . OF . THIS . CHURCH . AND . CHAPLAYNE . TO . HIS

SACRED . MATY. . KING . CHARLES . THE . FIRST . ON . THE . 30 OF . JANUARY . 1663 . FELL . ASLEEPE . EXPECTING . THE RES(S)URRECTION .

SHE . WAS . NOBLY . BORNE .
SHE . WAS . VERTVOVSLY . BRED .
SHE . LIVED . PIOVSLY .
SHE . DIED . PEACEABLY .
SHE . CARRIED . A . GOOD . CONSCIENCE . WITH . HER .
AND . HATH . LEFT . A . GOOD . NAME . BEHIND . HER .

SIC . SIC . IVVAT . IRE . SVB . VMBRAS .

FOR . PITY . AND . FOR . PIETY .
FOR . CHASTITIE . AND . FOR . CHARITIE .
FOR . PATIENCE . AND . HUMILITIE .
SHE . WAS . RARELIE . EXEMPLARY .

HIC . TENDIMUS . OMNES .

On the narrow right hand slab adjoining, the inscription is:

Arms—Same, without cherub and wreath.

VXOREM . SEQVITVR .
THOMAS . BRADLÆVS .
AD . VRNAM . CŒLVM .
ANIMAS . CINERES .
HÆC . HABET . VRNAM .
SVOS.

I : KINGS : 19 : 4 :

I . AM . NO . BETTER
THEN . MY . FATHERS .

OBIT .
HOMO . ZTIO . DIE .
IOBRIS . AN . DOM .
1673.

The floor of the vestry, nave, and aisles of the Church are covered with memorial slabs, bearing inscriptions for the most part nearly obliterated, or unimportant, except perhaps as name indicators. I have noted the following names and dates:—

Burford, 1781. Daniel Hepworth (no date). Austwick, 1778. Howitt, 1755. Parker, 1769. Ann Ramsden, (aged 90), 1763. Ann Sly (aged 87), 1611. Samuel Anthron, 1789. Wise (?) Rishforth, 1732. Baynes, etc.

There are others, but they are covered by the organ and other fittings.

Sir Roger Hopton's tombstone, which was discovered under the seats now allotted to the occupiers of Ackworth Park, when the Church was restored in 1852, is in excellent preservation, is by far the most interesting and important relic of its kind in Ackworth Church, and may now be seen in the south aisle. In the centre is a large floriated cross, flanked by the arms of Hopton and Savile, the whole surrounded by the following inscription:—" Orate pro animabus, Rogeri Hoptonis, militis, et Annæ uxoris suæ, qui obiêrunt, Anno Domini 1506." It is, therefore, the oldest tombstone in Ackworth Church. A sketch is here inserted. *Coat of Arms.* Hopton—two bars, each charged with three mullets, in dexter chief a mullet for difference. Savile—on a bend three owls. The name Roger is common in the Hopton family. This Roger was probably the same who, in 1492, was nominated by William Scargill as trustee of a charity founded by the latter at Rothwell, and who in 3 Henry VII. (1487), was gentleman usher of the King's chamber.

In the vestry, there is another slab, the inscription upon which, so far as it is legible, is interesting:—

Hoc sub marmore Reponuntur
Mortales Reliquæ,
Matronæ Nobilis & Lectissimæ
Dme. Elizab. Lowther,

Hopton=Savile Tombslab.

Quæ Filiæ quondam Joh Hare
de Stow Bardolph in Comitat.
Norfolciæ Equit Aurati
Primum Woolley Leigh Armig Nupta
Demum Honorabili Viro.
DNO. JOH LOWTHER de Lowther in
Agro Westmort Baronetto:
Multum Natalib: plus virtulib: inclaruit
Honorificas Nuptias,
hinc una nide senâ sobole beavit:
tribus nempe Filiis totidenq Filiabus
Familiæ LOWTHERINÆ Additis
Venultum speciem mente plane divinâ
Decoravit:
———sas deniq Faculates Effusissima
———assitate, charitate, munificentia,
———um impendit magis honorifice
an audauxit.
———ihter Beatam vitam utpote.

The remainder is hidden beneath the masonry which encloses the vestry. The following names also appear on the vestry floor.

Jonathan Seaton, 1762, Mary Lowther,
1753, and Margt. Baynes.

The mural monuments are few and unimportant. In the south aisle, upon a fine slab of white marble:—

Arms of Gully.

Motto — Vix ea nostra voco.

Sacred
to the memory of ROBERT GULLY, son of John Gully, Esq.,
of Ackworth Park, who, after suffering the horrors
and privations of shipwreck on the island
of Formosa, in the Brig, "*Ann,*" on the
night of the 10th of March, 1842,

in which vessel he was a passenger,
was, together with the rest of the crew, taken
prisoner by the Chinese, and suffered the greatest
privations and hardships, which he bore
with the most exemplary fortitude,
manly and cheerful resignation
to about the 15th August,
when he, together with about 300 British subjects, was
most barbarously murdered in cold
blood by the Chinese authorities in the
town of Ty-wan-foo. He was endeared to a
large circle of friends for his manly
virtues and kindness of heart.
This tablet is erected by a bereaved and afflicted father.

Know thou, O stranger, to the fame
Of this much loved, much honoured name,
For none that knew him need be told
A warmer heart death ne'er made cold.

Under the tower, on white marble and grey granite:—

Robert Heptinstall,
Died June 1st, 1726. Aged 43 years.

Upon a white marble slab, flanked with columns with floriated capitals, supported by flying cherubim, and surmounted with the Lowther coat of arms:—

RALPH AND ROBERT LOWTHER, of Ackworth Park, Esqrs.,
Sons of Sir John Lowther, of Lowther, in
Westmorland, Bart., by Elizh. daughter
of Sir Ralph Hare, Bart. Issue of Ralph
Lowther, by Mary his wife, daughter of Godfrey
Lawson, of Leeds, Esq., one son and eight daughters.
Died 1724. Aged 69.

ROBERT LOWTHER, died without issue, 1720. Aged 57.
John, only son of Ralph, Died without issue
1729, 45. Dorothy Norton, Grand-daughter

of Ralph Lowther, and daughter of William Norton,
of Sawley, Esq., Died 1729. Aged 12.
Monument erected by Mary, only surviving of
eight daughters, 1735.

On a stone slab :—

Near this place lieth the Body of the Revd.
Charles Pearse, of Ackworth, who died July
8th, 1776. Aged 80.

On a white marble slab :—

Richard Mason, died 22nd July, 1760,
Aged 67 years.

George Mason, his son, died 22nd Novr., 1747,
Aged 28 years.

Rebecca, wife of Richard Mason, died June 19,
1769, Aged 72 years.

On white marble and granite :—

Anthony Surtees, Esq., J.P., Lieut. Col. 2nd W. Y. M.
Died Jan. 12, 1807. Aged 65 years.

In same vault :—

Frances Dorothea Surtees, wife of the above,
Died March 27, 1802. Aged 64 years.
She was daughter of Penelope, wife of John
Price, Esq., who afterwards married
Timothy Lee, D.D., Rector of
this Parish.

Before the restoration on the south side of the altar rails:—

Here lyeth interred the body of the Lady
Margt. Aubrey, wife of St. John
Aubrey, Bart., of Lantrithidge,
in Glamorganshire in South Wales, who departed
this Life the 13th June, 1868—aged 31 years.

Underneath on the same stone :—

Also of Robert Lowther, Esq., youngest
Son of the Honble. St. John Lowther,
of Lowther, Bart.
Who departed this Life the 24th day of
August, 1720, in the 56 year of
his age.

The following inscriptions appear in the Churchyard : *

Henry Mitton, died Nov. 20, 1791, 81 years.
Elizabeth, wife of above, died March 22, 1802,
76 years.
John Beaumont, died June 19, 1798, aged 76.
Mary, wife of Joseph White, died Feb. 5th, 1776,
aged 65.
Mary, wife of John Burford, died Feb. 2, 1795,
aged 67.
William, son of John and Mary Burford, died April
30, 1781, aged 20.
Catherine, wife of Wm. Sikes, died 4th August,
1742, aged 48.
Robert Sikes, son of above, died 4th January,
1746, aged 2 years.
William Sikes, husband of Catherine, died
June 25th, 1764, aged 55.
Major John Goldsworthy,† of Hon. East India
Co.'s Madras Army. Died June 1, 1884, aged 80.

(*Skull and Crossbones.*)

Samuel, son of Mr. Samuel Turner, A.M., late Vicar
of Blyth, by Frances, his wife, daughter of
Mr. Hacksup, of Finniley, afterwards

---

* Facts only are here given, such as names, dates, and ages.

† Major Goldsworthy was a very pronounced Conservative, and declined the use of his pew to the Duke of Gloucester, when that nobleman attended Ackworth Church, because he was a Liberal.

wife to Robert Mason, of Ackworth,
Gent. died 26th December, 1706,*
aged 18.

John, son of Wm. Heptinstall, died 4th Sept. 1726,
aged 21.

William, second son of above William, died
27th Feb., 1735-6, aged 29.

And as an early token of his pious inclinations and the true honour he bore to God's house, did (with the consent of his dear mother) give ten pounds towards the building of a vestry to this Church.

Rev. Thos. Bell, late of East Hardwick,
Died Nov. — 18— aged 77 years.†

On the west side of the Churchyard, near the Church—
William Robert Hay, M.A.,
Rector of this Parish
37 years;
Died
10th December, 1839, aged
78.

On the other side of the tomb—
Mary Hay,
Wife of the Rector
of this Parish,
Died
18th Feb., 1832,
aged 71.

Further north—
Here lies the Body of Ann, Relict
of the Rev. Kingsman Baskett,
of Pocklington,
She died 26 March, 1826, aged
81 Years.

* Vide sub datum, Ann : 1712. The young man's wish was probably only carried out six years after his death.

† Date obliterated.

On the north-east side, separated by a high wall from the Churchyard, there is the mausoleum of the Gully family, formerly of Ackworth Park. It stands in its own grounds, which are kept in beautiful order.

John Gully,* Died at Durham, March 9th, 1863, 79 years.

There are also two daughters of Mr. Gully buried here, both of whom died in infancy.

East end—
Captain R. S. Adams (14th Foot), Died August 5, 1837, aged 47.
Wm. Clark, Surgeon, Died July 22, 1861, 55 years.

North side—
Ann Clareborough, Died April 19, 1832, 60 years.
John Petty, Esq., of Ackworth Park, Died Oct. 4, 1826, 68 years.

East end—
Lucy, wife of Wm. Peel, of Ackworth Park, Died April 14, 1869.

Stained Glass.

Ackworth Church is rich in memorial windows, all of them, except two, being filled with stained glass of elegant tints and appropriate designs. The east window is a fine specimen of decorative art. Five figures are depicted therein, three are designed to represent ecclesiastical saints, and two regal; emblematical of the union and co-operation which should exist between the Church and the Throne. S.S. Cuthbert, Augustine of Canterbury, and Paulinus, were Bishops, and S.S. Edmund and Oswald, were Kings. The ancient prediction of

---

* A memoir of John Gully will be found herein, under the head of Biographical Sketches.

Isaiah: "and Kings shall be thy nursing fathers, and their Queens thy nursing mothers," is no contradiction of the more recent saying of our Divine Head, "My Kingdom is not of this world." St. Edmund is represented in the first light as holding in his hand the instrument of his martyrdom. The second light contains a figure of St. Augustine of Canterbury, vested in episcopal habits, and holding in his left hand a banner, upon which is inscribed an emblem, or picture, of the Crucifixion of our Lord. The centre figure is a representation of St. Cuthbert (to whom the Parish Church of Ackworth is dedicated), with the head of St. Oswald in his hand. Above is St. Cuthbert's cross. In the cinque-foil on the north side is depicted the incident of the young Cuthbert keeping watch over his flock by the river Leder. On the other side is portrayed St. Cuthbert administering the Holy Communion to the dying Boisil, monk of Melrose. In the next light is the figure of St. Paulinus, attired in archiepiscopal vestments, and the figure in the fifth light represents St. Oswald, King and Martyr, crowned, and holding in one hand a sceptre, and in the other a cross. Along the bottom of the window appears the following inscription:—
"In memory of Elizabeth Harriet (Kenworthy), the wife of the Rector of this parish, who departed this life March 2nd, 1853, aged 32 years."

There are four other windows in the *Chancel*, all filled with stained glass. The first on the *south side* is a two-light, containing full length figures of S.S. Hilda and Ebba; and the other is a single light representation of S. Alban. The first of these saints was the virgin founder of Whitby Abbey; the second was the daughter of Ethelfrid, King of Northumberland, sister of S. Oswald, and abbess of Coldingham, in Scotland; and the third is known as the proto-martyr of Britain, all three, however, were martyrs. On the *north side* of the *Chancel*, which at Ackworth is a continuation of the north aisle, the windows are both two-light memorial ones. In the first window are representations of Christ bearing His Cross, and the legendary incident in the life of St. Veronica ; below is the following inscription :—" In memory of Clara, the beloved wife of John Hardy Thursby. Born 24 March, 1839, Died 21 March, 1867. Ætat 27." The other window depicts Monica's visit to S. Augustine, and S. Paulinus baptizing in the Swale. It was inserted to the memory of "Henry Cockerill Leatham, Deceased 6 Aug. 1852 aged 75 years," and "Lucy Leatham, his wife, Deceased 18 Feb. 1866, aged 78 years."

East end of South Aisle.

Three-light window representing the Crucifixion, Resurrection, and Ascension of Christ, and underneath the following inscription :—"In memory of John Pearson, who deceased May 9th, 1843, aged 63 years ; also of Emma his wife, who departed this life May 11th, 1842, aged 54. They rest on the east side of this window."

South Aisle.

Two double-light windows. The former contains a representation of Christ in Gethsemane, and on the road to Calvary. The inscriptions below are as follows :—" In memory of William Grubb, who departed this life April 2nd, 1854, aged 79 years." "In memory of Hannah Grubb, who departed this life 3rd Augt. 1876, in her 92 year." The latter depicts Christ being crowned with thorns, and scourged. This window was put in to the "memory of Mary Plowes, of this parish, who departed this life on the 14th day of December, 1857, aged 84."

West end of South Aisle.

Two-light window, representing Christ being baptized, and blessing little children. Inscription:— ✠ Basil Anthony Kenworthy ✠ Born F : of the Epiphany ✠ Deceased Eve of All Saints, 1854 ✠ Aged 9 months. ✠ "The Lord gave and the Lord hath taken away ; blessed be the name of the Lord." ✠

The upper or tracery portion of the large west window only is stained, the rest is tinted.

West end of North Aisle.

Two-light window, corresponding with west end of south aisle, one light depicting the annunciation to the Shepherds, and the other the Presentation of Christ in the Temple. Inscription:—" In memory of Jane Yates Wilson, who deceased 13th December, 1842, aged 28; also Anna Maria Wilson, who departed this life May 25th, 1846, aged 24."

North Aisle.

Three double-light windows. (1) Mercy and Charity. Inscription:—" Mary Munkhouse Barnett, Deceased 2nd May, 1864, aged 78 years." (2) Manifestation to the Shepherds and Magi. Inscription:—" Francis Augusta Bland, Deceased Dec. 26, 1855, aged 75 years." (3) The flight into Egypt and the Herodian massacre. Inscription:— "Judith Selina Bland, Departed this life July 16, 1847, aged 66 years."

The window at the east end of the north aisle is like the west window in the nave, stained in the upper portion and tinted in the lower.

It will easily be imagined that so much stained glass creates a "dim religious light," which in itself is both depressing and undesirable, making the use of artificial light frequently necessary in the winter months, during the greater part of the day. In this instance convenience must give way to art, for it would be difficult to obtain a faculty for their removal, and the only way to obtain "more light" would be either to restore the clerestorie, or insert Dormer windows in the roof.

The Parish Registers.

These valuable records, which begin 10th February, 1558, are in a good state of preservation from the first, with the exception of a few places in the earliest book, where the entries have almost disappeared; but this defect is remedied to a great extent by a page for page paper copy on interleaves bound with the original parchment. During the rectorate of Dr. Timothy Lee (1744-77), more than ordinary care was shewn in keeping the books. It was the Doctor who caused the copy to be made of the first book; and in his time the numbers of births and deaths, ages at death, and causes of death, are tabulated yearly, males being distinguished from females, and the entries being signed by him and the Churchwardens periodically. The death tables are interesting as shewing the disorders most prevalent in the village. Consumption appears to have been peculiarly fatal. In one year, out of twelve burials of children from the Foundling Hospital, eleven are stated to have died from this cause. In the second volume, which extends from August, 1687, to March, 1732, entries are made of the fact of pregnancy of women at the time of marriage,—"being with child." Sometimes, when a birth occurred too soon after marriage, the words "begotten in fornication" are added to the entry of its baptism. We also perceive evidence of the existence of the Foundling Hospital* in the following entry: "June, 1705, Thomas, a child brought to the parish in the night, (was) baptised." The prevalence of the plague is shewn in this register, as well as at Wakefield and others, thus— "Richard Pickeringe and Frances Ledsome, married June 25th, 1645, in which year there dyed of the plague in Ackworth 153 persons; Richard Pickeringe being then Constable." The following surnames, which still exist here, or in the neighbourhood, or have, in a few instances, lately disappeared, are found in the registers from 1558 to 1717. The earliest are: Pearson, Austwicke, Heptonstall, Simson, Wormald, Becket, Roberts, Newell, Broadlaye, Huntingden, Briggs, Scolaye (now Scholey), Roades, Hepworth, Horncastle, Grenfield 1579, Heaton, Shillito, Fernlaye, Brears, Tompson, Thacker, Warde, Rishworth, Newsam, Jackson, Lightfoote, Howitt 1618, Turner, Beamond, Collett, Patrick 1641, Ryder after 1652, Warde, Sayll, Battye, Crossley

* Probably a small building in connection with London.

about 1710, Spink, Wrath, Nelstrope, Towning after 1726, Birkett, Haggar, Wofendale, Townend, Hollins, Hattersall, Duffins. Marriages in 1654 (only) took place before "Jo Warde" and "John Ramsden." The following is a descriptive list of the Parish Registers, extracted from the Parochial Magazine of December, 1859, and brought down to the present time.

The Registers of this Parish consist of 15 volumes up to the present time.

VOL I.

Vol. 1 is a parchment book, interleaved with paper. It would appear to consist of two parts, and, considering its antiquity, is in excellent repair. The writing is, however, in some instances, nearly illegible. Dr. Timothy Lee, who was instituted to the Rectory of Ackworth in 1744, employed an expert in writing to copy each page. That copy is interleaved with the original. The volume is bound in calf with brass clasps.

The 1st part is from 1558 to 1648.
The 2nd part „ 1648 to 1687.
The first Baptism is February 10th, 1558.
„ „ Marriage „ October, 1558.
„ „ Burial „ January 8th, 1561.
The last Baptism „ May 5th, 1686.
„ „ Marriage „ January 5th, 1686.
„ „ Burial „ March 20th, 1685.

On the first page of parchment is this entry, "Thomas Hartyndon, Rector, presented to this living by Queen Mary, April, 1554."

Amongst the Baptisms for 1558 and 1559, are to be found the still familiar names of "Austwicke" and "Heptinstall."

In this volume are many entries worth transcribing. We can only find space, however, for the following: "Richard Pickeringe and Ffrances Ledsome, Married June 25th, 1645, in which year there dyed of the Plague in Ackworth, 153 persons—Richard Pickeringe being then Constable."

"Baptismes 1663."

"Charles the Sonne of Mr. Danyell Godfrey, By Barberry the Daughter of Dr. Thomas Bradley, Rector of Ackworth, Chaplayne to His Majesty King Charles the First, and Prebendary of Yorke, and the Lady Ffrances his wife, daughter to the Right Honourable John Lord Saville, Baron of Pontefract, &c., was baptized the 24th of November, Anno 1663: being the first that was baptized in the ffont newly sett up after the antient ffont was destroyed and broken downe in the late Civill Warrs. On Candlemas Day imediatly followinge, was The Honourable the Lady Ffrances above-mentioned here, honourably inter'd, who died the Saturday before, being the 30th Day of January, the day wherein his late Majesty, of blessed memory, was put to death, and the very same hour (as neere as may be conjectured) wherein His Majesty suffered, did she breath her last, and returnd her Spirit unto God that gave it."

VOL. II.

Is a folio parchment Book, bound in calf, with brass clasps. Here also two volumes appear to have been bound up into one.

The first part is from 28th August, 1687 to 1732.
The second „ „ 25th March, 1732 to 1754.
In the first part the first Baptism is 28th August, 1687.
„ „ Burial „ 28th May, 1688.
„ „ Marriage „ 16th Nov. 1687.
the last Baptism „ 9th March, 1732.
In the first part „ „ Burial „ 22nd Feb., 1732.
„ „ Marriage „ 20th Dec., 1731.
In the second part the first Baptism „ 24th May, 1732.
„ „ Burial „ 21st April, 1732.
„ „ Marriage „ 10th April, 1732.
the last Baptism „ 13th Feb., 1754.
„ „ Burial „ 9th March, 1754.
„ „ Marriage „ 12th Feb., 1754.

In the beginning of this volume, it is worthy of note, that in marriages, where the woman is in the family way, the fact is recorded both in the entry of marriage and also in that of the baptism.—Thus, in 1695, " William Simpson and Grace Howitt were Marryed Nov. 21, *being with child.*" " Abraham Walker and Mary Usher were marryed Feb. the 25th, *being with child.*"

In 1696, we find this entry:—"Wm. ye Son of Wm. Simpson and Grace his wife, begotten in fornicacion, born March ye 20, baptized eodem Die."

We do not remember ever to have met with, or heard of, an instance of similar discipline.

VOL. III.

Is a bound parchment folio. It contains the entries to the end of 1788. Into this Dr. Lee (who was inducted 4th Dec. 1744) seems to have brought forward the entries from the time of his induction.

From June, 1754, the publication of banns is entered. From 24 Nov. 1754 to 6th Feb. 1759, (both inclusive,) the entries of the marriages are made in the form prescribed by 26th George II. From thence to the end of 1788, the marriages are entered agreeably to the substance of it, but not in the exact form. On the 18th March, 1753, *Births* as well as *Baptisms* begin to be registered.

VOL. IV.

A parchment folio. Bound in Calf.

Births, Baptisms, Deaths, Burials and the publication of Banns } are entered to the end of 1812.

The marriages are entered to the end of 1802.

VOL. V.

Is a paper Book, bound in Calf. It contains the entries of Marriages from 1802 to the end of 1812.

VOL. VI.

Is a parchment volume, bound in calf, with clasps. It contains the entries of Baptisms from 1812 to Dec. 21st., 1834. All the entries from 1812 are made in accordance with the Act 52nd George III, cap. 146.

VOL. VII.

Is also a parchment folio, bound in calf, with clasps. It contains the entries of Baptisms from 21st Dec., 1834, to the present time.

VOL. VIII.

Is a parchment folio, bound in calf, with clasps. It contains the entries of Burials from 1812 to 27th May, 1851.

VOL. IX.

Is a paper book, ruled agreeably to the directions of the Marriage Act of 52 George III., cap. 146. It contains the entries of Marriages from 1812 to June, 1837.

VOL. X.

Is also a paper book, bound in boards, and ruled in accordance with the Act 6th and 7th Guelelmi IV., cap. 86. It contains the entries of Marriages from June, 1837, to present time.

VOL. XI.

Duplicate of above.

VOL. XII.

Contains the Burials at Ackworth from June, 1851, to Novr., 1882. Parchment leaves. Bound in leather, with brass clasps. It records 778 Burials, but contains no title-page.

VOL. XIII.

Register of Baptisms, from June, 1868, to March, 1885. Paper leaves, bound in leather. It records 800 Baptisms, and from the year 1875 the date of birth is also generally recorded. The words, "By whom the ceremony was performed," in the last column, are altered into "By whom the Sacrament was administered."

VOL. XIV.

Register of Burials from Jan., 1883. Paper leaves, bound in leather. The word "ceremony" in the last column is altered to "service."

VOL. XV.

Register of Baptisms from March, 1885. Paper leaves, bound in vellum. Date of birth recorded, and words in last column altered as in Vol. XIII. The last four volumes are neatly and carefully kept.

The name "*Austwicke*," spelt differently, occurs one hundred times in eighty-three years; and "*Howett*," eighty-seven times in a hundred years. After these, "*Wormald*" and "*Scholey*" appear more frequently than any other name. Some very curious Christian names also occur, instance the following: "*Beersheba* Burton," baptized in 1794; and "*Sindonia* Belcher," mother of Mary, baptized in 1796. The former was meant by the parents to have been christened *Bathsheba*. "*Hephzibah* Heptinstall," baptized in 1751, only survived her baptism two months; "*Septima* Asquith," baptized in 1752; "*Gamaliel* Patrick," in 1762; "*Hezekiah* Parsons, a foundling," buried in 1762; "*Cassandra* Waller," buried in 1763; "*Magdalen Foundling*," buried from the Foundling Hospital in 1764. She is described as an "orphan," and her surname was evidently given to indicate her original condition. The son of William and Elizabeth Freeman, (the father being described as a "labourer,") was actually baptized in 1765 by the name of "*Doctor Willia!*" shall we say as a compliment to the medical man who assisted to bring him into the world? "*Debora* Blackbeard, *Lucretia* Drake, *Amor* Baker, *Bona* Crew, *Camilla* Grove, *Samuella* Sykes, *Silvester* Harrison, *Benedict* Hall," all foundlings, were buried in Ackworth Churchyard between the years 1765 and 1772. "*Epaphroditus* Hattersley," yeoman, was buried in the latter year. The Registers are well worth perusal.*

---

* The earlier portion (1558-1648) is reproduced verbatim in "*Yorkshire Notes and Queries*," Parts II.-X.

The Chantry.

There was in the Chapel of St. Mary, in Ackworth Church, before the Reformation, a Chantry of our Lady, founded by Isabel de Castleforth, value at the dissolution, £4 16s. 4d. per annum.

Mr. Torre gives the following catalogue of the Chantry Priests:—*

Temp. Inst.	Capellan.	Patrons.	Vacat.
	Willm. Eltham		Resig.
1407. 18 Aug.	Robertus Briggs, Pbr.	Tho. De Whiston, Rector Eccles. Act.	
1420. 19 July.	Tho. Handrys, Pbr.	Tho. Balne, Rector de Ackworth	
1433. 28 Aug.	Tho. Hoderode, Pbr.	Prior and Convt. of Monk Bretton	
	Tho. Pond, alias Jonet		Death.
1480. 26 May.	Tho. Reynolds, Chaplin	John Winter, Rector of Ackworth	Death.
1521. 2 Oct.	Jno. Thompson, Pbr.	Assignee of Rector of Ackworth	

This account of the Chantry will remind the reader of the field and croft adjoining, on the north, a portion of glebe called the Stone Style Acre, traversed by the footpath from Ackworth to Hessle. This piece of ground was, and is still, called the "Chantry Close," and there can be no doubt that it formed part of the endowment of the Chantry above-named. Indeed, this is almost certain, from the fact that about one hundred and forty years ago this field was the property of Sir Rowland Winn, of Nostel, in whom seems to have centered all the estates of which the Church in this neighbourhood was robbed at the Dissolution.

The Rectory.

The Church, having had the good fortune to escape being appropriated, remains a Rectory, heretofore appendant to the manor, and in the patronage of the several Lords thereof—the Laceys, and Dukes of Lancaster—but not passing in the grant to the City of London, is now become an advowson in gross

---

* Extracted from Mr. Torre's Books in the Library of the Dean and Chapter of York.

remaining to the Duchy of Lancaster, the several Chancellors, for the time being, being patrons. In Henry VIII. a payment was made in exchange with the Archbishop of York for other lands, but for all that the King presented to the living, and not the Archbishop.*

Value and taxation of Ackworth Rectory in the King's Book:—

	£	s.	d.
First Fruits	22	1	8½
Tenths	2	4	1¼
Procurations	0	7	6
Subsidies	1	18	0
Synodols	0	6	6
	4	16	1¼
	£26	17	9¾

The present value of the living, according to *Crockford*, is Glebe 152 acres, let for £258; T. R. C. £150; Consols from Glebe, £19; Gross Income, £447 and house.

Soon after the foundation of Nostel Priory, the brethren of that monastery acquired the advowson of various livings in the neighbourhood, including Ackworth, which, at the dissolution, revolved to the Crown. Many of the early Rectors of Ackworth were brethren of Nostel.†

The present Rectory was built upon the site of an older edifice, in 1842. It would seem from the relics which still remain, and which were used in the construction of the modern building, that the fittings of the old Rectory were of an elaborate and durable character, notably the carved oak mantlepiece in the dining room, and the *en suite* mouldings which surround the doors and windows. There are also two interesting bust portraits in oil of two former Rectors—the Rev. Dr. Bradley, and the Rev. Dr. Timothy Lee. They are in good condition, the latter is painted by *Killingbeck*, but by whom the former is not known.

* Vide Torre's MSS. York.
† Vide Boothroyd's Hist. Pont., p. 82.

Arms of Nostel Priory.

Annals.

The earliest mention of Ackworth to be found in ancient documents is probably that contained in the Domesday survey, to which reference has already been made. A verbatim extract of the entry will, therefore, be both interesting and valuable.

[DOMESDAY, 316, col. 2.]

In ACEVVRDE. Erdulf & Osulf habuer'. vi. car' t'ræ
II ad g'ld'. ubi poss'. e'e'. v. car'. N'c h't Hunfrid, de Ilb'to.
Ipse ibi. i. car' & dimid'. & xiiii. uill'. & ii. bord'. cu'. vi.
M, car'. Ibi eccl'a & p'b'r'. un' mold'. xvi. denarior'. T.R.E. val'
iiii. lib'. m°. iii. lib'. D.B. 107. Terr. Ilb'ti d' Lac'.

A.D. 1087.
Domesday Survey.

The following is a translation, for the benefit of those who are not versed in old documentary Latin:

"Manor in Ackworth. Erdulf & Osulf have six carucates of land to be taxed, where there might be five ploughs. Humphry now holds it of Ilbert. [Humphry] himself has there one plough and a half, and fourteen villains, and two boors. There is a Church there, and priest; one mill, of sixteen pence. Value in King Edward's time four pounds, now three pounds. Domesday Book 107. Land of Ilbert de Lacy.*

There is a local tradition that Standing Flat Bridge, the northern boundary mark between the parishes of Ackworth, Badsworth, and Pontefract, was the scene of an encounter between a fugitive soldier from the battle of Stamford Bridge, and one of the victorious Norwegian army, who had relentlessly pursued his victim up to this place. Whether, by feigning flight, the wary Saxon had purposely drawn his enemy away

1066.
Battle of Stamford Bridge.

* Vide Ackworth Manor.

A.D. 1066.   from the main body of the army, we do not know, but it is said that, having gained the bridge, he turned like a stag at bay, and, after a fierce encounter, succeeded, like the heroic Horatius,

"Who kept the bridge in the brave days of old,"

in slaying his antagonist, but only to be himself overcome and slain, after a most desperate struggle, by a body of Normans in search of fugitives. From this incident the bridge is said to have derived its name; but Boothroyd, one of the historians of Pontefract, has taken upon himself the responsibility of giving the tradition a semblance of truth, by saying that Standing Flat Bridge actually was the scene of the battle of Stamford Bridge (*Pons belli*). But, of course, he has no ground whatever for the statement, except the tradition above alluded to.

1081.
Great
Survey.

We learn from Domesday that in Saxon times there were two Manors in Ackworth, now perhaps represented by High Ackworth and Low Ackworth, but these had been united before the Conquest, when, out of 2,643 acres, the taxable area was six carucates, capable of employing five ploughs. At the time of the Great Survey, the Manor was in the hands of Ilbert de Lacy, whose tenant was one Hunfrid or Humphrey, He held 1½ carucates, that is, a quarter of the whole Manor, in his own hands, as demesne, employing 14 villains in its cultivation, while the rest of the Manor was apportioned between two borderers, or farmers, as his under-tenants, who employed six ploughs. There was a mill paying xviijd., but the township was so purely arable, that there was neither taxable meadow nor taxable wood.*

Circa.
1100.
Hundfridus.

Hundfridus (a name more familiar in the form of Humphrey) was a vassal of Ilbert de Laci, holding manors and lands in Snidal, Newton, and two in Ackworth. As "Umfredus de Villeio," we find him not long afterwards (i.e., before 1100) giving two garbs (from the harvest yearly) at the first two places, towards the endowment of the Chapel of St. Clement, in Pontefract

* Vide Arch. and Top. Journal, Part XXXVIII., p. 256.

ITS HISTORY AND ANNALS. 43

Castle,* founded by Ilbert de Lacy. He must have come from one of the places called Villy, in the department of Calvados, in which Lassy also is situated.†   A.D. 1100.

Osulf (a contemporary of Hundfridus), who held a manor in (High) Hoyland, and now holds it of Ilbert de Laci, was perhaps, the same Osulf, whose manors in Methley and Ackworth, Ilbert also had, but retained in his own hands. To Roger de Busli were given the lands of Osul(f), in Barnborough, Bolton-upon-Dearne, and other places near Doncaster.‡   Osulf.

Ex Rotulo pl'itar in dorso ter Pascha, II. John Roll 7.   1209.

EE. 20. [Vol. 124.] Between Roger Constable, of Chester, plf. & Guilbert de Aquila & Isabell his wife, of one Kts. fee in the wood of Roinhay (Roundhay). Isabella disponsata fuit in Hoiland in alio Com. Robto. de Lascy filio Henrico de Lascy quem p. fuit dos huius Isabellæ het in dotem in Warmefield, Croston (Crofton) in *Akeworth* & in Roindhay quo Robtus habuit.§

About this time a Charter was granted to Margaret, Countess of Lincoln, free warren in the demsne lands of Wrangle, Riby, Scarthro, Wayth, in Lincolnshire; Bradenham, in Norfolk; Halton, Thoresby, Sedgebrook, in Lincoln; Kneesall, in Notts.; Beaghall, *Ackworth*, Cridling Stubbs, and Warmfield, in Yorkshire.   1216-72. A Charter.

"Henry de Akeworth, clerk, who had a pension of xls. (in the name of the parson) from the Ch. of Akeworth, being dead, at the presentation of the King, as guardian of the land and   1226. Institution.

---

* Vide Old Mon., Vol. I., p. 160.
† For Yorkshire Tenants named in Domesday Book, see Ellis's " Biographical Notes."
‡ Vide Ellis's " Biographical Notes."
§ "This is," says Mr. Holmes, "an exceedingly important deed. The childless widow of Robert de Lacy, by her marriage with Gilbert de Aquila, became the mother of a daughter, Alice, who ultimately became the first wife of John the Constable, son of the present plaintiff." *Vide Arch & Top. Journal. Part XXXVIII, page 256, foot-note.*

A.D. 1226.   heir of the late Earl of Lincoln, we institute Th. de Noketon, clerk, to it.*

1294.   *Pl'ita de quo warranto, A° 22 E. 1, ter Pascha.*

D.D. 50. [Vol. 122.]   For free warren in Rockesden (als Ridlesden) Keswicke, *Ackworth* & Hagenworth, comonly Haworth, in the County of York.†

1301. Presentation.   *Out of the Register of Thos: Corbrigg, Archbp. of Y.*

B [Vol. 28] 37. 29. E. 1.   Henry de Lascy, E. of Lincolne, p'sents to the Church of *Ackworth.*‡

1310. Reversion of Ackworth.   Fourth, Edward II., Henry de Lacy, Baron of Pontefract, Earl of Lincoln, etc., died seized of this manor, with the advowson of the Church there.§ Upon the death of Henry de Lacy, Ackworth, as part of the Barony of Pontefract, passed, with other great estates and honours, by the marriage of Alice, his only daughter and heiress, to Thomas (son of Edmund Crouchback, brother of Edward I.), Earl of Lancaster.

1315.   Thomas, Earl of Lancaster, was returned as Lord of the Manor of Ackworth, in the ninth year of Edward II.

1318. A fine.   Twelfth, Edward II. There was a fine levied to the manor of Monk Bretton of a mess; and sixty acres of land at Ackworth.

1321.   In 1321, Thomas, Earl of Lancaster, took up arms against his cousin, Edward II., and was defeated at Boroughbridge, in the fifteenth year of Edward the Second, brought back to his Castle of Pontefract, tried, condemned, and beheaded there, and his estate (including the Manor of Ackworth) seized into the King's hands as forfeited.

1323.   Sixteenth Edward II. Joan, widow of Henry de Lacy, released to the King her rights in this manor (of Ackworth) and the park there.

---

* Vide Abp. Gray's Register, 1215-55, and Surtees Soc., 1470, col. 56.
† Vide Dodsworth's MSS.
‡ Vide Dodsworth's MSS., and Harl MS., 800.
§ Vide Inquis. post mortem.

ITS HISTORY AND ANNALS.

At the Revolution, Henry (brother of Thomas), Duke of Lancaster, recovered all his estates. These passed again, by the marriage of Maud, heiress general of the first family of Lancasters, to John of Gaunt, third son of Edward III., and founder of the second family of Lancasters, and created by his father Duke of Lancaster.   A.D. 1327.

Out of Melton's Register, fo. 197.   1333.

B [Vol. 28] 95. Phillippa the Queen p'sentes to the Church of
7. E. 3.   Ackworth. 1333.*

Poll Tax, 2 Ric. II. At this date there was a taxable population in Ackworth of 83, of whom 77 paid fourpence, and 6 paid sixpence. These last were 3 tailours, 2 wrights, and 1 smith. The remainder were *villains* (labourers) and *borderers* (farmers).†   1379.

Wappentagium de Osgodcrosse.   Villate de Ackeworth.

		Poll Tax Returns.
Richard Brande and Matilda his wife, Taylour	...	vj.d.
Johanna his daughter	...	iiij.d.
Robert del Hill and Isabella his wife, Smyth ...	...	vj.d.
John Horner and Johanna his wife, Taylour ...	...	—
Wm. Carter and Magota his wife, Wright	...	—
Edmund Amyas and Isabella his wife, Taylour ...	...	—
Rich. de Thornehill and Johanna his wife, Wright	...	—
John Nurre and Agnes	...	iiij.d.
Robt. del More and Cecilia ...	...	—
John Paileben (?) and Agnes ...	...	—
Johanna his daughter ...	...	—
John de Wollay	...	—
Robert Cooke	...	—
John Faythe and Alicia	...	—
John his son	...	—
Thos. Maundrell and Elenor	...	—
John his servant	...	—

* Vide Dodsworth's Yorkshire Notes, and Harl MS.
† Vide Poll Tax Returns.

A.D. 1379.	John Bakester and Johanna	vj.d.
	Adam Raynald and Magota	—
	John Rylle and Avicia	—
	John Johnson and Agnes	—
	John Couper and Elenor	—
	Peter Gange and Avicia	—
	Robert atte Hole and Alicia	—
	Wm. Raynald and Johanna ... ...· ...	—
	Matilda their servant	—
	Adam Darkyn and Alicia	—
	John Waleys and Johanna	—
	Thos. Harman and Agnes ... .: ...	—
	Thos. Shephird and Johanna	—
	Henry Crofton and Magaret	—
	Wm. Taylour and Matilda	—
	Robt. Shephird and Katherine	—
	John Marre and Constance	—
	John Shephird and Alicia	—
	Thos. Carter and Magota	—
	Wm. Waleys and Alicia	—
	Robt. Smyth and Johanna	—
	John de Wodhous and Alicia	—
	John Smyth and Johanna	—
	Adam Whytchead and Clara	—
	Hugo de Fetherstan and Emma	—
	John Long and Johanna	—
	Rich. de Fenton and Emma	—
	John Wryght and Alicia *	—

John de Acworthe, mercer, and Idonia his wife paid the tax of vj.d., in the ville of Wakefield and Wapentake of Agbrigg.

1399.   Henry, the son of John of Gaunt, coming to the Crown, on the deposition of Richard II., brought Ackworth in the honour of Pontefract, and other great estates into it, as parcel of the

* See " Yorkshire Archæolog. Journal." Part XXI., p. 36.

Duchy of Lancaster, in which it continued until the time of James I. *A.D. 1399.*

Henry Forrester had the manor of "Hesill," near Ackworth and Pontefract, to him and the heirs male of his body, the remainder belonging to the King, which manor first came to the hands of the King after the death of Edmond de Flockton.* *1402. Manor of Hessle.*

Twenty-fourth Henry VI. John Swillington, of Swillington, Esqr., devised lands at Ackworth (inter alia) to trustees, to the use of Jennet, his wife, for life, with a remainder in fee to Margery, his sister, wife of Henry Hunt, of Carlton, near Rothwell. *1446.*

Wapentake of Agbrigg. In the writing of Richard Beaumont, of Whitley, Knt. and Bart., 20 Aug. 1629. John Hopton, of Armley, Esq., gave to Wm. Scargill, of Thorp; Roger Hopton,† of Ackworth; John Scargill, of Roche, Esq.; and William Talbot, his chaplain; his messuage of Gawkethorp in Sefton, in the parish of Heton, with Stages and Arkilcroft, together with 2s. rent going out of one messuage called Nickhouse, in Mirefielde, etc. Witness, Sir John Savile, Knt., etc. Dated at Armley, nr. Leeds 27th May, 16th Edw. IV., 1477.‡ *1477. Deed of Gift.*

Fourth Henry VII. In this year there was a great insurrection in this County, occasioned by a large subsidy then granted by Parliament for carrying on the war with France. This tax the people said they neither could nor would pay. The Earl of Northumberland, then Lord Lieutenant, enforcing the payment of it in a harsh manner, they attacked him in his house at Cocklege (?), near Thirsk, and killed him. Upon this, Thomas Howard, Earl of Surrey, was sent down with forces to subdue them, which he did, and caused Jon. à Chambre, and others, to be hanged. But it seems that this did not wholly end the disturbance, for, the next year, the insurgents gathered *1488. Battle at Ackworth.*

* Vide Dodsworth's Yorkshire MSS., in the Duchy Office; 4th Henry IV.
† Buried in Ackworth Church. Vide p. 22.
‡ Vide Dodsworth's Yorkshire MSS.

A.D. 1488. together again in the western parts of the County. The Earl of Surrey marched against them a second time, fought, and subdued them at Ackworth, took and hanged their leaders, obtaining the King's mercy for the rest, which greatly endeared him to them.

1510. Second Henry VIII. Roger Ward died, seized (inter alia) of a messuage and eight oxgangs of land at Ackworth, held of the King as of his Castle of Pontefract, and Roger Ward, his son, heir.

1532. Fines were very generally used in former days as a means of transferring property, and from the many details which they give, both of genealogy and topography, and from the long period which they cover, they may be well said to be among the most valuable of all the public records. The plaintiff was the new possessor, and the deforciant the old one.

Twenty-fourth Henry VIII. Easter Term. John Rawson, Plaintiff, John Segutpole and Ann his wife, deforciants, for land in Ackworth, called Burnell Houses.*

1536. "Pilgrimage of Grace." It is generally supposed that the rebel forces, headed by Robert Aske, styling themselves "The Pilgrimage of Grace," passed through Ackworth on their way to Pontefract, the Castle of which they afterwards captured. Several inhabitants of the village were compelled to join the expedition, "as they would answer for it at the day of judgment." The insurgents were subsequently defeated, and the instigators executed, notably, Nicholas Tempest, of Ackworth.†

1545. Yorkshire Fine. 1545, Easter Term. 37 Henry VIII. The King, plaintiff; and Robert, Archbishop of York, deforciant, for the Church of Ackworth, in Ackworthe, etc.‡

* Vide Yorkshire Records, Vol. II., p. 241.
† Vide Cassell's Hist. Eng., pp. 236-7.
‡ Vide Yorkshire Records, Vol. II.

The Priory of St. Oswald, at Nostel, founded by Robert de Laci, son of Ilbert de Laci, first Norman Lord of the Castle and honour of Pontefract, surrendered to Dr. Thos. Leigh and others, the Royal Sequestration Commissioners, by Robert Ferrar, the last Prior, who afterwards became Bishop of St. David's, and was burned at the stake at Carmarthen, in 1555.

<small>A.D. 1540. Nostel Priory.*</small>

Archbishop Holgate's Grammar School, at Hemsworth, was founded by Robert Holgate, 59th Archbishop of York. On October 24th, 1546, Letters Patent were granted to him by Henry VIII., authorising him to found three Grammar Schools, in York, Hemsworth, and Old Malton. Hemsworth is supposed to have been the Archbishop's native place. On May 24th, 1548, the Archbishop by deed poll prescribed rules and ordinances for the school at Hemsworth. He endowed it with property of the value of twenty-four pounds a year (which amount he afterwards increased), appointed John Thurleston to be first master, and reserved the patronage to himself and his successors in the see of York; providing that if the Archbishop failed to appoint within 20 days of a vacancy, the appointment should lapse to the Dean and Chapter of York, and if they failed to appoint within another 20 days, to the householders of Hemsworth with the Curate. The master was ordered to pay ten pounds a year to each of six "poore scollers," between the ages of 8 and 18; but a scholar born in the parish of Hemsworth might, if he were then fatherless, retain "ye same anuitie untill he shall be xxii. yeares of aige." These scholars were to be chosen of "poore men's childeren being husbandmen or men of occupac'ons inhabitinge in the p'ishes of Hymseworthe, Felkirke, Southekirkebye, Ackworthe, Royston, and Wragbie." Provision was made for the removal of these scholars, after two public monitions in Church, " if anye of them be not studious to learne, or be not apte to take learning, or doe not kepe the scole and lerninge there, but absent

<small>1546. Archbishp. Holgate's Grammar School, Hemsworth.</small>

---

* For detailed history of the Priory, see Paper read by Rev. R. E. Batty to Yorkshire Architectural Society, in August, 1855.

A.D. 1546. themselves by the space of one fortnighte in a quarter of a year wthout lysence of the Scolm^{r,} or be a comon drunkard, or a comon player at unlawfull games, or do use or exercise anye notable offences or crimes."

In 1861, a new scheme was made by order of the Court of Chancery. The Trustees of Archbishop Holgate's Hospital in Hemsworth were constituted Trustees of the Grammar School. A grant of £300 a year was made to the School from the Hospital, for a period of 36 years, from 1857; if, at the end of that period the school was not, in the opinion of the Trustees, in an efficient state, they might apply to the Court of Chancery for leave to discontinue the grant. The School was to be divided into an Upper and Lower School. New buildings were erected for both, and the Lower School, or Parish School, is now a Boys' Public Elementary School under Government Inspection.

In January, 1868, the New Grammar School was occupied by the Head-master (Rev. C. Andrew), and his boarders. Accommodation was provided for 20 boarders and 20 day scholars. The highest number of boys in that year was 36. Mr. Andrew died in the following year, and the Revd. S. W. Earnshaw was appointed master. In 1875, the numbers were found to have fallen off considerably, and in 1877 there were 10 boys in the School, including the free-scholars. During the negotiations for the appointment of a new Head-master (Rev. C. S. Butler), the Charity Commissioners became aware of this state of affairs, and announced their intention to make a new scheme. In July, 1878, an Assistant Commissioner met the Trustees, and made enquiries. In March, 1879, the Commissioners suggested to the Trustees that the School should be removed, but they did not fall in with the suggestion. Eventually, in 1881, they being under the impression that the Commissioners had absolute power to remove the School, gave a qualified assent to its being removed to Pontefract, under certain conditions. These conditions Pontefract failed to comply with, but Barnsley was successful in raising the required sum of money. In 1883, the Commissioners published a scheme for removing the School to Barnsley: the Trustees having taken legal opinion as to the powers of the Commissioners, and having regard to the improved state of the School, and the rapid increase of population in the neighbourhood, resolved to oppose the scheme for removal. A.D. 1546.

In 1885, there were 36 boys in the School. In 1886, the Trustees appealed to Her Majesty on certain legal points, but the decision of the Judicial Committee of the Privy Council given in March, 1887, was unfavourable to the appeal. The scheme was, on March 18th (according to the provisions of the Endowed Schools Acts), placed upon the table in the House of Lords and the House of Commons. Unless within two months of that date an address to Her Majesty is carried in either House, praying her to withhold her consent from this scheme, the scheme will receive Her Majesty's assent in due course, and the School will be removed to Barnsley as soon as practicable.*

1550. Mich. Term, 4 Edw. VI. Thos. Reynolde, Esq., plaintiff; & Wm. Halyday, gent., & Alice his wife, deforciants; for lands in Pontefract & Ackworthe.† 1550. Yorkshire Fine.

"Thomas Hartyndon, Rector, Presented to this Living by Queen Mary, Apr., 1554."‡ 1554.

1554. Mich. Term, 1 & 2 Philip & Mary. James Crofte, plaintiff, John Brayton & Agnes his wife, with Richd. & Roger Brayton, deforciants; for messuage with lands in Hessyle, Wragbye, & Ackeworthe.§ Yorkshire Fines.

Robert Ferrar, D.D., Bishop of St. David's, was born at Ewood, near Midgeley, in 1505. He was the last Prior of Nostel, and the first English monk who became tainted with Lutheran opinions. He was arrested on the most frivolous 1555. Martyrdm. of St. Robert of Nostel.

---

* I am indebted to the Rev. C. S. Butler for the above particulars. The scheme of removal has now been carried out.
† Vide Yorkshire Records, Vol. II.
‡ Vide Parish Register, Vol. I.
§ Vide Yorkshire Records. Vol. II.

A.D. 1555. charges, fifty-six in number,* and condemned by Gardiner, Bishop of Winchester, and Morgan, of St. David's, to be burnt alive on March 30, 1555. On the day appointed, the Saturday before Passion Week, he was brought out of prison to the market place, near Carmarthen Castle, and there, on the south side of the market cross, he was bound to a stake, and heroically endured the martyrdom of fire.† Monuments are erected to his memory in Carmarthen and Halifax Parish Churches, and also at St. Florence's Church, near Tenby.

1559.   The Rev. George Ackworth, D.D., Public Orator to the University of Cambridge in 1559, was most probably a native of Ackworth, near Pontefract. He was incorporated L.L.D., at Oxford, in 1568; became Rector of Ellington and Prebendary of Southwell; and was author of the "Life of St. Augustine, the first Archbishop of Canterbury," the MS. of which is in the possession of Mr. Wharton, by whom it was prepared for the press.‡

1560.
Yorkshire
Fines.

1560. Mich. Term, 2 & 3 Elizth. Margaret Wilcock, plaintiff: George Wilcocke, gent. and Elizth. his wife, deforciants; for land in Ackworthe.

Nicholas Levett, gent., plaintiff, George & Richd. Talinsall, gents., deforciants, for two messuages with lands in Hutton, Morehouse, Ackworth and Auston.§

1561.
Edward
Rustbie.

In the first volume of the Ackworth Parish Registers, the following entry appears under the head of marriages celebrated at the Parish Church, in 1561.||

"Edwarde Rustbie and Grace Alline (?)
Julie 5."

This refers without doubt to the marriage of Edward Rusby, who was Mayor of Pontefract in 1582.¶ It is most likely that

---

* Vide Harleian MSS. Brit. Mus.   † For full account of him, see Biographical Sketch by J. W. Conway Hughes, 1884.
‡ Vide Tanner's "Bibliography," p. 3; and Wilson's Historical MS.
§ Vide Yorkshire Records, Vol. II.
|| Vide "Yorkshire Parish Registers," in "Yorkshire Archæological Journal," Part VI., p. 109.
¶ Vide Civic Roll.

he was, both before and after his marriage, an influential resident of Ackworth. He certainly resided at Hundhill in 1570. In the Subsidy Roll for Pontefract, in 1543, his name occurs as "*Edwardus Rusbye*," and two years later (1545) as "*Edwardus Rusby* in terr. *xxijs .. ijd.*" Later on we find him being dispossessed of land. "Fine. Hilary, 6 Eliz: (1563). Jonathan Grant Guest, & Edward Rustbie & Grace uxor deforct. of 4 acres of land in Balne," and in 1570 we find him acquiring land by Royal Patent. "13 Eliz. (1570) one acre in Hundall in the parish of Ackworth in tenure of Edwd. Rusby." Thus we have a short, but very interesting family history, capable of considerable expansion by those who are fond of genealogical research. There can be no doubt that Edward Rustbie was a man whom the people of Pontefract delighted to honour, and of whom the people of Ackworth ought to be justly proud.

A.D. 1561.

1562. Mich. Term, 4 & 5 Elizth. John Kaye de Okenshawe, gent., plaintiff, Robert Bradford, deforciant, for Manor of Preston Jaclyn, & five messuages and four cottages with lands in the same, & in Ayeton, Fetherstone, Ackworthe, Warmfield, Heathe, and Kyrkethorpe.*

1562. Yorkshire Fines.

1563. Easter Term, 5 Elizth. Richard Thorpe, plaintiff, Wm. Wentworth, Edwd. Clytherawe, gent., & Thos. Wentworth, Esq., deforciants, for land in Burnel houses & Akeworth. Wm. Broke, plaintiff; & Robert Walker, deforciant, for messuage and three cottages with lands in Pontfrett, Preston Jacklyn, Derryngton, Feytherstone, Ackeworth, Carleton, Hardwyke, & Hundell.*

1563.

1564. Hilary Term, 6 Elizth. Thos. Smythe, plaintiff, Henry Wyathbothame, & Johanna his wife, deforciants, for a messuage with lands in Wragby & Ackworth.*

1564.

Ralph Snaith, by his will dated sixth Elizabeth, leaves to the Church of Ackworth a vestment that wants an alb, and vjs. viijd. to buy an alb with.†

* Vide Yorkshire Records, Vol. II.
† Vide Test Ebor III. 45.

A.D. 1566. Yorkshire Fines.	1566. Easter Term, 8 Elizth. Edwd. Wright, plaintiff, and Henry Halley, gent., deforciant, for a messuage with lands in Baddysworth, & Ackworth.*
1568.	1568. Easter Term, 10 Elizth. Edwd. Wright, plaintiff, Chas. Jackson, gent., & Dorothy his wife, deforciants; for two messuages & a cottage with lands in East Hardwycke, Pontefrett, Tanshelff, Carleton, Hundell, & Acworthe.*
1578.	" Barnab. Shepheard, Rector; presented to this Living by Abp. York, Jany. 1578."†
1585.	"Simon Buck, Rector; Abp. York, Patron, January 1585."†
1589.	Thirty-first Elizabeth. Thomas Wentworth, Esq., was found to hold divers lands and tenements here, of the Queen, as of her honour of Pontefract, for military service. James Wilcocks was found to hold three pasture closes here, called Burnell Houses, of the Queen, for service unknown.
1594.	"Will: Lamb, Rectr: presented to this Living by Queen Eliz. in January 1594."†
1599.	Henry Huntingdon and Ann Smithson, both of Ackworth, were married in the Parish Church of Ackworth.‡
1600.	Roger, son of Richard Pickering, of Ackworth, was married to Grace Midgley, of Addle, at the Parish Church of Addle. Also, Richard Ransley, of Wakefield, to Mary Parkhurst, of Ackworth, in the Parish Church of Ackworth.‡
1603. Ackworth Mortgaged	About this time, Ackworth, together with the greater part of the Honour of Pontefract, was mortgaged to the City of London.
1611. East Hardwick Manor House.	This building was renovated in 1846, at which time the original stone lintel over the front entrance, bearing date 1611, was removed. The house is now used as a ladies' school.

* Vide Yorkshire Records, Vol. II.
† Vide Parish Register, Vol. I.
‡ Vide Paver's Marriage Licenses.

Aggbrigg Wapentake, 17th James. Out of Queen Anne's joynture, the King granted   *   *   all our Manor of Pontefract, in the County of Yorke, and other Counties wheresoever that Honor extendeth, and all the demesnes, castles, manors, &c., being part of the said Honor of Pontefract, or to the said Honor of Pontefract any way belonging, with the appurtenances in the said County of Yorke, viz., all those our towns of Pontefract, and all those our manors of Tanshelfe, Carleton, *Ackworth*, Allerton, Altofts, Kipax, Warnefield, Barwicke, Scoles, Roundhay, Elmershall, Camsall Ouston, Knottingley, Credling, Beghall, Rothwell, Leedes, Marshden, and Almonbury, &c. Dated at Westminster, 11th Oct., 17th James.*

A.D. 1619.

On June 14th in this year, Ackworth was granted outright to Ditchfield, Highlord, and others, their trustees or committees, under the reservation of an annual fee farm rent of £39 2s. 2d.

1627.

On February 24th, 1628, Ditchfield, and other original grantees, assigned the Manor of Ackworth, in the honour of Pontefract, to Mark Pickering, of York, Robert Claphamson, of York, and John Redman, of Water Fulford.

1628.

"Dan: Fawkner, M.A., presented by K. Charles ye first ye 14 Aprill 1634; and ye 25th of September following he was succeeded by Samuel Carter, M.A., being presented thereto by K. Charles ye 1st."†

1634.

Hessle is a hamlet of a dozen houses, lying at the extreme north of the parish of Wragby, and within its ecclesiastical boundary. It is evident that this northern boundary between the parishes of Wragby and Ackworth is the ancient one defined by the Domesday Survey, and confirmed in later years by the Ecclesiastical Commissioners, on the recommendation of H. M. Ordnance Surveyors in 1859. A delimitation is, however, necessary, whereby the hamlet of Hessle would come within

1641.
Old house.

* Vide Dodsworth's Yorkshire MS., and Yorkshire Arch. Journal, Part XXIII, p. 426.
† Vide Parish Register, Vol. I.

A.D. 1641. the boundaries of the parish of Ackworth, and the village of Brackenhill within the parish of Wragby. In the 17th century, Hessle would probably be a village of some forty or fifty houses, boasting of its squire's residence in the midst. This edifice still exists, and is undoubtedly the only remnant of the 17th century village. It is in the Elizabethan style of architecture, and is still known as "*Hessle Hall.*" Over the front entrance may be seen the figures and letters, 1641, S.P. The house was either built, or passed very soon after its erection, into the hands of the Winns, of Nostel, in whose possession it has since remained. The old Hall at Ackworth was most probably built about the same time.

1642.
Loyal Clergy.
When Charles I. was deserted by nearly all the kingdom, the castle of Pontefract remained faithful, and was garrisoned by the nobility and gentry of the town and adjoining villages, amongst which Ackworth is conspicuous. Their names are handed down to us in a MS. of the Rev. Dr. Samuel Drake, at that time Rector of Hemsworth and Vicar of Pontefract. These gentlemen volunteers were enlisted into four divisions, commanded by (1) Col. Grey, (2) Sir Richard Hutton, (3) Sir John Ramsden, (4) Sir G. Wentworth; the whole being manœuvred by Colonel Lowther. Among the volunteers in Sir John Ramsden's division we find Mr. Pickering, the parson of Ackworth, and father of Mr. Alderman Pickering, of Leeds, acting probably as one of the chaplains of the division; and in Sir G. Wentworth's division we find the Rev. Thos. Bradley, D.D., parson of Ackworth and Castleford, who warmly espoused the cause of royalty. He lived a long time after the restoration.*

1643. "Thos. Bradley, Rector. His Patron K. Charles 1st. He died & was buried at Ackw. Decr. 17th, 1672."†

1645.
Civil Wars
In or about this year, there was a severe skirmish between

---

* Fox's Hist. Pont., p. 173.
† Vide Parish Register, Vol. I.

the royalists and roundheads, at the top of the large field crossed by the footpath from Ackworth to Hundhill. This pasture is still called "Burial Field," because, as some think, those who fell in the battle were buried on the spot.

A.D. 1645.

The following entry occurs in one of the Parish Books:—
"In the year 1645 there died of the plague in Ackworth 153 persons, Richard Pickering being then Constable. 30, May." The Plague Stone, on Castle Syke Hill, dates from this period. Food for the inhabitants of Ackworth, who were not allowed to travel beyond the precincts of their own parish, was brought by their neighbours and placed on the stone above-named in return for their value in money, previously placed in a cavity full of water, to prevent infection. Those who died during this plague were buried, some say, in the "Burial Field," which is very likely, especially as it was already strewn with the bodies of the slain."

The Plague. Plague Stone.

On St. Bartholomew's Day, August 24th, 1645, the Rump remaining of the Parliament passed an ordinance, subjecting to a year's imprisonment those who should dare to use the Book of Common Prayer, even in a private house, or at family prayers. They had just martyred the Archbishop of Canterbury on a public scaffold, and proceeded to turn eight thousand Church of England Clergy out of their homes, consigning them to beggary and ruin. Those treated most leniently were told to get a pension from their Puritan successors, if they could. Dr. Bradley, Rector of Ackworth, was one of these unfortunate eight thousand.*

Puritan intolerance.

On the 9th October, the Parliamentary troops, under Sir H. Cholmley, entered Pontefract, having previously occupied the villages of Ackworth, Featherstone, and Ferrybridge.†

1648. Ackworth a military rendezvous.

Cawood's Old Chapel is supposed to have been built about this time. An entry in the Pontefract Church Books states

1653. EastHardwick old Chapel.

---

* Vide "Walker's Sufferings of the Clergy."
† Fox's Hist. Pont., p. 246.

A.D. 1653. that on February 19th, 1653-4, "Stephen Cawood, of East Hardwicke, within this parish, yeoman, departed this life, and his corps was interred in his owne ground in East Hardwicke, aforesaid, the twentieth day of the same moneth." This Stephen Cawood had in the previous month executed a deed of gift, vesting his property, after his decease, in trustees, for the erection and endowment of a Chapel and Free School in East Hardwick, a dole to the poor there, and a contribution of an equal amount towards the repair of a road in Ackworth. The latter place as well as East Hardwick is benefitted by this Charity, and by the Foundation Deed, the Free School is open alike to children of the two townships. From the fact that Stephen Cawood is said to have been buried "in his owne ground," it is evident that the Chapel was not then built, but it is probable that its erection took place as soon as the necessary arrangements could be made, for the building bears evident signs of the Cromwellian decade. Thirteen years after Mr. Cawood's death the building certainly existed, for in 1667, the Pontefract Church Books contain another entry, recording that on "Oct. 26th, Mr. Lawrence Addam was buried in ye Church of East Hardwick." There is unfortunately no record of its Consecration or Dedication, but from the fact that at the time of Stephen Cawood's death the See of York had been vacant nearly four years, and that the vacancy was not filled up until 1660, it is probable that the Chapel erected in the interval was never consecrated at all. About the year 1845, efforts were made to obtain Consecration for the building, but Archbishop Musgrave saw some impassable barrier to it, and no further attempts were afterwards made. A description of the building will be found in a pamphlet published in 1871, from which the above particulars have been obtained.

1654. According to an entry in the Parish Registers, marriages in in 1654 (only) took place before "Jo. Warde" and "John Ramsden," who would probably be Royal Commissioners appointed for the purpose, or Justices of the Peace.

This large house known as East Hardwicke Hall was built about the middle of the 17th century. Its style and the "banker-marks" on the surface of the ashlar both inside and outside of the building are sufficient evidence of its antiquity. It was formerly the seat of W. Lambe, Esq., whose monument may be seen inside Pontefract Parish Church. In his time four powdered servants were kept, and it is said that one of them, a footman, was accidentally killed by falling down stairs.

A.D. 1660.
East Hardwick Hall.

On Brackenhill common there stands a small house which was formerly a lodge at the southern end of Nostel Park. It is an interesting structure, and dates probably from the 17th century. Its exterior walls are about two feet thick, the small lancet-shaped windows being deeply pierced. Access to the upper story was originally obtained by means of a trap door and ladder. The rafters are of old oak, and the general arrangement of the interior indicates an ancient origin. At the south end of the house, is an old pear tree, which has long since ceased to bear. The old coach road from Doncaster to Wakefield may still be traced, and altogether the site is one which, as an ancient land-mark, is worth observation.

circa 1660.

Barnsley, xvi. January, Anno xiiii. Caroli Regis. Present: Sir Francis Wortley, Knt. & Bart., Sir Geo. Wentworth, Knt., William West, Robt. Rockley, and Thos. Jobson, Esquires.

1662.
A fire.

On certificate that Thomas Cliffe, of *Ackworth*, being a man of honest life and conversation, and painful in his vocation and calling, by a sudden, vehement, and fearful fire, happening in one Anthony Birlison his neighbour's house, adjoining upon the said Thomas Cliffe his dwelling-house, upon Wednesday, the nineteenth day of December last past, about nine o'clock in the forenoon of the said day, the said house was suddenly burnt, three kyne of good value, corn threshed and unthreshed, and all other his household goods to the value of three score pounds and upwards; and the said Anthony Birlison, and likewise all his goods and household stuff burned. The Court

A.D. 1662. desires ministers and curates in the Wapentake of Osgoldcross to read, order, and make a collection towards relief. Mary Blagburne, widow, owner of the houses, to have some allowance out of the moneys collected, as Sir Thos. Wentworth and Sir Edw. Rodes, or either of them, shall think fitting, towards the re-building of the said houses.*

1663. "Charles, the sonne of Mr. Danyell Godfrey, By Barberry the daughter of Doctor Thomas Bradley (Rector of Ackworth, Chaplayne to his Maty. King Charles the first, and prebendary of Yorke) and the Lady Ffrances his wife, daughter to the right Honble. John Lord Savile, Bar of Pontefract, &c., was baptized the 24th November, Anno: 1663: beinge the first that was baptized in the ffont newly sett up after the antient ffont was destroyed, and broken downe in the late civill warrs; On Candlemas day imediatly followinge was the Honble. the Lady Ffrancis afour mentioned here Honourably inter'd, who dyed the Satturday before beinge the 30th day of January, the day wherein his late Maty. of blessed memory was put to deathe and the very same houre (as neere as may be conjectured) wherein his Maty. suffered, did she breathe her last, and returned her spirit unto God that gave it."†

1664. "This Doctor Bradley being instituted and inducted into this Ackworth, Anno 1643, was driven hence by the troublesome tymes caused by the Civill Warrs 1664 (margin—suppose this 1664 should be 1644) and so remayned till this yeare, and at the Kings returne he returned to his liveinge agayne, beinge one of the Chaplaynes to the Kings Majtye."†

1665. An appeal was made on behalf of the sufferers to the clemency of Cromwell, who was then firmly established in the Protectorship, and had just issued his famous but most inhuman Declaration, depriving them of all possible means of obtaining a livelihood. This appeal stated that "above half of the

---

* Vide West Riding Session Rolls.
† Vide Parish Register, Vol. I.

Ministers and Scholars of England and Wales had been, upon one account or other, sequestered from their livings, besides fellowships and free schools;" and that many others also had been wholly deprived of their prebendaries, deaneries, bishoprics, and highest dignities in the Church; in all amounting to at least six or seven thousand persons. Truly it was a fearful spoliation. A more grinding and intolerable tyranny than that of the Puritans was never set up. They stifled freedom of thought, waged war upon opinion, persecuted conscience, confiscated private property, and rigorously abolished all amusements. *A.D. 1665.*

30 May : 1673. Jeremiah Bolton, M.A., was presented by K. Char : 2d.* *1673.*

In the house occupied by James Findlay, Esq., of High Ackworth, there is a very handsomely carved oaken bedstead, very massive and evidently very antique. The oak is nearly black, and the date on the footboard is 1674. The canopy, which is elegantly carved, is attached to four disconnected massive posts, on the foot of which is carved the coat of arms of the Butler family. The whole piece is well worth the inspection of the antiquarian. It belongs to the family of the late John Hepworth. *1674. An old bedstead.*

The most ancient existing house in Ackworth next to the Old Hall (circa 1641), is the building now known as the "Mason's Arms" Inn. The following inscription may still be seen upon the lintel of the front door: *1682. Old house.*

I. A.
1682.

The letters I. A. are supposed to stand for "John Askew," who it is said, opened out the first stone-quarry in the parish of Ackworth. The "Boot and Shoe" Inn and posting house is also of considerable antiquity.

* Vide Parish Register, Vol. I.

A.D. 1694.   "In 1694, Jordan Tancred was presented to ye Living by ye Duke of Leeds, Chancellr. of ye Duchy of Lancaster."*

1695.   "In 1695, Benj. Rentmore, M.A., was presented by D. of Lancaster."

"Wm. Simson & Grace Howitt marryed Nov. 21, beinge with child."

"Abraham Walker & Mary Usher marryed feb. (?) ye 25th, being with child."*

1696.   "Elizabeth the Daughter of Benjamin Wrentmore, D.D., & Rector of Ackworth, and Elizabeth his wife borne March the first on a monday morning about ten of the clocke and baptized March the 14th, 169$\frac{6}{7}$."†

1698. Curious document.   "Aprill ye 10th, 1698. Whereas Thomas Howitt, late of Ackworth, deced. did (upon leave given him by William Lambe, Esq., late owner of the Mannour House and demeasnes of Ackworth aforesaid) erect and build one seat or pew in ye north quire in Ackworth Church, ye said quire belonging then to ye said William Lambe, and since then sold with ye aforesaid Manner house and demesnes to Robert Lowther of Ackworth aforesaid, Esq., which said seat or pew is yet standing, and continued in ye said quire. And whereas Robert Mason of Ackworth aforesaid, having bought an estate in Ackworth aforesaid and living in ye said parish is desirous to have loan of ye said Mr. Robert Lowther for himself and family to sitt in ye said seat or pew soe built in ye north quire of ye said Church on Sundays and other dayes of divine service. Ys is therefore entered in ys booke as a memorandum betwixt ye said Robert Lowther and Robert Mason that ye said Robert Lowther doth give ye said Robert Mason and his family leave to sitt in ye said pew or seat aforesaid during ye pleasure of him ye said Robert Lowther, and ye said Robert Mason doth hereby

* Vide Parish Register, Vol. II.
† Vide Register of Baptisms, Vol. II.

acknowledge that he hath not or claims to have any right in ye said seat or pew but only to sitt there by ye leave of ye said Robert Lowther and not otherwise. In witness whereof ye said Robert Lowther & Robert Mason have sett their hands to ys memorand. and agreement in ye presence of ye witnesses following.

 Witnesses.
B. Wrentmore, Rector.   Robert Lowther.
Edm: Abbott.   Robert Mason.*

1698.

"In 1700 Ph. Hollings, M.A., was presented by Ld. Gower."*

1700.

"Epaphroditus, ye sonn of John Hattersall & Prudence his wife was baptiz'd Novr. 2d."†

1703.

"In June, 1705, "Thomas," a child brought to the parish in the night, baptized."‡

1705.

There is in Low Ackworth, at the bottom of Lea Lane, a square enclosure surrounded by a high wall, which has been used for nearly two hundred years by the Society of Friends as their place of interment. Inside, the smoothly cut sward, the parallel rows of small uniform slabs, and the neatly trimmed shrubs and beds, impress the visitor with a transient desire to select it as his last resting place. On the north side of the entrance gate inside is the following inscription:—

"Philip Austwick gave for a Buriall place to the People called Quakers in 1707, 12 yards square of this ground."

And on the south:—

"228 square yards of this ground was purchased of John Bartlin, 1780."

The tomb of the original donor has been carefully preserved.

1707.
Friends' Burial Ground.

---

* Vide Parish Register, Vol. II.

† Vide Register of Baptisms, Vol. II. Another son, "Paul," was baptized on September 26th, 1705, and "Amram, their sonne," July 6, 1707.

‡ Probably a foundling. The Hospital was not then erected, but foundling cottages existed.

A.D. 1707. It is situated near the centre of the ground, and is in shape a large "table tomb," the inscription thereon being quite legible: "Here lyeth the body of Philip AVSTWICK, who died April 21, 1710."

A considerable period elapses between this and the next earliest slab, which in common with all the rest is a small square slab laid down in a slightly inclined position.

The following is an excerpt from the Register of interments. James Harrison 1828, Jane Peacock 1843, Mary Rous 1843, John Pilmor 1845, Mary Pilmor 1852, William Sykes 1857, Mary Sykes 1863, Elizabeth Sykes 1830, Rachel Sykes 1834, Richard Sykes 1825, Mary Sykes 1866, Mark Blake (a scholar)* 1841, Jane Simpson (a scholar) 1837, Mary Dumbleton 1828, Mary Heptinstall 1845, Elizabeth Armstrong 1837, Rachel Pumphrey † 1842, Thomas Pumphrey 1862, Leonard Thistlethwaite 1837, Benjamin Donbavand 1833, Caroline Smith (a scholar) 1854, Bernard Knowles 1835, Hannah Knowles 1841, Anne Cooper 1826, Joseph Donbavand 1831, Sarah Reid 1824, Joseph Donbavand Junior 1825, John Donbavand 1824, Sarah Donbavand 1824, Elizabeth Donbavand 1825, Robert Donbavand 1858, Isaac Levitt 1862, Mary Levitt 1875, Robert Whitaker ‡ 1848, James Morley 1848, Henry Beaumont Fryer 1875, William Wilson 1875, James Fisher 1871, Jane Fisher 1881, Hannah Thorchill 1847, Henry Brady 1828, Ann Linney 1862, Hannah Linney 1872, Esther Linney (infant) 1854, Elizabeth Linney 1882, George Linney 1867, Elizabeth Linney 1834, Mary Linney 1875, Leonard West 1830, Joseph Cowell 1843, George Haskhurst 1835, Joseph Johnson 1830, Jane Oakes 1824, Mary Thistlethwaite 1833, Samuel Thistlethwaite (infant) 1839, Agnes Thistlethwaite 1857, Thomas Robinson § 1878, Thomas Atkins 1847, Lydia Donbavand 1821, William Donbavand 1821, Ann

---

* From the Friends' School. No ages are inscribed upon the slabs.
† Wife of Thomas Pumphrey, the then Superintendent.
‡ Superintendent.
§ An old tomb dated 1844 was removed to make room for this interment, vide plan.

ITS HISTORY AND ANNALS.

A.D. 1707.

Ranson * 1847, Elizabeth Martha Peacock 1848, Rebecca Brown 1849, Elizabeth Briggs 1879, Ann Marshall 1854, George Dawson Peacock 1848, Michael Pilmor 1828, Elizabeth Pilmor 1829, Lydia Burley (a scholar) 1845, Jane Bennell (a scholar) 1845, Sarah Adlington (a scholar) 1842, Henry Snowdon 1842, Sarah Ann Watson 1834, Eleanor Dickenson (a scholar) 1839, Joseph Benson 1831, 3 infants of James Wood—James 1831, George 1831, Thomas 1833; Margaret Binns (a scholar) 1830, Richard Weatherall (a scholar) 1831, Mary Hannah Drewitt (a scholar) 1828, Mary Clemesha (a scholar) 1828, Mary Baynes (a scholar) 1828, Hannah Farrer (a scholar) 1828, Charles Hustler (a scholar) 1824, Mary Ianson (a scholar) 1825, Occupied, name not known, Occupied, name not known, James Ianson (a scholar) 1866, Thomas Thistlethwaite 1879, Mary Thistlethwaite 1867, Mary Fryer 1886, Arthur Stacey Fletcher 1875, William Boardman (a scholar) 1848, Constance Reckitt (a scholar) 1847, Ann Newby 1847, Marianna Cooper (a child) 1846, Mennel Stickney (a scholar) 1845, Samuel Stanfield Holmes (a scholar) 1840, Alfred Bracher (a scholar) 1841, William Whalley (a scholar) 1835, Thomas Wood (a scholar) 1839, Jane Stickney (a scholar) 1831, Cuthbert Watson (a scholar) 1831, Ellen Webster (a scholar) 1829, Lucy Stevens (a scholar) 1830, Samuel Graham (infant) 1845, Richard Oddie 1835, Hannah Baker (a scholar) 1825, Joseph Gray (a scholar) 1827, Elizabeth Jacobs (a scholar) 1827, John Farden (a scholar) 1824, Thompson Pumphrey (a scholar) 1823, Richard Shipley Dix (a scholar) 1823, Joseph Thompson (a scholar) 1822, Isabella Brown (a scholar) 1822, Arthur Sketton (a scholar) 1876, Mary F. Jackson (a scholar) 1877, Samuel Satterthwaite 1865, William Marsland 1850, Mary Doubleday 1854, Eliza Gulielma Taylor (a scholar) 1859, Arthur L. Harrison (a scholar) 1863, James Chapman (a scholar) 1863, Emily Brightwen (a scholar) 1862, Louisa Wallis (a scholar) 1860, Lucy Pumphrey (a scholar) 1859, Charlotte Morley (a scholar) 1863, Mary Williamson 1867, Sarah Wadham 1870,

* Another old tomb, dated 1844, removed, vide Plan.

A.D. 1707. Ann West Brown (a scholar) 1877, John Newby 1877, Maria Newby 1869, Elizabeth Bennington 1857, Elizabeth Yeardley 1854, Robert Graham 1857, Mary Graham 1864, Ann J. Kaye 1875, John Walker 1877, Alfred J. Greenwood 1880, Frederick William Kitchen 1873, Harold Kitchen 1878, Martha Thornhill 1856, Joseph Wright 1858, Martha Hodgson 1859, Lydia Sparker 1860, Henry Wright 1861, Henry R. Neave 1864, Arthur L. Leicester 1871, Herbert J. Evans 1877, William Cammage 1878, William Douthwaite 1867, Ellen Pollard 1858, Sarah Pearson 1853, Joseph Storrs 1850, Isaac Briggs (an infant) 1853, Sarah Pilmor 1864, Michael Pilmor 1863, Guilelma Mason, Lucy Mason, Eliza Mason 1864, Harriet Smith 1875, Elizabeth Forth 1876, S. Radford (no date), John N. Airey 1872, Leonard A. Airey 1872, Sarah Wood 1870, James Wood 1861, Elmira Wood 1863, Jane Clemes 1850, Betsy Willis 1865, Susan Clemes 1850, Mary Hoskin (an infant) 1861. There are spaces for fifty more graves, in which a hundred and fifty persons could be interred. The ground was last enlarged in 1848, by the purchase from John Barff or Barfin of 270 square yards. The total contents of the ground is 642 square yards.

1712. A missing link. Over the door of the old vestry before the restoration of the Parish Church, a small stone slab was inserted bearing the following inscription :—

Samuel Turner
with the consent of his mother F. M.
erected this Vestry, Anno. Dni.
1712.

The above slab was removed from the ground by Mr. J. Hepworth of Ackworth House, where it may still be seen!

1721. "Anne ye Daughter of William Addy labr, July ye 9th, begotton in ffornicacion."*

1724. "Ralph Lowther, Esq. (of Ackworth Park) buried August 15th."†

* Vide Register of Baptisms, Vol. II. This crime was punishable by excommunication. Vide Canons 26, 109, Homily XI., and Article XXXIII.
† Vide Register of Burials, Vol. II.

Illegitimacy of birth, when not expressly stated in the register of baptisms in use at this time, is frequently indicated by an index finger, and occasionally by both, thus :— A.D. 1727.

☞ "Prudence (?), the *Bastard* child of Mary Nelstrope, was baptiz'd May ye 4th."*

"Margarett the wife of Phil: Hollins, Cler: Rector of this Parish was Buried March the 20th."†

Defoe, writing in 1727, in his account of the Roman Roads of Yorkshire, says: "I must go back to Pontefract, to take notice that here again the great Roman highway, which I mentioned at Doncaster, and which is visible from thence in several places on the way to Pontefract, though not in the open road, is apparent again; and from Castleford Bridge it goes on to Aberforth, a small market town famous for pin-making, and so to Tadcaster and York." This Roman road cuts across the north-eastern corner of the parish of Ackworth, near Rigg Farm, so called from *ridge* = raised, the Roman roads always being raised above the level of the surrounding country. Roman Road.

"In 1728, Will. Key, M.A., was presented to this Living by ye D. of Rutland."‡ 1728.

"John Lowther, Esqr. (of Ackworth Park) buried July ye 12."† 1729.

"The Revd. Mr. Fleeming, Vicar de Thornor, and Mrs. Martha Barman, married (at Ackworth Church) with license granted by Mr. Drake, Vicar of Pontefract."§ 1732.

New mansion built at Nostel, by Sir Rowland Winn, and a new bridge over the lake erected. The Architect was James Paine. 1740.

"July 26, Doctor Winteringham, York. widower, and Mrs. Catherine Bright, Badsworth, spinster (?)."§ 1742.

"Tim: Lee, Rector. Instituted Decr. 8th, 1744. Presented to this Living by Ld. Edgcumb."‡ 1744.

---
* Vide Register of Baptisms, Vol. II.
† Vide Register of Burials, Vol. II.
‡ Vide Parish Register, Vol. II.
§ Vide Register of Marriages, Vol. II.

A.D. 1749.
Curious Bargain.

By Indenture dated July 6th, 1749 (23 Geo. II.), between Ann Beaumont,* of Brackenhill Quarry, in the parish of Ackworth, and Abstrupus Danby, of Kingston-upon-Hull, merchant, it was agreed that in consideration of the sum of five shillings, the said Ann Beaumond would sell to the said Abstrupus Danby, a cottage at Brackenhill Quarry for the term of one year, and the said Abstrupus Danby agreed to yield and pay to the said Ann Beaumond therefor the "rent of one Red Rose in the time of Roses (if the same were lawfully demanded) etc."

The witnesses to the signing and sealing of the above document were Thomas Slater and Wm. Kirkby, and the deed was duly registered at Wakefield, on July 10th, 1749, by J. B. Leng, Deputy Registrar.

1754.
Latin Formulas.

Upon the front cover inside the Register of Banns for the years 1754-84, are two quaint Latin formulas, both of them being certificates of publication of Banns. The phraseology employed is an official Latin which is generally used in all early legal documents, and so easy to discipher, that there is no necessity to append a translation.

"Mem. Banna matrimonialia ter publicata fuere in Ecclesia nostra parochiali de Ackworth inter Clement Cryer de Ackworth et Annam Oldfield de Featherston et nihil objicitur quo minus sancto matrimonij vinculo conjungantur. Ita Testor. T. Lee, July 3, 1754."

"Scias per certo (Vir Reverende) Banna matrimonialia inter Gulielmum Wager et Mariam Crawshaw de Pontefract ter pronunciata fuisse secundum Leges ecclesiasticas in Ecclesia Parochiali de Ackworth, nimine contradicente, in cujus hic testimonium subscribitur nomen. T. Lee. Ex musœo nostro, 10 mo. Die Novembris, 1754."

1758.
Forbidden Banns.

The Banns of marriage were published between "John Longstaff, of Ackworth, and Elizabeth Littlewood, of Snaith,

---

* Daughter of Thomas Beamond, of Ackworth, yeoman, and grand-daughter of Thomas Beamond, of Ackworth, labourer.—Vide Indenture.

on ye 11th of June, but discontinued because she was his wife's sister's Daughter. T. Lee."* A.D. 1758.

1759. Boundary Bridge. The Boundary Bridge which marks the place where the parishes of Hemsworth and Ackworth meet on the Hemsworth Road, bears an inscription which informs the traveller that the bridge was erected in 1759 and enlarged in 1770.

Foundling Hospital. This hospital (now the National School of the Society of Friends) was built in 1757-59, at a cost of £13,000, partly by voluntary subscriptions, and partly by Parliamentary Grant, as an appendage to the Central Institution, which had a few years previously risen in London, a third house being opened in Shropshire, and both the secondary establishments being supplied with children from London. The register, cash, and other books, relating to this hospital, are still kept at Ackworth School, as also are several interesting documents of an earlier date concerning foundlings sent into the country several years before the house was built. Captain Coram started his benevolent schemes about 1739,† and there is a book headed "Accounts with the Foundling Hospital, begun Mar. 30th, 1741," containing particulars of receipts and payments in respect of children, six in number at first, shewing that a return was made to the London institution once a quarter. At this time infants were lodged in the villages of Ackworth, Kippax, Empsal, Hemsworth, Hoyland, Midgley, and Crigglestone. * * * It seems, too, that originally nurses and infants were sent down by stage waggon; but after that a "hospital caravan" was provided, a minute being made that no more were to be sent by waggon. All this was prior to the erection of a hospital. On the hospital books is a stamp bearing the representation of the finding of Moses; and on a circle the words, "Hospitium Infantum Expositorum." The full style of the Corporation was, "The Governors and Guardians of the Hospital for the maintenance and education of exposed and

* Vide Register of Banns, Vol. III.
† The Royal Charter is dated 17th October, 1739.

A.D. 1759. deserted young children." The hospital at Ackworth was open for sixteen years, namely, from 19th August, 1757, to 25th July, 1773, and in that time 2,665 children were received into it; and of these 169, or 6⅓ per cent., died there. The causes of death are summarised at the end of the hospital register, and their burials recorded in the parish registers of Ackworth Church. The first master of the hospital appears to have been Richard Hargreaves, and the first money he received was from Dr. Timothy Lee, the Rector of Ackworth, amounting to £49 14s. 4½d. The obstacles, however, to the hospital's success were so great as to cause Parliament to interfere.* Reference is made elsewhere to the mortality of the Institution.

1761. By an Indenture of purchase dated 1761, certain lands at Flempton, in Suffolk, were sold by Dr. Timothy Lee, Rector of Ackworth, in the County of York, and others, to Sir William Gage, of Bury St. Edmunds, in the County of Suffolk, Bart.

1765. Indenture of lease and release between the Rev. Timothy Lee, D.D.,† on the one part, and William Sykes, Gentleman, on the other, made the 28th and 29th May, 1765. Extract from schedule referring to the Ackworth Park Estate.

1766. Interesting record.

The following is an extract from Dr. Lee's papers :—

ANN APPEW,

Daughter of Zachariah. Baptized at Ackworth, 22nd May, 1683, and, being a spinster, was buried at Ackworth, 28th December, 1776.

There were at the Funeral the following persons, all at Ackworth.

Mary Burgess	... aged 89.	Mary Atheron	... aged 70.
Mrs. Minton	... „ 82.	Fanny Cryer	... „ 70.
Susn. Smith	... „ 81.	Nanny Slack	... „ 64.
Mary Wilson	... „ 78.	Molly Beetham	... „ 66.

* Banks's " Walks about Yorkshire," pp. 294-8.

† It is said that Dr. Lee kept a pack of hounds (probably harriers) for the amusement of his parishioners.

Jane Moor	...	aged 77.	Mrs. Pearson	...	aged 64.	A.D. 1766.
Fanny Wager	...	„ 76.	Dolly Grice	...	„ 64.	
Mary Himsworth	...	„ 75.	Molly Addy	...	„ 73.	
Jane Standish	...	„ 73.	Betty Harrison	...	„ 71.	
Widow Heptinstall		„ 72.	Betty Smith	...	„ 68.	
			Ages of 18	...	1313.	

The Rector was at the Funeral, and, considering the great ages of the Parishioners, on the 11th of January, 1767, he invited the above 18 to Dinner, and, it being the great snow, only 13 were present, whose ages equall'd 958, 5 absent, Total, 1313.

Richard Woodhead, aged 88.			Robert Heptinstall, aged 78.		
Wm. Heptinstall	...	„ 79.	Francis Howitt	...	„ 65.
Wm. Nelstrup	...	„ 79.	Thos. Lockwood	...	„ 64.
Jon. Thompson	...	„ 75.	Benjn. Clark	...	„ 64.
Richard Briggs	...	„ 75.	Mr. Swan	...	„ 67.
Wm. Wager	...	„ 71.	Mr. Furniss	...	„ 66.
Richard Nelstrup	...	„ 71.	Thomas Slater	...	„ 65.
Rev. M. Pearse	...	„ 71.	Richard Hepworth		„ 65.
Mr. Benj. Turton	...	„ 71.	Wm. Scratcher	...	„ 64.
John Wainwright		„ 71.	Wm. Wood	...	„ 64.
John Beetham		„ 68.			
			Ages of 21	...	1471.

On the 8th of February, 1767, the Rector invited the above 21 men to dine with him, and there were present 19, whose ages = 1328, and 2 absent = 143. Total, 1471. The ages of the 32 who dined, 2,286. The ages of the 39 invited = 2,784. And all the above are now alive at Ackworth, this 12th Sep., 1767. Besides the above, there were at this time living at Ackworth, but not thought of for the funeral, Dr. Watkinson, aged 74, and Mrs. Watkinson, aged 68."

Dr. Lee says that "the corpse was carried to the Church by eight young women, who were all clothed in white, and two of them carried a garland in the old style."

A.D. 1767. Marriage frustrated.	"N.B. Thos. Burton & Margaret Backhouse, both of Ackworth, pubd. 10 & 17 May, but Margt. was transported for Felony before Mar: T. Lee."*
1769. Banns forbidden.	The Banns of Marriage were published between James Hey, of Ackworth, and Mary Lightowler, of Pontefract, "on ye 9th, but stopt by M. Lightowler in Person, ye 15th July, 1769.—T. Lee, Rector." Mary Lightowler was evidently a very prudent young woman.
Foundling Hospital.	This Institution was closed by order of Parliament, after a comparatively useless existence of 12 years. It is said that a majority of the children admitted to the house at Ackworth, died before they were at an age to be put out as apprentices, which was usually at about eight years of age. This mortality, the difficulty of obtaining proper nurses, and of providing humane masters, with the frequent contests from the opposition of parishes, and the cruelty of masters where they were apprenticed, proved such insurmountable obstacles to the well-conducting of the Charity, that the house at Ackworth was finally abandoned as a Foundling Hospital, and remained unoccupied and on sale for eight years.† An excerpt from the Parish Registers will throw some light upon the internal management of the Hospital:—

1765, Buried. *Inhabitants*, Males 8, Females, 8. *Foundlings*, Males 27, Females 25. The disproportion is seen at once.

Analysis of cause of death. Inhabitants: Dysentery, 1; Small Pox, 3; Fever, 2; Consumption, 3; other causes, 7. Foundlings: Dysentery, 23; Small Pox, 18; Fever, 4; Consumption, 2; other causes, 5.

1771. Quadruple Birth.	The year 1771 will ever be a remarkable one in the annals of Ackworth, on account of a quadruple birth which occurred there. A poor woman, whose name cannot be ascertained, was safely delivered of four children.‡

---

* Vide Register of Banns, Vol. III. † Vide Baines' Hist. York. p. 441.
‡ Vide Ross' Topographical Index of the "Annual Register." There is no mention of the incident in the Ackworth Parish Registers.

From the "Annual Register" we learn that a woman named Elizabeth Rainbow, of Ackworth, was murdered by her master, Lieut. N. Bolton.*

<small>A.D. 1774.</small>

The Banns of Marriage were published between William Atick, of Crofton, and Elizabeth Crossley, of Ackworth, on the 3rd of November, but forbid by Elizabeth Crossley on the 4th. J. Beevor, Curate."† It would seem that the youths of that time were too often in the habit of taking "silence for consent," or else the maidens were pressed against their will, and, naturally, took the earliest opportunity of revoking their promise. In this instance, however, Elizabeth Crossley could not summon up courage to forbid the banns publicly, but went privately to the Curate on the following day, and we are not surprised to find the reverend gentleman willing to accept the girl's protest, although the course he saw fit to adopt was somewhat out of order.

<small>1776. Banns forbidden.</small>

Foundling Hospital purchased by Dr. Fothergill and three others for £7000.

<small>1777. Friends' School.</small>

The following are extracts from the diary of the late Mr. N——, of Ackworth:—

<small>1778.</small>

"Wednesday, August 5th, went to Leeds, to the Conference, was not so lively in the meeting as I could wish. I heard Mr. Wesley preach from Luke 13, verses 23-4, and was found wanting under his sermon.

"Thursday, 6th. I had the pleasure of hearing Mr. Wesley preach at five o'clock this morning, from these words:—'And to him that ordereth his conversation aright will I show the salvation of God.' I was found wanting, yet glory be to God, I got fresh desires, and I trust, through grace, to be made more and more like unto the Lord."

This Hospital was erected in Northgate, Pontefract, in 1778, out of the personal estate of the late Edward Watkinson, Esq.,

<small>Watkinson's Hospital.</small>

---

* Vide Ross' Topographical Index. Elizabeth Rainbow's Burial is not recorded at Ackworth.
† Vide Register of Banns, Vol. III.

A.D. 1778.   M.D., of Ackworth.* The Rector of Ackworth for the time being is one of the Trustees of the Hospital.

1779.   The following extracts from Mrs. N———'s diary are interesting :—

"January 28th, 1779. Went to Badsworth to-day to my brothers, they had company, all carnal people, I found an awful sense of the Lord and fear of offending him. Before I came away I thought if I did not take up my cross, and go to prayer with them, I should go home in distress. I asked for the hymn book, and as soon as I began to give out the hymn I found the Lord was with us, and for ever blessed be His Holy Name, He enabled me to go to prayer, and it was a blessing to my soul, and may the Lord grant it may be a blessing to all the souls that were present, and glory shall be given to Him."

"April 28th. Much afraid of sinning to-day, and much drawn out in prayer, heard Mr. Wesley preach at Wakefield,† the word was a feast to my soul, may I never more grieve His Spirit."

1780.
Banns forbidden.

Between "Joseph Bayldon, Ackworth, and Hannah Field, Womersley, on the 23rd, 30th January, 1780, but forbid by Joseph Bayldon and John Bayldon." This looks as if the *girl* or her friends, had put up the banns, which were forbidden by the young man and his brother, or perhaps his father.

1784.   Between "George Hattersley and Mary Wood, both of Ackworth, on the 2nd, 9th, and 16th of September, 1784, but forbid in the Church, on ye 16th, by Thos. Wood," probably the girl's father.

1788.   Between "John Hargrave, Leeds, and Mary Issott, Ackworth, on the 15th, 22nd of June, and were forbid on the 29th of the same month, by Mary Hargrave, who says she is the wife of the above John Hargrave, 1778, by P. Heaton, Curate."‡

---

* For Dr. Watkinson's Will in extenso, see Fox's Hist. Pont., p. 344.
† Mr. Wesley never seems to have honoured Ackworth with a visit.
‡ Vide Register of Banns, Vol. III.

Two persons, both males, aged respectively 81 and 48, died of this disease, at Ackworth, in 1790, and a woman, aged 49, in 1793. It is probable, however, that this "Palsy" was what is now known as paralysis. A.D. 1790. Palsy.

A very bad case of Leprosy occurred at Ackworth School in this year, a disease which seldom appears in this country. As soon as its real character was known, the boy was removed into the village, until he could be suitably sent home.* Leprosy was very common in England in the 16th century, imported principally no doubt by itinerant Jews; and for the special treatment of such cases, Lazar Hospitals were erected in several of the large towns. The frequency of leprous and other loathsome diseases, is referred to by Spenser, "The Sunrise of English poetry," in his "Faëry Queen," (Book I, Canto IV. 3.) "Like loathsome lazars, by the hedges lay." 1791. Leprosy.

The following entry appears in the Parish Register of Baptisms:—"Mary, daughter of Joshua Bryer, Soldier, born at sea, Oct. 20th, baptised Nov. 24th."† 1793.

A characteristic epitaph of the old time may be read upon a slab on the north side of the Parish Church. It would seem as though the glorious doctrine of the Resurrection had entirely been lost sight of, so dolorous is the tone of the epitaph. 1795. Epitaph.

> "Hark: from the Tombs a doleful sound,
> My friends, attend the Cry:
> Ye Living men, come view the Ground
> Where you must shortly Lye.
> ——— this clay must be your Bed—
> The Spire of all your Tow'rs
> Must fall: the Wise the Rev'rend head:
> Must lye as Low as ours.

The inscription above, informs us that William Burford's remains are deposited beneath the stone.‡ He was born June 25, 1760, and died April 30, 1781. Mary, his wife, died Feb. 2nd, 1795.

---

* Vide "Hist: Ackworth School," p. 75.
† Vol. IV.
‡ Some of the grave-stones were brought out of the church-yard into the Church, when it was restored, for the purpose of pavement.

A.D. 1796. Dearth.	"This was a year of dear bread, and we find it raising the wages of the chief shoemaker at Ackworth School, (Samuel Whalley) to eighteen shillings a week, in consequence of "the high price of the necessaries of life." Wheat sold from 96/- to 112/- per quarter, and Henry Hipsley records in his journal, that it was "doubtful whether corn would be found in the country at any price," and that when he went to Pontefract to buy corn, he had to place his hand in the farmer's sack, in order to secure the wheat, the moment the bell rang for the market to begin.*
1798.	Charles Butter, Curate of Ackworth, died Jan. 5th, 1798, aged 74, and was buried at Ackworth. He was succeeded by George Hendwick.
1803. Sykes Family.	Indenture made the 10th August, 1803, between Francis Sykes, as Sir Francis Sykes, Bart., and Dame Elizabeth, his wife on the one part, and Thomas Taylor, Gentleman, on the other part. Francis Sykes, Esq., of Ackworth Park, was born in 1732, and amassed a considerable fortune in India, whilst Governor of Cossumbazar, in Bengal. He was created a Baronet on the 24th March, 1781, and married first, Feb. 7th, 1766, Catherine, daughter of John Ridley, Esq., and had issue, two sons, 1, Francis William, who succeeded, and 2, John, R.N., who died on board the *Grampus*. Sir Francis married secondly, Sep. 2nd, 1774, Henrietta Elizabeth Monckton, oldest daughter of William, second Viscount Galway.
Suffocation.	Under date May 7th, the "Gentleman's Magazine" for 1803, records the following :—"At Ackworth, near Pontefract, Mrs. Townley and her son, who resided at that place, had removed to a new house,† and, in order to dry their bedrooms, which had been newly plastered, they burnt in them during the night, a chafing dish with charcoal. In the morning they were both found dead. Both were illegitimate, and both died intestate, in

* Vide "Hist: Ackworth School," p.p. 86, 96.
† The house formerly occupied by the late Mr. John Haigh.

consequence of which a house, maltkiln, and seven acres of land, lately purchased by one or both of them, near the Rectory, resolved to the King as Duke of Lancaster, and from him to the Trustees of the Manor of Ackworth, to whom the manor and its privileges had been granted in the reign of Charles I.

A.D. 1803.

Martha Chapel, of Ackworth, aged 19, says the "Annual Register," was executed at York in this year, for the murder of her illegitimate child.*

ACKWORTH PARK.

Old sale bill.

TO BE
SOLD BY AUCTION
TOGETHER, OR IN THE FOLLOWING LOTS,
AT THE HOUSE OF
Mr. ROBERTS, THE ELEPHANT AND CASTLE, IN PONTEFRACT,
ON THE ELEVENTH DAY OF APRIL NEXT,
Between the Hours of Two and Six in the Afternoon,
Unless previously disposed of by private Contract, of which due notice will be given;
Subject to such conditions as will be then and there produced.

LOT I.

Consisting of Two Closes, Tithe-free, in Ackworth, containing Eight Acres, One Rood, Six Perches, and now in the Occupation of James Waite.

LOT II.

A Good House, Dove-Cot, Barns, Stables, Coach-House, &c., together with Five Pieces or Parcels of Land adjoining thereto, called the Hemp Yard, the Hall Close and Garden, the Larger Hemp Yard, the Plantation, and the New Close, containing together Fifteen Acres, Three Perches, and now in the occupation of John Gill.

LOT III.

Five Closes, Pieces, or Parcels of Land, in Ackworth aforesaid, called the New Close, the Plantation, the East End of Smithy Butts, containing together Five Acres, Two Roods, Six Perches; the Near Lodge Hill, and the Lodge Hill, containing together Twenty Acres, Two Roods, and now in the Possession of the said James Waite and John Gill.

LOT IV.

Three Closes, Pieces, or Parcels of Land, in Ackworth aforesaid, called the Farr Lodge Hill, the Fourteen Acres, and Two Acres at the West End of Smithy Butts, containing together Twenty-five Acres, One Rood, Nineteen Perches, and now in the Possession of the said James Waite and John Gill.

LOT V.

Three other Closes of Land, in Ackworth and Purston, called the Lower Wood Slack, the Broom Close, and the Upper Wood Slack, containing together Twenty Acres, Three Roods, Fourteen Perches, and now in the Possession of the said James Waite and John Gill.

* Vide Ross' Topographical Index. There is no record of this at Ackworth.

A.D. 1803.

LOT VI.

The Coal Hill Close, Tithe-free, containing Forty Acres, Thirty Perches, in Ackworth aforesaid, and now in the Possession of the said John Gill.

LOT VII.

The Park Close, containing Eleven Acres, Ten Perches, in Ackworth aforesaid, and now in the possession of Michael Cuttle.

LOT VIII.

A Good House, Barns, Stables, and Outbuildings; together with Nine Closes, Pieces, or Parcels of Land adjoining thereto, called the Twelve Acres, the Sixteen Acres, with Plantation, the Far Four Acres, the Six Acres, the Under Close, the Two Castle Syke Closes, the Jackson Close, and the Near Four Acres, in Ackworth aforesaid, containing together Seventy-three Acres, Two Roods, Two Perches, and now in the Occupation of the said Michael Cuttle.

LOT IX.

Two Closes of Land, in Ackworth aforesaid, called the Castle Syke and the Jeffry Close, containing together Fourteen Acres, Three Roods, Six Perches, also in the Possession of the said Michael Cuttle.

LOT X.

Two other Closes of Land, in Ackworth aforesaid, called the Three Acres and the Near Close, containing together Twelve Acres, Twelve Perches, and also in the Possesssion of the said Michael Cuttle.

LOT XI.

The Mansion-House, Good Gardens, well stocked with Fruit Trees; Barns, Stables, with Fifteen Stands for Horses; Coach-Houses, Dove-Cot, and other convenient Outbuildings, all in Good Repair; *with Three Pews in the Church*, and about One Hundred Acres of Land, lying in a Ring Fence adjoining to the said Mansion-House, and now in the occupation of Lady Dowager Mexbro', Michael Cuttle, John Gill, and John Thompson.

The Whole of the Estate is supposed to be full of Coal.—Ackworth Park is situated in the most desirable Part of the West Riding of the County of York. The Mansion is modern-built, in good Repair, and fit for the Reception of a large Family. It is within Two Miles of Pontefract, Four from Ferrybridge, Seven from Wakefield, and Fourteen from Doncaster.

Mr. Michael Cuttle of Ackworth will shew the Premises, and further Particulars may be had of Mr. Richard Mitton, Pontefract; or of Messrs. Sykes and Knowles, Solicitors, Boswell-Court, London.

The Estate in Ackworth is subject to a Fee Farm Rent of 11l. 3s. 5d. Is exonerated from the Land Tax; and such Part thereof as is not Tithe-free, is subject only to 2s. per Annum, in Lieu thereof; but the Lands in Purston are subject to Tithe in Kind.—There is some fine thriving Wood on the Estate, which must be taken by the Purchaser or Purchasers at a fair Valuation.

—:—

Pontefract. Printed by John Fox, Market-Place.

This old Sale bill is preserved in the Main-Guard Historical Museum, Pontefract.

A.D. 1805. Old sale bill.

SALE
OF VALUABLE FURNITURE,
BY AUCTION,
AT ACKWORTH GROVE,

The Residence of JAMES BUCK, on THURSDAY, the 21st of FEBRUARY, 1805, and the following days till all be sold, the Sale to commence (each day) at 10 o'clock in the forenoon.

Consisting of a great variety of elegant Mahogany Sideboard, Dining and Card Tables, Chairs, Chests of Drawers, Wardrobe, Feather Beds of the best Quality, Mahogany and other Bedsteads and Bedding, Pier and Swing Glasses, Floor and other Carpets, Kitchen, Brewing, and Dairy Utensils, a Capital Mangle, Melon & Cucumber Frames, Hand Glasses, &c.

Horses, Cows, Haystack, a neat Tax'd Cart and Harness, a Curious American Sledge, Carts, Plow-rollers, Harrows, a great variety of Farming Utensils and Husbandry gear, also a stout modern built Whiskey Vat on curricle spindles and patent axletree.

N.B.—The live Stock and Husbandry gear to be sold the first day.
Feb. 12th, 1805.
Pontefract: Printed by J. Fox, Market Place.

John Donbavand, one of the masters of the Friends' School, when in his twenty-first year, suffered a month's imprisonment in the Wakefield House of Correction, for refusing to serve, after having been "drawn" on the local Militia! Four years later he was "drawn" a second time, and, with two others, was imprisoned at Wakefield for twenty-four days.* This must have been an unmitigated hardship to one whose principles were essentially those of peace, the very idea of war being odious to the Quaker mind. Members of the Society of Friends were, however, not legally exempt from military service, so that Donbavand's conduct was, in reality, contumacious, and he was punished accordingly.

1810.

Henry Mitton, of Ackworth, yeoman, by his Will, dated 10th October, 1809, and proved at York, 16th February, 1810, ordered and directed his Executors to lay out £20 in building a Hearse for the conveyance of corpses from the confines of the Parish to inter at Ackworth Church. The Hearse was afterwards to be placed under the management and direction

Parish Hearse.

* Vide Hist. Ackworth School, p. 129.

A.D. 1810. of the Churchwardens. A Hearse was accordingly built, and the present Hearse-house, at the corner of the Pinfold, erected to keep it in. For many years this Hearse was very useful, and served the ends intended by the Testator. In 1872, however, it was worn out, and could no longer be used. Subscriptions were therefore raised, amounting to over £40, to procure the Hearse at present in use, which is let out by the Churchwardens for the interment of any bonâ-fide parishioner, whether buried at Ackworth or any other Church.

1811.
A windfall.

In the month of March in this year, a young man came to the "Brown Cow" Inn, at Ackworth, then kept by a Mrs. Howitt, and took up his abode there. He declined to give any account of himself, except that his name was W. Wilson. Whilst staying at the "Brown Cow," he died, and property was found upon him amounting to nearly £100, which, after the payment of funeral and other expenses, was reduced to £85 14s. 9d. Subsequent enquiries elicited the information that he was a felon, who had escaped from Lincoln Castle in the month of December preceding, whilst lying under condemnation for burglary, and that his name was Robert Warff. According to custom, the money was appropriated by the Lords of the Manor of Ackworth, for the benefit of the freeholders, to be invested where and how the said Lords for the time being should think fit.* Every effort, however, was made by the Rector (Mr. Hay) and the Churchwardens to discover the friends of the young man, as the following entries testify.†

	£	s.	d.
1872, Oct. 1st. By the Rev Mr. Hay, p. Acct. for advertizg. for Warff's Friends, etc.	5	4	8
By a letter			11
By George Fairburn, two journeys to Wakefield to speak to Mr. Carr about Warff's property, as Mr. Hodgson claimed it		6	0
By a letter to Mr. Hay from old Warff			10

* Vide Manor Minute Book, p. 4.
† Vide Manor Accounts.

		£	s.	d.	A.D. 1811
By Hardin to pack the young man's cloths in to old Warft			1	6	
By Mr. Pearson, journey to York to Mr. Carr, for him to inspect the Deed of the Grant of the Manor, and Mr. Hodgson gave up his claim...			14	1	
1813, May 1st. By balance in hand of George Fairbarn		84	10	9	

From the above statement it will be seen that all was done, that could be done under the circumstances, and that in a most satisfactory and straightforward manner.

During the year, no less than £47 18s. 3d. was recovered by the Lords of the Manor from various persons in Ackworth as compensation for encroachments upon lands belonging to the Manor. A Mr. Pearson paid 18s. 9d.; Geo. Fairbarn, for an encroachment upon Long Lane, £2 15s.; Richd. Smith, do. against his garden, £6 15s.; Ackworth School, £6 11s. 3d.; Nelly Heptinstall, £2 10s.; James Camplin, £8 12s. 6d.; Thomas Howitt, £8 0s. 0d.; and John Heaton, £11 16s. 3d.* {1813. Interesting Statistics.}

There can be no doubt that the Trustees of the Manor, for the time being, can legally claim any amount they may think fit, from any person, who may so encroach.

This Court, which is really the only method recognized by law of bringing together the Lords of the Manor and Freeholders of Ackworth for the transaction of business, has not been convened for many years, but the little business to be transacted is now disposed of by an informal meeting, attended by the Rector and two or three "lords in waiting," called together by the Clerk of the Manor, or rather Secretary, whose duties, I am informed, are peculiarly onerous. One reason why these Ancient Courts Leet and Baron have not been holden was probably the expense connected with such Sessions, the jurymen and officials of which seemed to enjoy, according to the accounts, an extraordinarily good time of it. Such Courts were not held at stated times, but were called only when {The Court Leet.}

* Vide Manor Accounts.

A.D. 1813. occasion required, generally by a public notice given out by the parish clerk in the Church.* The last Court was held in 1862.

Spiritual condition.

From a small faded memorandum book which has come into the compiler's possession, some idea may be formed of the spiritual condition of Ackworth in the year 1813. The contents of the book purport to be the result of a house to house canvass of two members of the Ackworth Branch of the British and Foreign Bible Society. The record is a most interesting one. Out of 112 poor families visited in the parish, 65 were destitute of Bibles, and 75 of New Testaments. Out of an aggregate of 430 individuals, 200 were reported as unable to read. Some of the entries are worth re-producing. One family possessed a piece of a Bible, and another a piece of the New Testament. One Bible was in parts, seven of which, however, were wanting; another was destitute of beginning and end; and the inhabitants of one cottage stated that when they wanted a Bible, which was not very often, they borrowed one! A sixth family produced "a small tattered piece of a Bible; and two doors further on it was said that there was a small piece of a Testament in the house, which they were unable to find. A lady who has resided for many years at Ackworth says she has a distinct recollection of her father saying that when he, in company with the Rev. Geo. Maddison, made a canvass on behalf of the Bible Society in the hamlet of Brackenhill, they found the inhabitants in a very uncivilized state, and that the canvassers were really alarmed when they were met at the door of a cottage by a woman holding a carving knife menacingly in her hand.

1817. Oct. 27. By E. Patrick, for giving notice in the Church for 6 years Court Day, 3s.

1819. On Sunday, May 9th, 1819, the following notice was publicly given out in the Parish Church: "This is to give notice. The Trustees of the Manor desire the attendance of the Freeholders in the Vestry immediately after Divine Service." The Free-

* Vide sub datum, 1817.

holders accordingly attended (how many is not known) and it was agreed that the business which had called them together so extraordinarily should be left to the Overseers of Highways. The business, it appears, was this. The Lords of the Manor by their Clerk had, in the first instance, considered it their duty to serve the following notice upon Miss Hannah Mary Horton: "We the undersigned being Trustees for the Manor of Ackworth do hereby discharge (sic) you from diging up or leading away the earth or soil, from the waste land upon the said Manor, otherwise an Action at Law will be immediately commenced against you." (Signatures.)* This notice was read by the Clerk, and a subsequent meeting was held in the vestry on the following Thursday at 11 o'clock in the forenoon, to take into consideration the most effectual means to put a stop to Miss Horton's proceedings upon the waste land in Houndhill Lane. There is no record as to what course the Lords adopted; probably Miss Horton had wisely obeyed the injunction, or the Lords ultimately decided that the matter was of too trivial a nature to be further prosecuted. The unbiassed reader will, however, at once perceive in what a "cart-before-the-horse" fashion the business of the Trust in this instance was transacted.

A.D. 1819.

Stage coaches ran daily from Ackworth to Scarborough at at nine o'clock in the morning; to Sheffield at five in the evening; to Lincoln on Monday, Wednesday and Friday, at ten in the morning; and to Wakefield every Tuesday, Thursday, and Saturday at three in the afternoon.† Children, as a rule, were not favourite "fares" with the drivers and guards of the old stage-coach. They were not *au fait* in "tips," or clever in providing the little warming treats which were so highly esteemed. It is related that on one occasion, three children were being escorted from Ackworth to Wentbridge, by a wide-awake matronly Friend, who overheard the coachman describing the young travellers to a companion on the box, as nothing better than "tag-rag and bobtail." On appearing at

1822. Stage Coaches.

* Vide List of Lords, in Appendix.
† Vide Baine's Hist: York:, p. 442,

A.D. 1822. the door of the coach on its arrival at Wentbridge, to solicit his *douceur*, the humorous lady presented him with three small coins, which she described as being one from "Tag," another from "Rag," and the third from "Bobtail."*

A Sporting Curate.   J—— H————, Curate of Ackworth, is said to have been passionately fond of fox-hunting, which in those days was considered in society an essential accomplishment for a clergyman. The pastime, however, was eyed askance by "Hodge," because of the rough-shod manner in which the huntsmen rode across country, taking not only hedges and ditches, but crops and gardens in their mad career. To the rustic daysman it is well known that in Yorkshire the "hunting parson" is an odious and despicable personage. One Sunday morning the Curate in question was accosted during an impressive pause in his sermon, by one T——W——d loudly vociferating "Thou's preachin' ta day, an be fox-hunting to-morrow!" The truth of this statement did not prevent the man from being summoned for brawling, and fined 10/- and costs.†

Population.   The population of Ackworth this year according to a recent census, was (including Low Ackworth,) 1575. The chief residents were—Ackworth Park, John Petyt, Esq.; Ackworth House, John Goldsworthy, Esq.; Ackworth Villa (now the Court), Thomas St. Quintin, Esq.; Ackworth Lodge, The Rev. George Maddison; Ackworth Moor-Top, Thomas Gee, Esq.; Ackworth Grange, Richard Wilson, Esq.; and at Ackworth, D'Oyley Saunders, Esq.

Mr. Thomas Wilkinson, of Ackworth, was at this time Chief Constable and Subdivision Clerk for the Osgoldcross Division of the West Riding of Yorkshire.‡

1823. Ackworth Gazette.   A little newspaper promoted and circulated by the Society of Friends in Ackworth. The first number appeared on the 9th September, 1823. "It was," says Thompson, "a current

* Vide "Hist: Ackworth School," p. 34.   † Communicated by G—— S——.
‡ Vide Langdale's Top. Dict. 1822, p. 465.

register of events, chiefly in the great world outside," although from time to time local events of interest were duly chronicled.*

A.D. 1823.

During the month of November in this year, Ackworth was honoured by the visit of a noble of royal blood, viz.: His Grace the Duke of Gloucester. The event is thus celebrated in rhyme by a lady who was resident in the village at the time :—

Royal visit

> "I trust my muse will not refuse
>   To celebrate the happy day
> When Gloucester's duke his Court forsook,
>   And to the country sped his way.
>
> 'Twas *Cantley*† *Hall* which first of all
>   Received this most illustrious guest ;
> What there befel I cannot tell,
>   I must proceed to speak the rest.
>
> All in the dark to *Kippax*‡ *Park*
>   The royal stranger sped amain ;
> Perchance that he disliked to see
>   On *Pomfret's* wall the bloody stain.‖
>
> All dangers past, arrived at last,
>   He finds a noble party there,
> The welcome said, the board is spread
>   With fish, and soup, and viands rare.
>
> And fowl and game, both wild and tame,
>   Were all in tasteful plenty given,
> And fruit so fine, and choicest wine,
>   From every country under heaven.
>
> Each day and night, with rapid flight
>   In gay succession sunk and rose ;
> The time is flown, the Duke is gone,
>   I must pursue him as he goes.
>
> A friendly call at *Houndhill*§ *Hall*,
>   Impedes him in his hasty course ;
> He there would stay the Sabbath day,
>   That day of rest for man and horse.
>
> Soon in the morn to Church ¶ he's borne,
>   But not in car of royal state ;
> To lay aside all thoughts of pride,
>   Full well becomes the rich and great.

* Vide " Hist. of Ackworth School," p. 165.
† Norfolkshire.
‡ The object of the Duke's visit was to stand sponsor for the twelfth child of Thomas Davidson Bland, Esq., of Kippax.
‖ Pontefract Castle thrice beseiged, and the scene of civil discord and bloodshed.
§ At Houndhill Hall lived Mrs. Bland, mother of T. D. Bland, Esq., and two or three unmarried daughters. It was said that she had been kind to the Duke when he was a young officer in the army, hence his intimacy with the family.
¶ Ackworth Parish Church.

The Rector's* seat, as his most meet,
  Receives him with a train of friends,
The bells have rung, the hymn is sung,
  The congregation, mute, attends.

"God save the King,"† or some such thing
  Is sung with ready glee and art;
Then out they pour forth from the door
  And for the Quaker's school depart.‡

All in amaze with steady gaze,
  The assembled crowd astonished stare;
Take a last look at Gloucester's Duke,
  Then to their several homes repair.

The school is seen, so neat and clean,
  The boys and girls prepare to eat,
The dinner brought, the grace is thought,||
  Who would not relish such a treat?

The meal is done, the clock strikes one,
  The noble party onward passed;§
'Twas pleasure all at Houndhill Hall
  That even,¶ but it was the last.

The noble guest awakes from rest,
  And takes his leave with grief so true;
The coach and four are at the door,
  Adieu, Adieu, Adieu, Adieu!"

—:—

Although several hiati are apparent, the rhyme is a tolerably good specimen of the Yorkshire Ballad.**

* The Rev. W. R. Hay, M.A. Tradition says that a very eccentric member of the congregation, into whose pew the Duke was first shewn, refused his Grace admittance, not knowing who the illustrious stranger was.

† The "National Anthem," says an old inhabitant, was sung on the occasion.

‡ There is an error in Chronology here. The visit to Ackworth School, took place on Monday morning. Vide "Ackworth Gazette," December, 1823.

|| After the manner of the Quakers.

§ "On the 30th November, 1823, at half past twelve o'clock at noon, the Duke of Gloucester and his suite, arrived in two carriages at the entrance of the Friends' School. His Grace was conducted through the various buildings, and shewn everything calculated to interest him. Then, having seen as much of the establishment as time and weather would permit, the day being very wet, the Duke at half-past one o'clock returned to his carriage, expressing himself highly gratified with his visit, and hoping that the Institution would long continue to prove a blessing to the Society." Vide "Ackworth Gazette," December, 1823.

¶ Monday evening. A ball was held in honour of the Duke, with other festivities.

** Vide "Yorkshire Notes and Queries," Jan. 1886. I am indebted for the MS. of the above lines to Miss M. Whittaker, of Ackworth. J. L. S.

The following extract is taken from a published letter of the late R―― H――――, to a friend at T――――. "Our attention has been very much occupied * with the subject of Dame Schools, and the means of improving them. * * The Moor-Top School is my favourite object of attention. The Mistress I found in great repute, surrounded by nearly forty children: and seeing that she had some talent, I thought it best to direct my views to that school, on account of the number. When I first looked in upon them, last year, it was quite a problem to me to discover *how they learnt* anything;— scarcely any books to be seen, except a few spelling books, which had lost their first pages—some loose leaves of what seemed to have been a Geography, and some Children's Tales: but I afterwards found that the Tracts from the [Lending] Library were in great request. Still, I pitied the Mistress, condemned to sit for three hours incessantly engaged in hearing lessons, and obliged, at the same time, to attend to sewing, marking, and writing: it was almost enough to distract her. And then the poor children are obliged to sit still most of the day, doing nothing; unless they invent some amusement, by pulling their clothes to pieces, or tying and twisting a few coloured threads: and so packed that they could hardly sit down altogether—in fact, learning to be dunces! Well, I immediately thought, what an advantage the Lancasterian system would be here! The Mistress fell in with the proposal." The system was ultimately introduced, and the school carried on for many years, until superseded by a school more in accordance with the requirements of the times.

<small>A.D. 1826. Dame School.</small>

John Petyt (formerly John Petty), Esq., of Brunswick Square, in the County of Middlesex, and Ackworth Park, died 4th October, 1826. His will bears date 7th August, 1826. The Petyt family have a vault in Ackworth Churchyard.

To some, the following old Sale Bill, copied from the "*Doncaster, Nottingham, and Lincoln Gazette,*" of Friday,

<small>1828. Sale Bill.</small>

A.D. 1828. March 24, 1828, will doubtless be interesting.

ACKWORTH PARK.

Shortly will be exposed for SALE by PUBLIC AUCTION, unless previously disposed of by PRIVATE CONTRACT,

ALL that capital MANSION HOUSE and ESTATE called ACKWORTH PARK, situate in the Parish of Ackworth, in the West Riding of Yorkshire, comprising an excellent Dwellinghouse, with all requisite conveniences, for the residence of a Nobleman or Gentleman, and 355 acres of LAND or thereabouts, with suitable Farm Houses, all lying in a ring fence.

The above Estate is freehold and tithe-free, (being subject as to part, however, to a perpetual annual payment of 2s. an acre, in lieu of tithes, settled by Act of Parliament,) and the land-tax is redeemed. Ackworth Park is distant two miles from Pontefract, eight from Wakefield, * * * * * * and is delightfully situated in a remarkably fine part of the country, and in the centre of the Badsworth Hunt. The Glasgow mail coach passes within a mile of it.

For further particulars, and for tickets to view the place, (without which it will not be shewn,) apply if by letter, post paid, to Messrs. Smithson and Ramskill, Solicitors, Pontefract.
Pontefract, March 17, 1828.

The price of the "*Doncaster, Nottingham, and Lincoln Gazette,*" was 7d.

1830. Reform Bill.

At the time of the disturbances in London respecting the Reform Bill, the late E——— H———, of Ackworth, whose correspondence was published after her death, in a letter dated Nov. 4th, 1830, writes as follows—" J. was to have come home at half-past four, and it is now nearly six, and I am still alone; and I feel that, if I stitch, stitch, all the evening, I shall be very nervous before he comes, for really I do not like *mobs* and *tricoloured flags.** You will hear as much from the papers, and more, probably, of what is going on, than we could tell you. 'Tis strange work, and were I to waste all the evening about it, I could neither tell you what the mob wants, nor what those above them are afraid of. One cannot but look with some eagerness to see the end of it, though very probably it may, after all, end in nothing."

Wonderful calf.

On the 3rd of October, 1830, a cow belonging to Mr. Sudbury, of Pontefract, brought forth a full grown calf with two heads, two breasts, two necks, four fore-legs, two hearts, two

---

* Pontefract has always been the arena of political animus—and very often tumult and strife. The Reform Bill although passed in 1831, did not operate 'until 1832.

livers and lights, two back bones, which are separated as far as the sixth rib from the issuing bone, where they became joined into one back, two tails, and only two hind legs, each body possessing separate intestines quite perfect.* Mr. Sudbury was well known at Ackworth, and the story is still related at the fireside of farm house kitchens. x A.D. 1830.

Boy killed at Ackworth School, by the fall of some cart-shelvings, whilst he was assisting the farmer.† 1831. Fatal Accident.

This periodical was published at Ackworth School, and circulated chiefly amongst the Masters and pupils, although a few copies found their way into the village.‡ Ackworth Review.

Writing from the "Villa" (now known as the "Court"), on May 1st, the late R—— H———, in her published correspondence says—"A shower of cherryblossoms brought over the house by the north wind, from the two great trees in the yard, has twice deceived me, to-day (May 5th), into the apprehension that we were going to have a snow-storm. Very little surprise would be felt if the phenomenon should occur, so very cold is the season. Yet vegetation comes on very well; and we understand the farmers have no fear for their crops." 1832. Interesting records

May 3rd. "I have begun to drink the Spa ‖ before breakfast, and generally step in at the Grices', where there is sure to be some business about the School."

On June 21, she thus writes to a friend,—"Our High Ackworth neighbours have just been having their "feast."§ It was a sad time—a scene of dancing and riot, all night, I believe! * * * * We were seriously threatened with bull-baiting, which was put a stop to by a good deal being said about it. My father went to the "Boot and Shoe," and Capt. W., and others, to the Beer-shop in the Quarry, to speak Ackworth Feast.

* Vide "Wonders of Nature and Art," pp. 114-15.
† Vide "History of Ackworth School," p. 248.
‡ Vide "Hist: Ackworth School," p. 214.
‖ Tan-house Lane.
§ Beginning May 31, and lasting about four days.

A.D. 1832.   against it. We have set our faces against the children's having "holidays" at the Schools, and *seeing* all these things; for which, I expect, we shall get plenty of ill-will; but I am convinced that it is quite right so to do. I wish we had carried opposition a little further. I *do* want a good tract against "Feasts" for circulation."*

The Derby and St. Leger.   Both these famous races were both won this year by a horse, the joint property of Mr. Gully, of Ackworth Park, and a Mr. Ridsdale.†

1834. A religious enthusiast   In a published letter to her sister, dated June 15th, 1834, Mrs. R—— H—— writes—"I had an entertainment [this evening at Low Ackworth] which I did not expect—a sermon on the Millenium! It was from a middle aged man, with a serious countenance and a long beard, who had taken his station on the top of a wall opposite Farmer Lee's; from whose garden I heard great part of it. People call him a Joannaite, and set him down for a deceiver. I neither saw nor heard anything deceptive, but, on the contrary, much evidence of sincerity. He appeared to be sound in the faith, and to have a remarkably comprehensive knowledge of Holy Scripture, especially on the subject of Redemption. His allusions to the Atonement were particularly satisfactory; his declarations of the Scripture doctrine of the resurrection of the body remarkably clear; and his anticipations of the Redemption completed, by the glorification of the Saints at the Last Day, to me, quite animating. But when he proceeded to proclaim the near approach of that day, and told us we were no longer to prepare for death, but for life eternal, I felt as if I could not go along with him. . . . His facility in quoting Scripture by memory (chapter and verse), and the seriousness yet friendliness of his manner, impressed me very agreeably, though he spoke too rapidly for [the comprehension] of the ignorant. From the theological

* "Memoranda of Rachel Howard." Part III. p. 274.
† Vide Memoir of John Gully, in Appendix.

terms he used, he must be a well read man. My father conjectures him to be a Seventh-day Baptist.* A.D. 1834.

This historical event was commemorated at Ackworth by a display of bunting, and the ringing of the Church bells. At Ackworth School, the 18th of August was observed as a gala-day, and the children were stimulated to write verses appropriate to the occasion, for the best of which prizes were offered. A large meeting of all the children, and numerous visitors was held in the Meeting House in the evening, presided over by Luke Howard, F.R.S. Various congratulatory resolutions were passed, one of which, proposed by William Fisher Sim, and seconded by John Bright,† was—"That this meeting unites in the feeling of humble gratitude to the Author of all Good, who has condescended so to bless the efforts of all Christians of every denomination in this Country, that the curse of slavery throughout the British Empire is this day ended, and that all the slaves are free." Slavery Emancipation Commemoration.

The "*Telegraph*" succeeded the defunct "*Ackworth Review*," but, like its predecessor, had but a short existence. It died in 1838.‡ 1835. The Telegraph.

Ackworth Mechanics' Library established Nov. 15th, 1836. 1836.

In addition to the festivities at the Friends' School, a sumptuous dinner was provided for the working poor of Ackworth, by Mr. Gully of Ackworth Park, and other gentlemen. It was laid out in a large tent in a field at the rear of the Post Office Buildings, and was followed in the evening by an equally substantial tea. Merry peals were rung all day, and the ringers liberally supplied with refreshments from the neighbouring public house. 1837. Coronation.

* More probably an itinerant separatist from Irvingism, who, in common with many others, had adopted the more advanced views of Joanna Southcote, respecting the Millenium and second Coming of Christ, afterwards promulgated by Dr. Cumming.
† John Bright, Esq., M.P., was educated at Ackworth School.
‡ Vide Hist. Ackworth School, p. 214.

A.D. 1837. Introduction of gas.

The Committee of Ackworth School were the first to substitute for the dismal oil-lamp and the glimmering dip, the then suspicious illumination of gas; and it was not for several years afterwards that gas was introduced into their houses by a few of the more venturesome inhabitants of the village. Even now the primitive obscurity of the dark ages lingers tenaciously in the lanes of the village, and strange to say the people love to have it so.

Epitaph.

Hannah Camplin must have been a most estimable young person, if the following epitaph upon her gravestone in Ackworth Churchyard accurately describes her qualities:

> "Her manners mild, her temper such,
> Her language good, and not too much."

She died August 18th, 1837, aged 27. She was evidently too good for this world; had she lived, the manners, temper and language of Ackworthians might have been leavened into something very differently; but "Those whom the Gods love, die young."

1839.

Died at Ackworth, Elizabeth, relict of the Right Rev. T. Middleton, first Bishop of Calcutta, aged 64.* Mrs. Middleton (née Miss Maddison) was buried at Wragby, and formerly resided at Ackworth, in what was once the residence of the Plowes family, additions to which were made for Miss Maddison's reception in 1827.

Mrs. Middleton was the sister of the Rev. Geo. Maddison, who resided at Ackworth Lodge, and came to Ackworth because the district in which his Lincolnshire living was situated did not suit his health. Mr. Maddison occasionally did duty for Mr. Hay, the Rector; and Miss Maddison before her marriage with Dr. Middleton, was deservedly beloved by the people of Ackworth.

* Vide Ross' Topographical Index of the "Annual Register."

Ackworth was certainly one of the pioneers of Horticulture. It is said that prior to the year 1833, horticultural shows were encouraged and held, but the oldest record in existence of such a show, is dated 1840, from which time horticultural shows were held annually for three years. From 1843 to 1863, the Ackworth Horticultural Show was in abeyance, but was revived in the latter year, and continued to be held regularly until 1867, when it again ceased, and no effort was made to recusitate it until 1880, since which time a show has taken place annually, and is much appreciated by the inhabitants and district.

1840. Horticultural show

During the vacancy which occured between the death of the Rev. W. R. Hay, and the induction of the Rev. E. G. Bailey, in February of this year, a most daring and desperate attempt was made to rob the Church. The miscreants were partially successful, but did not secure what they evidently wanted, viz.: the silver Communion plate, which at the time was fortunately lying in safety beneath the bed of the sexton's wife (Mrs. Greenfield). In their search for the hidden treasure, they forced open the Parish chest, and burnt the contents; endeavoured to break into the iron safe, evidence of which was afterwards found in broken shovels, and bent pokers; smashed off the lid of the wine chest and drank the contents of the one bottle remaining; scattered over the vestry floors a quantity of Queen Anne coppers which they found in the drawer of the vestry table, but which were too cumbersome to carry away; maliciously gashed the pulpit cushions, and altar cloth; smashed chairs and benches; and carried away all the keys, the hearse driver's cloak, two surplices, a B.A. hood, and black preaching gown. In addition to all this, they collected a large quantity of the service books lying about in the pews, barricaded the vestry door, and carried the books into Topham's close, where they emptied them down in a heap under an oak tree. No trace of the delinquents could afterwards be found, although two neighbouring churches experienced the same fate in the same week.*

1840. Sacrilege.

* The above details were elicited from the Sexton's wife herself, who was an eye-witness of the depredation.

A.D. 1841.
Population.
The population of Ackworth according to the census of 1841, was 1,828.

1844.
July 30. "The body of a newly born male child, name unknown, buried by order of Coroner."†

British School.
The school in the old Wesleyan Chapel ceased to exist, when the latter was taken down to make room for the new Chapel which stands on the site of the old one. The insufficient accomodation thus produced was met by the establishment in 1844 of a British School on the Lancasterian system, for boys, in a room below the Public Assembly Room, which was erected in the same year. The school is supported by voluntary contributions, and accommodates about 70 boys.

1845.
Magnificent oak felled in Bell Close, and sold for £22 12/-‡

Fatal accident.
A most melancholy accident occurred this year at Ackworth School. One of the girls, it is supposed, was playing with the fire in a room by herself, when her dress caught fire. She immediately rushed out into the passage, enveloped in flames, which were extinguished by counterpanes, but not before she was so fearfully scorched that she died within eight hours.‖

1846.
The Derby Race.
This year a horse named "Pyrrhus the First," the property of Mr. Gully, of Ackworth Park, won for his owner this celebrated race. Sam Day was the rider, and the race was won in two minutes and fifty five seconds.§ Another horse of Mr. Gully's won the Oaks race shortly afterwards.

1848.
Low Ackworth Burial Ground.
About forty years ago the Plymouth brethren* sect was somewhat numerous in Ackworth. At the rear of Mrs. Howard's School in Low Ackworth, there is a small burial ground, within iron railings, provided by Miss Howard's brother, Mr. Luke Howard, for poor persons of the above sect to which Mr. Howard, originally a Friend, belonged in the latter part of his life. The

† Vide Register of Burials. Vol. VIII.
‡ Vide Hist. Ackworth School. p. 350.
‖ Vide Hist. Ackworth School, p. 248.
§ Vide Memoir of John Gully, in Appendix.
* I am informed on good authority that on account of the diminution of Plymouth Brethren at Ackworth, aged and deserving poor people of other persuasions were allowed to be interred in this ground with their own rites. J.L.S.

register of burials in the ground is unfortunately missing, but it appears from the fourteen monumental slabs now standing, that at least a score of persons were interred within this little burial ground during a period of nearly thirty years. Of course there were other burials which are only indicated by raised mounds, but it is hoped that the names of those who lie beneath, are all written in the Book of Life. The following names, ages, and dates, found recorded upon the tomb-stones, may be interesting and useful to the curious in years to come. In 1848, Elizabeth Barker, 70, Martha Jackson, 55; 1850, Martha Mason, 72; 1851, Sarah Bowling, 39, Hannah Briggs, 74, William Briggs, 51; 1852, Mary Booth, 56; 1854, Maria Fletcher, 50, Ann Norton, 87; 1855, Jane Middleton, 50, Isabella Donbavand, 42; 1856, Ann Levitt, 90; 1861, Allan Mason, 84; 1865, Albert Simpson, 3; 1867, Ellen Allott, 37; 1869, Thomas Allott, 41; 1870, Ann Haggas, 71; 1877, Simeon Haggas, 79; 1879, Sarah Grice, 81.

A.D. 1848.

In Cathedrals and Collegiate Churches the verger's wand is a very imposing one of ebony and silver. In some churches it used to be carried, not only before the Bishop when he visited the church, but also before the Rector or Vicar, in his passage from the vestry to the reading desk, Communion table, or pulpit. Where this custom prevails, as at the Parish Church of Stockton-on-Tees, the duty falls to one of the vergers. But with the introduction of surpliced choirs, and the disappearance of "three deckers," the verger's wand also disappeared, and are now looked upon as relics of antiquity. There can be no doubt that the long "tip-staff" of the gaily caparisoned beadle, was the earliest form of these wands, and where, as at Ackworth, this important functionary's dignity was at one time further enhanced by the combined offices of village constable, and night watch-man, the "tip-staff" was supplemented or superseded by the short, but more widely mace-like wand, which served the double purpose of truncheon and wand. The ancient wand, a short staff painted green and white, still exists at

1849. Official Wand.

A.D. 1849. Ackworth, but it is not used. In 1849 it was superseded by a longer one, painted black, with a gilt knob, below which is inscribed in gilt letters, the following words:—"V.R. 1st (time used), 1849, (crown), J. JONES, W. BEECROFT, CHURCH-WARDENS." Although erected in the Churchwardens' pew, it is never used, two plain white wands being carried on special occasions, by the Churchwardens. Sometimes these wands are respectively surmounted by a crown and mitre, symbolising State and Church, as at Thornaby Church, Yorks.

Church rate.

The following is a copy of a notice posted upon the Church door at Ackworth in 1849:—"A Rate or Assessment of two Pence in the Pound upon all Occupiers of land and Tenements, within the Parish of Ackworth, in the County of York, for the repairs and other expenses of the Parish Church of Ackworth aforesaid for the Present year, maid (sic) this 8th day of November, 1849."

JAS. JONES,
WM. BEECROFT. } Churchwardens.

Cholera.

The village did not quite escape the cholera scourge which visited many of our large towns in the summer of 1849. The disease was brought into Ackworth in September, by a plasterer from Leeds, who was seized with the malady soon after his arrival, and whilst engaged at his work in a new house in Purston Lane. He was quickly conveyed to his lodgings, but died at four o'clock the next morning, notwithstanding the immediate application of hot baths, and blankets, mustard poultices and rum, and was buried at 9 o'clock. After this there were many cases, both mild and violent; as many as five deaths occurred in one week, the corpses being quickly buried whilst yet warm, with a very short service. It is said that in one case a coffin was ordered for a child supposed to be dead, but which ultimately recovered.*

* The above particulars were related to the compiler by a survivor.

ITS HISTORY AND ANNALS. 97

Towards the end of May in this year, a most destructive storm of hail-stones visited Ackworth and district. The stones were as large as pieces of lump sugar. The sails of the Ackworth wind-mill were much damaged, and an extensive destruction of conservatory and window glass took place. So violent and prolonged was the storm, that the cottagers, in great alarm, betook themselves to prayer.* {A.D. 1850. Hailstone storm.}

This year, also, the inside of the Ackworth Church tower was restored, at a cost of £116, defrayed by private subscriptions. {Inside of Tower restored.}

The place selected for the experiment, was "Washing Mill Field." On reaching a depth of 100 feet, a spring was tapped which projected its waters to within a few feet of the surface. The boring was continued to a total depth of 140 feet. {1851. Boring for water.}

The coveted distinction of the "blue ribband," was this year once more secured by Mr. Gully's "Andover," the rider on this occasion being Andrew Day. The race was run in the short time of two minutes and fifty-two seconds. {1854. The Derby}

The Parish Church was re-opened for Divine worship, after restoration, on Thursday morning, August 2nd, 1855. The preacher on the occasion was the Rev. Mr. Eden, Vicar of Aberford. The service was fully choral, including an anthem, very creditably rendered by the village choir, assisted by J. Spark, Esq., Choir-master of Bury Parish Church, who brought with him two of his choristers, and a bass songsman. Dr. Spark, of Leeds Parish Church, presided at the organ. The choir was surpliced on this occasion for the first time. The cost of the restoration up to this time, had been £2,629, towards which the Church Building Society had made a grant of £120, and the Yorkshire Architectural Society a grant of £10, the remainder had been raised by private subscription. {1855. Restoration Services.}

On February 19, an explosion occurred in the Lundhill coalpit, near Wombwell, in which four brothers, named respectively, Richard, Thomas, Charles, and Joseph Kellett, and three {1857. Explosion.}

* Description of one who witnessed it.

sons of the two former, of Brackenhill, were all killed. It is said that Charles, on the evening previous to his death, had a melancholy foreboding of something of an awful nature about to occur. Joseph was very fond of animals, and the night before his death, fed his favourite cat, which after his death went to the door mat, where she moaned piteously, refusing all food until hunger terminated her existence. The Kellett family were all steady and moral people, and much respected. Richard and Thomas both left widows, but Charles and Joseph were single, aged respectively 29 and 30.

1858. School Report.

The Government Inspector's Report of the work done in the Ackworth Church Schools, during 1858-9, and of the examination results, is as follows:—

> "The present master* came in November, 1858. He has made a good beginning. The reading of the lower classes is indistinct. The writing deserves commendation. The composition exercise of the First Class was intelligently done.
>
> The Mistress teaches gently and sensibly. A "Form and Colour box" is wanted.
>
> Thomas Sharp, an apprenticed Pupil Teacher in these schools, passed so good an examination, that the Lord President of the Council has given him one year of his apprenticeship."

"Tongues in Trees."

The following lament appeared in the weekly issue of a local paper:—

> Sir,—Your columns are, I dare say, open to the complaint of a distressed tree, as well as to the grievances of your own countrymen. Well, Sir, I must tell you that for many scores of years past I have looked upon the inhabitants of Ackworth, and have been looked at and admired by the fathers, and grandfathers, and great-grandfathers of the present people of Ackworth. I hardly know how old I am, but I think I may safely say that I was here when Anne became Queen, March 8th, 1702. Not that I care so very much for those who have not seen me, it is solely on account of the good people of Ackworth, that I am now in distress. Sir, I must tell you that I had hoped to have grown old, and died in peace, of natural decay in fact, to which trees are subject. no less than men. But I am, I fear, doomed to disappointment. The parish surveyors of the highways have been and cut off some of my principle roots, and I comsider myself much damaged by this cruel treatment. I certainly should

* Mr. E. Spencer.

have liked to have flourished as long as possible; I moan for myself; but chiefly am I stricken with sadness at the thought that with the loss of so much of the principle of life, I cannot expect to grow and look smilingly upon my Ackworth friends so long as I otherwise might have done. I have one consolation, however. I hear the sighs of those who come beneath my shade, and I thank them for their sympathy with me in the loss of my roots. No good can arise from this cruel treatment of me. Where there is mischief in the heart, and a knife in the hand, ancient village trees, like myself, may sing out, "Woodman, spare that tree;" but to little use if our friends among mankind won't come and protect us.

I am, Sir, with great respect and sadness at heart,

Your humble servant,

THE TREE ON ACKWORTH GREEN.

A.D. 1858.

The following interesting statement is extracted from the "Ackworth Parish Magazine":—

1859. Morality of Ackworth.

"In the ten years, ending 25th March, 1759, five bastard children were baptized, that is, one in twenty-eight.

In the ten years, ending 25th March, 1859, thirty-two bastard children were baptized, or one in 10.875.

In a recently published history of the Quaker's School, it is sneeringly remarked that "Catechisms of religious faith are not much in vogue at Ackworth."

A comparision of the morality of the religious practice of the periods under review, will tend, perhaps to make one wish that they were—at any rate for a return to the good old custom of our forefathers, when the head of every household enployed a portion of the evening of every Lord's day, at the least, in teaching his children and servants the Church Catechism.

We question very much whether that plan would not be more effectual towards the keeping of the Seventh Commandment, than the system which has been subsituted for it, evening meetings for religious (so called) preachings and scientific lectures.

Such meetings, we believe, are not unfrequently either places of assignation for young men and women, or they serve as pretexts for young people getting out at night, free from parental control.

All experience proves that, what are called religious revivals and practical moral evils, not unfrequently go hand in hand."

From January 1865, to January 1875, the number of illegitimate children baptized in Ackworth Church, was seven, or one in forty-six; and from January 1875, to January 1885, twenty, being one in 34.1. It will therefore be seen that

A.D. 1859. immorality in Ackworth is decidedly on the wane, especially when we remember that the population of the village has more than doubled itself since 1875.

Lords of the Manor

The following letter, which appeared in the Ackworth Parish Magazine, is worthy of re-production as a parochial record.

> Sir,—On the 7th of April last, three of the Trustees of the Manor, Messrs. Fairbarn, W. Nelstrop, and R. Nelstrop, if I understood them correctly, gave a large number of the Freeholders and Ratepayers, then assembled in Public Meeting, to understand that the Accounts and present state of their Trust should shortly be submitted to the Public.
>
> Finding that promise no nearer realization, I venture to ask you to print a Resolution on the subject, which was passed at a Vestry Meeting on the 3rd May, 1818 :—"That the Accounts of the Lords of the Manor be in future Audited in Vestry every year on the Sunday next after Saint Mark's day."
>
> If the Lords of the Manor were not as ignorant of the *nature* of their Trust as they, confessedly, are of its *duties*, this very reasonable direction would not have been allowed to become obsolete.
>
> A perusal of the Vestry Meetings, held on the subject of the Manor Trust from May 1813, to May 1818, will probably lead the reader to the conclusion that there existed at that time peculiar reasons for the Lords of the Manor not being anxious to court publicity.
>
> *I* do not charge the present Lords with similar conduct, but their evident reluctance to "give an account of their stewardship," might cause a less charitable judge to infer that there is something behind the scenes which they are ashamed of.
>
> I am, Sir, with grateful respect,
> *Ackworth,*   Your obedient Servant,
> *May* 14th, 1859.   A FREEHOLDER OF ACKWORTH.

Opening Services.

On Sunday, the 8th of August, 1859, sermons were preached in the new Wesleyan Chapel, by the Rev. S. D. Waddy, of Sheffield, when the collections amounted to £75. On the following Tuesday, the Rev. Dr. Guthrie preached,—afternoon and evening,—the evening sermon on Rev. xiv. 13. The following extract from Dr. Guthrie's autobiography, bearing upon his visit to Ackworth, has special interest :—" The Chapel in whose opening services I was called to take a part, is a perfect delight to preach in. Wonderful to see, in the afternoon of a busy harvest day, it was filled, and in the evening, crowded and overflowing. I never preached with more pleasure, seldom with so much, (to) a fine intelligent looking people; they had a deal of lively methodist feeling in their faces, and seemed ready often to burst out into an audible assent or expression of sympathy. I could not but envy the state of mind of one man especially, who was right before me. He sang the hymns with a face luminous as Stephen's, and as I preached, every feeling that passed over his heart was expressed on his countenance.* I was much gratified by not a few men and women coming up to shake hands with me, and thank me when the services were over."† {A.D. 1859.}

In July of this year, an indictment was entered and tried against certain members of the Society of Friends, for encroachment upon a highway, near Carr Bridge, in the parish of Ackworth, by enclosing a portion thereof. {Encroachment. Regina v. Johnson.}

Mr. Macauley, Q.C., and Mr. Field, were counsel for the prosecution; Mr. Sergeant Hayes appeared for the defendant.

There was little in the case, of general interest, beyond this, that it elicited the opinion of the Chief-Justice upon a mis-apprehension very widely entertained, that the owner of the soil of land, adjoining a highway, may enclose such a portion on the side adjoining as will leave fifteen feet clear on either side of the middle thread of the way. This notion, Mr. Macauley said, had arisen from a misconception of the effect of sections 64 and 69 of the Highway Act (5th and 6th William IV., cap. 50). The effect of this section was to give the justices at petty sessions, the power to convict and fine summarily persons enclosing or obstructing the road within those limits, and to compel the removal of obstructions.

The Chief-Justice, in summing-up, said that "when once a road had been set out and dedicated to the public, and had been occupied by the public, the owner of the soil of the road had no right to enclose any part of that road; it remained a road for ever, unless it be enclosed, or stopped, or diverted by law—that is, by putting into operation the provisions of the Highway Act for that purpose. The

---

* This man was a Mr. Ross, of Selby.

† Vide Pontefract and Castleford "Wesleyan Methodist Circuit Record," August, 1882.

A.D. 1859. lessening of the traffic along the road made no difference. When it was once a road, it was always a road, excepting it ceased to be so by act of law."

This would seem to settle, not only the Quakers', but the question of encroachments in general.

Dean Hook
On the second Sunday morning in November of this year, the pulpit of Ackworth Church, was occupied by the popular Vicar of Leeds, Dr. Hook, who had been asked by the Rector of Ackworth (Rev. J. Kenworthy,) to preach on behalf of a fund to complete the debt upon the church, consequent on its restoration. Dr. Hook's visit was a memorable one for two reasons :—(1) He pointed out with considerable warmth, the absence of much that was needed to make Divine worship what it ought to be, viz: reverent and decent; and (2) his sermon, which dealt with almsgiving as an act of worship, was considered by those competent to judge of such matters, a masterpiece of oratory and rhetoric.

Dr. Livingstone.
This eminent medical missionary and explorer paid a visit to Ackworth during his last furlough to England in the summer of 1859. The Dr. lectured at the Friends' School on his travels in Africa, and was much appreciated. Soon afterwards he returned to the scene of his labours, where he died.

1863.
Jan. 28. Miss Neilson, of Hundhill was this day married at Ackworth Church to Arthur Pemberton Lonsdale, Esq., of London. The Right Revd. Dr. Lonsdale, Bishop of Lichfield, Uncle of the bridegroom, officiated, and signed the marriage register with his episcopal signature "G. Lichfield."

Loyalty.
There are none more loyal than the people of Ackworth. On the occasion of the marriage of the Prince of Wales, the 10th of March, 1863, was observed in Ackworth as a general holiday. Banners were displayed; merry peals rung on the Church bells; and commemoration trees planted at Ackworth

School. The following formula was pronounced on the occasion:— A.D. 1863.

> "May the earth nourish their roots;
> May the dews cherish their branches;
> And may the sun ripen their fruits.
> May the union this day commemorated,
> be blessed with the fatness of the earth,
> the dew of heaven, and the refreshing
> beams of the Sun of Righteousness."*

March 10. Holiday. Marriage of Prince of Wales. Children assembled in the afternoon for buns, oranges, and medals. 1863. Festivities

March 11. Tea and cake in the afternoon.

March 27. The attendance this week has been unusally thin in consequence of more than half the children having the measles.

March 30. The visit of a Government Vaccination Officer to Ackworth, who examined each child's arm in the schools, caused quite a scare in the village.‡

In common with the rest of the nation, Ackworth was *en fete* on the occasion of the marriage of H. R. H. Albert Edward, Prince of Wales, and heir apparent to the English Throne, to the Princess Alexandra C. M. C. L. Julia, eldest daughter of the King of Denmark, March 10, 1863. Mrs. William Hepworth of the Lodge gave a dinner to all the aged people of the parish, from seventy years old and upwards, and the Church choir. A meat tea was enjoyed under canvas in Hague's Croft by the inhabitants of High Ackworth, and there were dinners at the "Boot and Shoe" and "Angel" Inns for the people of Moor Top; whilst the villagers of Low Ackworth were regaled with a meat tea in the Public Rooms. The cost of the festival was raised by subscription.

---

* These words were originally composed to be said at the planting of two trees, to commemorate the marriage of Robert and Hannah Whitaker, in 1812.

‡ Vide Log Book, National School.

A.D. 1863.
The village Stocks.

The primitive method of punishment by exposure in the stocks, ceased at Ackworth in or about the year quoted in the margin. They were placed originally near the pinfold which is itself in good condition but never used. They were subsequently removed to the vacant corner near the Church gates, and there stood until they were taken up and burnt. The last man confined therein was E———d T————m who was in the habit of imbibing a little too freely, and having allowed his whilom enemy to steal away his senses, he was consigned to "durance vile" to await their return. It is said that the sympathizing inhabitants of Vinegar Hill supplied him with an umbrella to shield him from the evening dew, and brought him beer and tobacco, wherewith to beguile his weary hours. But another instance is still remembered, and much oftener commented upon, viz., that of W————m P————r who it was said had three children christened, and was himself married and put into the stocks all in one day! It appears that the Rector had promised that if he would come to Church, have his three natural children baptised, and marry the woman with whom he had been living, no fee would be charged, and that a joint of beef from the Rectory would grace the marriage festivities. The neighbours unwisely but good-humouredly backed up this generous offer with a barrel of beer, which "Will" caused to be tapped before starting to Church. The consequence was that his courage was not only screwed up to sticking point, but his limbs were rendered very limp. The service concluded, Will, in stooping to pick up his hat, stumbled, and was quickly placed in the stocks by the Churchwardens, aided by the village constable. There he remained whilst the wedding party issued from the Church, and until his fond spouse returned with a substantial repast. All this occurred in March, 1849.

1864.
Fatal accident.

Henry Reynolds Neave, a pupil at Ackworth School, fatally injured by the breakage of a leaping pole, whilst vaulting over the horizontal bar. He lived twenty-eight hours after the accident, which took place in August, 1864.* A.D. 1864.

The Rev. A. S. Teutschil, Ph. D., appointed Chaplain and Schoolmaster of East Hardwick. 1866.

All the rivers of Yorkshire rising in mountainous or hilly districts, are subject to great floods, after heavy rains. The greatest flood in the Yorkshire rivers within recollection occured on Friday, November 16th, 1866, after a continuous rain of nearly twenty-four hours duration. In this great flood every stream overflowed its banks, and all the valleys were inundated. On the river Calder, near Dewsbury, a cart with three persons in it, was carried off the road into the river, and all three perished. At Wakefield, property to the value of £50,000 was destroyed. The number of persons drowned at Dewsbury by the overflow of the Calder, was ascertained to have been seven.† The river Went,‡ which flows through Ackworth, rose to an unprecedented height, and all the low-lying ground was submerged, both game and fish being drowned. Only the upper rooms of the houses at Carr Bridge were habitable, whilst all communication between Moor Top and the village was entirely cut off; even heavily built drays not venturing to stem the flood. The view of the surrounding country from the Church tower, presented the aspect of an extensive sea dotted with islands. Great Flood.

The Charity Commissioners having been requested by the late Mr. Henry Hill, of Ackworth Park, to enquire into the condition of the Manor Trust, reported as follows:—"The rents of the estate, which came to the Lords of the Manor by escheat,§ were applied for some time towards paying off a mortgage of 1867. An important opinion.

---

* Vide " Hist. of Ackworth School," p. 248.

† Vide Baines' " Yorkshire," Vol. I, p. 268.

‡ Baines says this river rises near Wentworth, but its actual source is at Syndale, near Normanton. It is about 20 miles long, and empties itself into the Don.

§ Forfeiture.

A.D. 1867.   £400,* to which the estate was subject, and they are now paid partly to the Surveyors of the highways and partly to the Overseers of the Poor.

The Manor appears to have been purchased for the use of the parishioners, and the rents and profits have accordingly been *always* applied for the public occasions of the parish, in the manner above-mentioned, and not as a charity for individuals of a particular class or description."

1868. Parish Poll

March 26th, 1868. At a public meeting of the inhabitants of Ackworth, rated and contributing to the Highway Rates thereof, in vestry assembled and convened by notice; it was moved by Mr. Brown, and seconded by Mr. Wade, that a person of skill and experience be appointed as paid Surveyor, at a salary of Twenty pounds per annum. Mr. Barratt proposed an amendment, which was seconded by Mr. Mason, that Mr. Brown's motion be negatived. The amendment, on being put, was carried by a considerable majority. Mr. Brown then demanded a poll, which was granted by the Chairman (Rev. J. Kenworthy), and fixed for the following Monday and Tuesday, March 30th and 31st, in Mr. Lowther's School Room, from 10 o'clock to 12, in the morning, and from 7 to 9 in the evening of each day. The following is an analysis of the result of poll.

	For Mr. Barratt.	For Mr. Brown.
On Monday morning.	2	76
On Monday evening.	50	26
On Tuesday morning.	4	44
On Tuesday evening.	58	39
Total number of votes	114	185

The poll was declared on Tuesday evening, at 9 o'clock. Majority for Mr. Brown, 71. The Rev. J. Kenworthy acted as Returning Officer, and Messrs. Atha and Spencer as Scrutators.

At a subsequent meeting of ratepayers held on the 2nd of April, "in order to settle all disputes and produce peace in the

* Vide List of Charities.

parish," the following compromise was made:— "That Mr. Fearnley be appointed Surveyor of the parish for the ensuing year at a salary of £20, which amount is guaranteed by Messrs. Brown, J. Nelstrop, R. Nelstrop, Waide, Simpson, Tempest and Satterthwaite, and the Rector.*

<small>A.D. 1868.</small>

The Church was in danger of destruction by fire on 2nd May, 1868, wilfully caused by a malicious, if not insane, man, who in a short time in the afternoon, ran from stack to outbuildings, and Church, and set all on fire to revenge some fancied slight about a gravestone. The pulpit and some stalls were first heaped together, the former filled with music books and other combustible materials, and ignited. Marks of the fire may still be seen inside the pulpit. Fortunately the fire was discovered before much damage was done. The offender was found in the Church and secured, and, at the ensuing assize at Leeds, was sentenced to twelve months' imprisonment.

<small>Arson and sacrilege.</small>

The following is another account:—

The Parish Church at Ackworth, near Pontefract, which was restored a few years ago at great expense, was set on fire May 1st, 1868, by a man named Wm. Chas. Wilson. He had removed into the pulpit various articles of an inflammable character, and had then deliberately ignited them. Fortunately the flames were observed by Mr. J. Fearnley and Mr. R. Nelstrop, who resided near, and who had been aroused by a stack-fire in the neighbourhood, also believed to have been caused by Wilson, who conducted himself very violently, kicking and striking the gentlemen named on their interfering with him. He was afterwards examined before the magistrates, and a medical certificate was produced showing that the prisoner had previously been in an asylum. He was committed to the West Riding Assizes for trial.†

<small>Fire at the Church.</small>

---

* In the following year Mr. Fearnley was elected without opposition, but in 1873 an attempt was made to eject him, in favour of Mr. Roberts. The result of the poll was: for Mr. Fearnley, 208; for Mr. Roberts, 76. Another attempt was made in 1874, with the following result: Mr. Fearnley, 156; Mr. Haigh, 137. In 1875: Fearnley, 208; Haigh, 154.

† "Annals of Yorkshire," Vol. III.

A.D. 1869.
Cawood's Charity.

By an order from the Charity Commissioners dated July 6th, 1869, the following gentlemen were appointed the legal trustees and administrators of the Cawood Charity:—

Rev. J. Kenworthy, Rector of Ackworth,
E. C. Waide,
Thos. Pearson, } of Ackworth.
Peter Watson,
Jervis Winn, } of East Hardwick.
Robert Bailey,
John Hope Barton, of Stapleton Park, Pontefract.
Joseph Nelstrop, of the Lodge, Ackworth.
Edmund Ernest Leatham, of Hemsworth Hall, and
Thomas William Tew, of Carleton.

1870. Fountain.

One of the felt wants of Ackworth is good water. The late Henry Hill, Esq., out of the munificence of his kindly heart, caused a high level boring to be made upon his estate, and piped water from thence to the entrance of the village. The parish was then asked to do its part, and the result was that subscriptions were quickly raised to purchase the appliances wherewith to bring the water into the centre of the village. The work was completed, and a handsome fountain erected at a cost of £90, but a very short time sufficed to prove the futility of the scheme. The water, which was little better than tincture of iron, quickly oxidised the filter, pipe, and nozzle of the fountain, and the fountain itself soon became what it has since continued to be, a useless ornament. Soon afterwards, Mr. Hill being convinced that the water of Ackworth contained chemical properties of considerable value, decided to pipe another stream from a field in Low Ackworth, known as "Assax," into the Tan House Lane, for the use of the Low Ackworth people. This fountain has since been known as the "Spa."

1872. Hardwick Church.

The foundation stone of this Church, dedicated to Saint Stephen, was laid by the Marquis of Ripon, October 23, 1872. The site selected whereon to erect the new building was only a few yards from the site of the old chapel, but on the opposite side of the road. Geologically the site is on the edge of the Pontefract Rock of Smith and Sedgewick, overlapping the Coal measures, the Stanley Main seam of Coal lying about 155 yards beneath.

A.D. 1872.

Mr. Thomas Baines, in his "Yorkshire, Past and Present," published in 1872, quoting from Mr. Charnock's report on the subject of the reclamation of waste lands in the West Riding, says, "I heard an intelligent farmer state that, since he entered on his occupation, the whole has been thoroughly drained; that on his first coming he found his neighbour's crops, on the higher ground around him, reached maturity a full fortnight before those on his farm; but that since the drainage has been completed his crops are invariably a week or two earlier than those in the immediately adjoining district. I refer" says Mr. Charnock, "to Mr. John Moore,* of Ackworth, near Pontefract, whose farming is an example to that locality."

A model farmer.

March 15. First Diocesan Inspection of Church Schools in Religious Knowledge, by Rev G. W. Kennion.

1873.

On Nov. 25th, the village of East Hardwick was *en fête*, on the occasion of the Consecration of their new Church, by Dr. Thomson, Archbishop of York. It is a pretty cruciform building in the Early English style of Architecture, the turret of which contains three melodious steel bells. The Parsonage was built and presented to the parish by Mr. T. W. Tew, J.P., of Carleton. The foundation stone was laid with masonic honours, and several emblems of the craft are carved outside the building.

1874. Hardwick Church.

The old organ having become dilapidated, the Rector and Churchwardens decided to have a new one built, and the work was entrusted to the late Mr. Booth, of Wakefield. The old

New Organ

---

* Mr. Moore died at Ackworth in 1887, after a long and painful indisposition, and was buried in Badsworth Churchyard.

A.D. 1874. organ was sold for £10. The new instrument cost £322, and was inaugurated in 1874, by Mr. Rogers, the Organist of Doncaster Parish Church. The new instrument, although small, contains some remarkably sweet pipes, and several stops, contained only in continental organs, the tones of which Mr. Rogers exhibited with considerable skill and taste.

1875.
New Rector's Manifesto.

After the death of the Rev. J. Kenworthy, the Rectory of Ackworth did not long remain vacant, for, in October, it was offered to, and accepted by, the Rev. W. M. Falloon, M.A., Vicar of St. Bride's, Liverpool, and Hon. Canon of Chester. Before coming into residence, the new Rector put forth the following manifesto :—

> To the Parishioners of Ackworth.
>
> My dear Parishioners,
>
> In God's good Providence, I have been appointed Rector of your Parish : the offer of it came to me from the Chancellor of the Duchy of Lancaster, unsought, and, by me, entirely unexpected: I am, therefore, comforted in the acceptance of it, by regarding it as a Divine ordering, for me and for you, and, in no respect, an accident for either of us.
>
> It is my earnest desire and Prayer to God, that I may come unto you in the fulness of the blessing of the Gospel of Christ: that, if spared, I may work amongst you, usefully; dwell in your midst lovingly; and, as far as lieth in me, live peaceably with all. I do not appear amongst you, altogether, as a young man, but as one who has had many years of opportunity, for learning something of the revealed will and Word of God; and for doing something in the work of God; on these grounds, therefore, I may fairly claim your confidence and forbearance; and I respectfully ask for these, at your hearts and hands.
>
> Believing the Church of England to be Catholic as regards truth; Evangelical as regards doctrine; Apostolic as regards order; and Protestant as regards error; it has ever been, and will continue to be, my effort, by God's assistance, to minister in accordance with such principles; and to serve, with fidelity and cordial obedience, in the safe and sure old paths, marked out by our honored Reformers.
>
> I invite your kind co-operation as Parishioners in all that may really concern the interests of our Church and Parish : and trust, that whilst thus duly mindful of our own things we may not selfishly forget the interests of others : "None of us liveth to himself, and no man dieth to himself." Let regular attendance at the House of God, and reverent worship there, each and all taking their part

therein, according to the intention and instruction of the Church of England, furnish one of the best evidences of the reality of our convictions and of the sincerity of our devotions. A.D. 1875.

I have learnt long since, that, without the blessing of God, nothing is holy, : I therefore earnestly and affectionately ask your prayers, your sympathy and your support : all these you can give : of these, *prayer* is the best, so, I ask it *first*; and, if you are led, by God's grace, to pray for him who is appointed to watch for your souls, I can have no doubt, that the other two will speedily follow.

I hope soon to be resident amongst you, and to do what I can to serve you, in ministering to you the glorious Gospel of the Blessed God ; in lifting up Christ as the sinner's only refuge ; trusting altogether to the present power of the Holy Spirit to apply the message savingly to your souls; and, in caring for the sick and the afflicted, according to the ability which God may give me ; and this, without any preference or partiality as regards rich or poor, there being no respect of persons with God. Meanwhile, allow me to subscribe myself, with all good will,

Yours very faithfully,
W. M. FALLOON, M.A.,
RECTOR (ELECT) OF ACKWORTH.

October, 1875.

This small, but at one time very important building, now converted into cottages, known as the "High Terrace," stands on a somewhat elevated position on the Ackworth Moor Top, at the right hand side of the road leading to Hemsworth. When first erected it stood some distance out of the village, but now it is almost surrounded by houses. After the passing of the Poor Law Amendment Act*in 1847, the old workhouse remained untenanted. At length it was bought by Mr. Jno. Simpson, of Ackworth, who soon afterwards sold it to Mr. Graham, formerly of Ackworth, by whom it was converted into four cottages, and mortgaged by him to Joseph Allbright, of Lancaster, in 1884. The old workhouse

On Sunday morning, December 5th, the Rev. W. M. Falloon, M.A., Honorary Canon of Chester, the newly-appointed Rector of Ackworth, admitted himself to the benefice, according to the usage, by reading the 39 articles of the Church of England, instead of preaching a sermon. In the evening Canon Falloon preached his inaugural sermon, to a crowded congregation, from New Rector.

* 10 & 11 Vict., c. 109.

A.D. 1875. Hebrews xiii, 8: "Jesus Christ, the same, yesterday, to-day, and for ever." The new Rector came to Ackworth from his late sphere at St. Bride's, Liverpool, well reported of, both for eloquence and good works.

1876. Mr. Fearnley resigned his position as Parish Surveyor, after eight years faithful discharge of duty, during which time he had encountered much opposition and unkind treatment from village agitators. Messrs. Cuttle, Child, Roberts, and Haigh were put forward as men of "skill and experience" to succeed him. The voting was as follows:—Cuttle, 0; Roberts, 7; Child, 8; Haigh, 10. In the second show of hands the numbers were Child, 8; Haigh, 13. Mr. Haigh was therefore duly elected Surveyor for the ensuing year.

1879. New Railway Opening. A new line of railway from Swinton to York was formally opened for general traffic on July 1st, 1879,—although the Company ran trains from York and Sheffield to the new station at Ackworth four days earlier, for the convenience of those who wished to attend the Centenary Celebration at Ackworth School. These were the first passenger trains which had ever reached the village. The first sod of this railway was cut on Octr. 12th, 1875.

Literature. Towards the close of this year, the following works, all connected with the Centenary Celebrations at the Friends' School, Ackworth, were published:—

1. List of Boys and Girls admitted into Ackworth School during the 100 years, 1779—1879. Published by the Centenary Committee, Ackworth School, 1879, pp. xxxix., 211, 8vo. There are nearly 9,500 names, or 1,300 surnames;[*] an invaluable record for Quaker genealogy, with an amusing 'Nominal' History by Thomas Pumphrey,—a play on the surnames. Printed at Gloucester.

[*] With the Friends, the first or baptismal name is really the *sur* or *added* name, being added to the patronymic when the child is registered according to law. J. L. S.

2. A narrative of the proceedings at the celebration of the Centenary of Ackworth School, 6th month, 1879; edited by James Henry Barber (of Sheffield). Also a sketch of the Life of Dr. Fothergill, by James Hach Tuke, and a short sketch of the History of Ackworth School, by John S. Rowntree, with a nearly verbatim report of the speeches delivered at the two meetings. Published by the Centenary Committee, Ackworth School, 1879, pp. iv., 212, 8vo. *Frontispiece*, Ackworth School, from a sketch by Mary Hodgson; Portrait of John Fothergill, from the cameo of Wedgwood; Car-end, near Semerwater, the birthplace of Fothergill, from a sketch by the late John Fothergill, of Darlington. [A.D. 1879.]

3. History of Ackworth School, during its first hundred years; preceded by a brief account of the fortunes of the house whilst occupied as a Foundling Hospital. By Henry Thompson (of Arnside, near Carnforth), with twelve illustrations from the pencil of Mary Hodgson, engraved on wood by Edmund Evans. Published by the Centenary Committee, Ackworth School, 1879, (Printed by Bellows, Gloucester,) pp. xxiv., 355, 8vo. *Views*—Ackworth School; Ackworth Village Green, shewing the Church, Lychgate, Village Cross, and Elm; Ackworth School Seed House; Great Garden; Car Bridge, River Went; Went Vale; Pontefract Castle; Ackworth School Temperance Inn; Brackenhill; Ackworth Mill Dam; Hemsworth Mill Dam; Nostell Priory and Lake; and the old Chalybeate Bath at Ackworth.*

The old Churchyard being found insufficient for the purposes of interment, steps were at once taken by the Rector to secure additional land wherewith to enlarge the old burial ground. Very soon he was able to issue a pastoral on the subject, from which I have gathered the following particulars:—" The Rector and Churchwardens, entirely convinced of the necessity of moving speedily in the matter, entered into communication [New Churchyard.]

---

* Vide "Yorkshire Notes and queries," Part I., pp. 8, 9, where also a Complete list of Educational and other works connected with Ackworth School are given, extracted from Smith's Catalogue of Friends' Books.

A.D. 1879. with Mr. Henry Hill, the owner of the land adjoining the Church, asking him to be good enough to arrange for the allocation of a certain portion of the field at the north side of the Church, for the purpose of adding to the present graveyard. Mr. Hill at once acknowledged the need there was for enlargement; said he had foreseen it for some time, and consented to take the matter into his immediate consideration. Accordingly, having fixed the day and hour, he met the Rector and Wardens on the ground proposed, a plan of which had previously been forwarded to him; the extent of land asked for is half an acre, along with about 200 yards of the Rectory garden, which the Rector is prepared to give to the Parish, in order to make the addition square. After consultation together, Mr. Hill declared himself prepared to sell the land required, for the sum of £200, and he undertakes to build a substantial wall around the New Grave Ground, to serve as a suitable fence to the same." Mr. Hill's offer was accepted and subscriptions quickly raised towards the amount required as purchase money, and on the 14th of March, 1879, the ground, levelled and walled round, was consecrated by the Right Rev. Rowley Hill, Bishop of Soder and Man, acting for His Grace the Archbishop of York.

Centenary of Ackworth School.

The Centenary of an Institution is in itself at once a guarantee of its utility and vitality, and of the public estimation in which it is held. When a person or institution attains the hundredth year of its existence, it is immediately crowned with an halo of awful veneration which has been chastely described as the "Majesty of time." Unlike the person however, we look upon the Institution as having arrived at the meridian of its greatness, and are apt to accord to it Divine honours, exultingly exclaiming—

Quod semper movetur æternum est!

The Centenary of Ackworth School therefore was an event which all Ackworth joined to celebrate, consequently to use the language of the historian of the Centenary Celebration "the 26th and 27th of Sixth month, 1879, were joyful and memorable days in the Annals of Ackworth School!"

With Mr. Barber's kind permission I propose to abstract from his comprehensive work a concise narrative of the proceedings, for the benefit of those who are not fortunate enough to possess the book itself. "Ackworth," says Mr. Barber, "had collected around her her sons and daughters from far and near to keep holiday, and commemorate her hundredth Anniversary.   *   *   And truly they were of almost every age, from the venerable old man in his ninth decade, to the young scholar not yet emerged from the first. Joyous youth, active manhood, womanhood, and grey-headed age were there all claiming the kindred tie of Ackworth scholarship."

In the afternoon of the 24th the General Meeting was held, which, "despite its formal examinations, is at all times a lively anniversary." This year "it was larger than usual," and "there was a Centenary atmosphere around it manifest from the first." The proceedings included an afternoon meeting of the Directors of the Friends' Provident Institution, a "somewhat elderly staid looking set of men, evidently full of facts." The capital of the Assurance Institution in 1879, according to the report, was £1,400,000, with 5,330 policies amounting to £4,237,914, and a yearly income of £151,927. In the evening, whilst the younger Friends mingle with the boys and girls in their sports, the "older ones, once scholars, wander to every familiar nook and recall their youthful days," moralising perhaps
———' On the decay
Of Ackworth boys in modern day;
and then "turn in for the night." Thus ended the doings of Third-day.

The morning of Fourth-day (25th) opened brightly and the proceedings of the General Meeting proper began at 10 a.m., with the meeting for worship; it was large, and an impressive and interesting occasion, partaking very much of a national character, being attended by ministers from various parts of the kingdom,—and one from the United States of America,—

A.D. 1879. the presence of the large number of children in a solid phalanx in the midst of the congregation, fitly symbolizing the care of the Church extended towards and around them. The General Report was then read, followed by a spirited discussion thereon, and then the Report of the Centenary Committee was read. The Meeting then adjourned until 2-30 p.m. the next day. The afternoon of the 25th and morning of the 26th was occupied with the Annual Examination. At 5 p.m., a meeting of a very enjoyable kind to the children, was held to hear the report of the Friends' Public Schools' Industrial Association, and to award the prizes to the successful exhibitors, and the day's proceedings were brought to a close by the Annual Meeting of the First-day School Association.

The morning of Fifth-day was inaugurated by a "meeting of an interesting character, for communion and united prayer at 6 a.m. There was something in the hour, the freshness of the morning, and in the feeling that those who had thus early assembled had come with an earnest desire after good, which contributed to the life of the meeting. The special subject for prayer was the work of the First-day Schools. The first meeting, however, in celebration of the Centenary was held at 6-30 p.m., at which, probably more than 1,000 persons were present. The meeting was presided over by Thomas Harvey, of Leeds, who opened the proceedings by slowly reading a few appropriate verses from the Psalms, followed by a short devotional pause. Letters of apology were then read, including one from the Right Honourable John Bright, who was educated at Ackworth, followed by an address by the Chairman, after which James Hack Tuke, of Hitchin, read a paper which he had prepared at the request of the Centenary Committee, being a sketch of the life of Dr. Fothergill, the originator, and at least the most active and liberal founder of Ackworth School.* Before the lecturer was placed, in view of the whole meeting, the beautiful Wedgwood bust of Dr. Fothergill, executed from

* Vide Biographical sketch of Dr. Fothergill, in Appendix.

a model by Flaxman. There were present at this meeting A.D. 1879. three collateral descendants of Dr. Fothergill, lineal descendants of Alexander Fothergill, one of his brothers. One of these, Samuel Fothergill, an old Ackworth Scholar, then addressed the meeting; after which Walter Wilson, the elder brother of the late Right Hon. James Wilson, Finance Minister of British India, who was educated at Ackworth, spoke. The remaining speakers were Henry E. Clark, the devoted missionary to Madagascar; and Joseph Simpson, a member of the Centenary Committee. The meeting then concluded, and it was felt to have been worthy of the occasion."

The devotional meeting on Sixth-day morning at 7 o'clock, was a much larger one than that on Fifth-day. It was a solemn prayerful time. Dr. Dougan Clark, Richmond, Indiana, opened the meeting by reading and commenting upon the 72nd Psalm. Soon after breakfast the *Great* Meeting took place in a monster marquee which had been erected specially to meet the requirements of the concourse of people which had been expected. At one end was the platform, close under which, sat the happy looking School children, and altogether it was a pretty and impressive sight. It is computed that there were about 1,600 persons present. The Chairman of the meeting was JAMES HENRY BARBER, of Sheffield, who took his place at ten o'clock, and opened the meeting by reading a few verses from the forty-eighth chapter of Genesis, being the account of Jacob blessing the sons of Joseph. His subsequent speech was a most felicitous one, bristling with history and narrative. ALFRED SIMPSON, of Manchester, one of the Secretaries, then read the Centenary Report, after which JOHN STEPHENSON ROWNTREE, was called upon to read his paper, entitled, "A sketch of the History of Ackworth School,"* the reading of which took up about an hour and a quarter, and was repeatedly and warmly applauded. The proposal of the reader to leave out a portion, at one period, was met by energetic cries of "No, no; go on." The whole

* Vide Ackworth Institutions.

A.D. 1879. company then rose to their feet and remained standing whilst the scholars sang the hymn—
"Abide with me, fast falls the eventide."
The next speaker was WILLIAM COOR PARKER, of Darlington, one of the Secretaries to the Centenary Committee, after which a number of old Ackworth scholars gave speeches of ten minutes' duration, the Chairman unflinchingly touching the bell at the expiration of nine minutes, so that the speaker might have one minute's warning in which to wind up his remarks. The names of the speakers were Henry Thompson, of Kendal; Henry Asworth, of Bolton; Thomas Puplett, of Ackworth; Robert Henry Marsh, of London; George Frederick Linney, of Croydon; J. S. Hodgson, of Manchester; J. F. Bottomley Firth; William Taylor, of Middlesborough; George Satterthwaite, for eleven years Superintendent of the School; William Jones, of Middlesborough; and lastly, by Frederick Andrews, the Superintendent, or "The Young Captain," as he was styled in a quotation by a previous speaker. Edward Gripper, of Nottingham, proposed a vote of thanks to the Centenary Committee and its two Secretaries, which was seconded by George William Binns, of Croydon. The motion was carried, with three cheers. William Coor Parker returned thanks, and the meeting was brought to a close.

After dinner, there was an interesting ceremony, viz.: the planting of two purple beech trees at the bottom of the Green, in commemoration of the Centenary, the one by the youngest child in the school, the infant daughter of the Superintendent, the other by one of the youngest boys in the school, Herbert Clark, of Manchester. The little girl's hand was guided by her mother, and a silver trowel provided for the purpose by Joseph Simpson, of Ashbourne, an old scholar, was presented to the little planter, and a commemorative inscription has since been engraved upon it. Both trees were presented by Robert E. Giles, of Derby, another old scholar. Commemorative medals were then presented to each boy and girl, the gift of Smith

FRIENDS' SCHOOL, ACKWORTH.

Harrison, of London; George Stacey Gibson, of Saffron Walden; and James Reckitt, of Hull. Medals in bronze, given by James Hack Tuke, were presented to each teacher in the School. This was followed by an aquatic entertainment in the large swimming bath, the sides of which were thronged with spectators. A number of prizes for skill in swimming and diving, were offered by visitors and received by the successful competitors. Robert B. Oddie, of Ackworth, was master of the Ceremonies. *A.D. 1879.*

The conclusion of the festivities consisted of an entertainment given by the children of the school to the Visitors, a detailed account of which, together with a verbatim report of the various speeches will be found in Mr. Barber's narrative of the Centenary proceedings.

A Church tower is scarcely complete without a clock, but it was not until 1879 that subscriptions were raised to purchase one. The present clock was supplied by Messrs. Potts and Son, of Leeds, and inserted by them in 1879. Its cost was £100, and the works were first set in motion by Miss Falloon, the Rector's daughter. *Church Clock.*

On Friday morning, March 14, Dr. Rowley Hill, late Bishop of Sodor and Man, held a Confirmation in Ackworth Church, for His Grace the Archbishop of York, and afterwards consecrated the new burial ground, as an addition to the old Churchyard, which had for many centuries been the only place of interment for the inhabitants of Ackworth. *Confirmation and Consecration.*

The old tenor bell had long been very much worn by constant and faithful service, so it was resolved to have it recast, the other bells tuned, and the whole peal re-hung on a perfectly new principle. The work was skilfully and speedily carried out under the direction of the late Mr. Mallaby, of Ripon, at the expense of Mrs. Peel, of Ackworth Park. The opening peals were rung on Sunday, December 19th, 1880, by eight gentleman ringers, on which occasion special collections were made on behalf of the National Schools. *1880. Re-opening of bells.*

A.D. 1880. Folk Lore.

A very beautiful custom, distinctly Norwegian in its origin,* has been observed for many years at Ackworth at Christmas. The following lines by "J.W." chastely describe it.

> At Ackworth Church, on Christmas Eve,
> Outside the porch is hung
> A sheaf of corn, to feast the birds
> That all the summer sung
> Around the Church their Maker's praise
> In many a joyous stave,
> And make them on Christ's birthday morn
> As blithesome and as brave.
>
> And is't not meet that we should keep
> Our Saviour's natal day
> In peace with all—man, beast and bird—
> That come across our way?
> Not making glad ourselves alone
> Beneath our sprigs of holly,
> But striving hard to make all else
> Around us, just as jolly.
>
> J.W.—Written in 1880.

The custom, however, has long been observed both at Christmastide and harvest.†

1882. New Burials Act.

The New Burials Act came into operation in 1880, but it was not until March, 1882, that its privileges were taken advantage of in Ackworth, and even then, the friends of the person interred were not, strictly speaking, Dissenters, but Roman Catholics. The burial was carried out in accordance with the provisions of the Act, that is to say, no bell was rung, the Church door was closed, and the name and address of the person certifying or having charge of the funeral, entered in the Parish Register of Burials. Since then, three burials have taken place under the provisions of the Act, viz: two Roman Catholics and a Wesleyan, and in each instance, the requirements of the Act have been carefully complied with.

1883.

At a public meeting of the Freeholders of Ackworth, held on the 3rd of April, it was resolved that the Lords of the Manor be requested to take steps for the planting of a tree somewhere on the Village Green, to succeed in due time the Grand Old Tree; and to be duly fenced for protection.

* Vide "Antiquarian Gossip of the Months" in "Leisure Hour" of 1879.
† I am informed that the custom was introduced into Ackworth by the Rev. Mr. Kenworthy, the late Rector.

In December of this year, a most unwelcome hurricane caused extensive damage in and around Ackworth. The Church suffered most severely. The pinnacles were blown down, one of them in its fall breaking through the roof in two places, and the battlements of the tower were shattered and displaced so seriously, that on two sides they required almost entire renewal, and general repair all round. A peculiar feature of this storm was that it brought with it a sleety brine from the north east, which left a sediment upon the windows resembling hoar-frost and which was distinctly saline to the taste.

<small>A.D. 1883. Great Storm.</small>

Paul Lindley was a familiar figure at Ackworth, and a great favourite with the market people who resorted every Saturday to the town of Pontefract, where he died in October of this year, aged 71. Notwithstanding the hurry and bustle of modern life, with its scientific progress, business activity, and political zeal, it is surprising how near we are still to a past in which existence was the reverse of feverish. For 22 years Lindley was honourably connected with the Borough police force in Pontefract, and for eleven years before he donned the constable's uniform he acted as night watchman and went about no doubt many-caped, and with his lantern, shouting the hour, "Two o'clock,—wet morn," unless fastened in his watch-box by the young dandies of the time. He was for 26 years Superintendent of the Fire Brigade, and at two fires at Fryston Hall rendered services such as to receive the thanks of the late Lord Houghton. On the occasion of the first fire at Fryston, the deceased recommended the late Lord Houghton to construct a receptacle for water supply in case of fire near the Hall. But the suggestion, unfortunately, was not carried out, and the mansion afterwards fell a prey to another fire. The deceased, who was an expert officer, was obliged through indisposition to resign his post about five years ago, and the Corporation granted him a pension of £1 1s. per week for life. Whatever his adventures, he did his duty faithfully, and died much respected.*

<small>1885. Death of an old watchman</small>

* Local Papers.

A.D. 1886.
Tenebræ
in luce.

On the evening of Friday, October 1st, a meeting of the ratepayers of the parish of Ackworth was held in the Public Rooms, "to take into consideration the desirability of lighting the village with gas." The Rev. Canon Falloon took the chair, on the motion of Mr. F. Andrews, B.A., seconded by Mr. W. F. Tempest, J.P.

The Chairman read the notice convening the meeting, after which he said that the meeting had not been called in a formal and legal manner, but simply to ascertain the opinion of the people on this important question. He had in this matter no private or individual interest to serve, and he was willing and anxious to carry out the wishes of the inhabitants whatever they might be. However, it was for the meeting to discuss the matter, and it was now open for any gentleman to state his opinions with regard to the question of lighting the village with gas.

Mr. Andrews said that the meeting had been called by no "ring" or clique, and he was there as the representative of no one but himself. He thought that in order to throw the question formally before the meeting he would move the following resolution:—"That this meeting of the ratepayers of the parish of Ackworth approves of the adoption of the provisions of the Lighting Act for the said parish, and appoints the following gentlemen as a Committee to take the necessary steps for carrying this resolution into effect." Mr. Jonah Barratt seconded the motion.

Mr. Tempest then proposed the following amendment:— "That this meeting of the ratepayers and inhabitants of Ackworth fails to see the necessity or expediency of lighting the village with gas, and thus adding to the burden of the existing rates." On being put to the meeting the amendment was carried by an overwhelming majority, the people of Ackworth thus deciding to remain in darkness.

During the summer of this year the compiler of this work has secured several very fine specimens of fragmentary fossil plants from the Ackworth quarries. They consist chiefly of large pieces of the trunk *Sigillaria*, and its root the *Stigmaria*, found in the quiet deposit of ragged stone above and below the stratas known as the Yorkshire Flag. The tuberous appendages of this flora denote it to be a mud plant. There are several pieces of deposit perforated with the tracks of *Annelides*, or as they are locally termed, the earthworm; one or two specimens of the scaly *Lepidodendron*, and one of the *Coniferæ* tribe having some faint traces of annual rings. The collection also contains a specimen of the red sandstone *Calamite*, and we may safely say that not a single piece in the collection had seen the light for at least six thousand years, and probably for a much longer period, as animal traces are altogether absent.

A.D. 1886. Fossils.

✗ Whatever links the present with the past is worthy of reverence, especially in the case of one who, having served his generation well and faithfully, has been gathered to his fathers in a good old age. Thomas Turton, commonly known as "Old Dr. Turton," died on Sunday evening, March 20, at the ripe old age of 93. With the exception of a little deafness, he enjoyed the full possession of his faculties up to the last, and, in many other respects, he was a wonderful old man. His memory was unimpaired, but, unfortunately, his disposition was reserved and taciturn. He was one of the very few remaining who practised the profession of Medicine before the year 1815, and was therefore a duly registered medical practitioner, although he had never gone through any regular course of training, or passed any qualifying examination. For many years he enjoyed considerable local reputation in the "bleeding" and "tapping" line, being known by many as the "Water-doctor!" He was supposed to possess the secret of many wonderful cures. ✗

1887. A worthy townsman

The very Rev. Canon Scruton died early on Monday morning, September 12th, at the Presbytery of St. Patrick's Roman Catholic Church at Bradford, in the 58th year of his age. He

Canon Scruton.

A.D. 1887. was born at York in July, 1830, educated at York Grammar School and at St. Cuthbert's College, Durham. He was ordained in 1856, and was consecrated by Bishop Briggs to the priesthood at Doncaster. He next went to Ackworth Grange as Chaplain to Mr. Roger Tempest. In 1862 he took charge, by the appointment of Bishop Cornthwaite, of St. Patrick's, at Bradford, and his devotion and energy since that time have been conspicuous.*

QUEEN'S JUBILEE.

1837.  1887.

Jubilee Festivities

A brief account of the rejoicings at Ackworth in commemoration of Her Majesty's Jubilee, will form a fitting conclusion to this section of the work. The initiatory steps were taken by the Rector, who called a representative meeting to devise the best means of celebrating the event, and it was decided that all denominations should join hands in doing honour to the Queen, on the completion of fifty years of her most illustrious reign. Canon Falloon was appointed Chairman of Committees; the Rev. J. L. Saywell, and Mr. Joseph Nelstrop, Secretaries; and Mr. Lean, Treasurer. A sum of over £60 was soon collected in the village, and before the auspicious day arrived, all was in readiness for the occasion. The money had been well and judiciously expended, as will be seen from the following account of the proceedings. The 20th and 21st of June were brilliant days of veritable "Queen's weather," and the inhabitants did their duty right loyally and well; indeed all were joined in hand and heart to do honour to her to whom honour is due. Scarcely a house failed to hang out its symbol of affection for the Queen. Flags, banners, festoons, arches, and all kinds of decorations were visible in every direction, those of the cottages being sweetly touching tributes of loving loyalty. Early on Monday, the 20th, the bells of the Parish Church (from the tower of which floated a handsome Royal Ensign,) rang out a merry

* Yorkshire Post, September 14th, 1887.

peal of gladness, which was continued at intervals throughout   A.D. 1887.
the day. In the evening a hundred old people sat down
together in the Public Rooms, Low Ackworth, to supper, and
happiness reigned supreme. Their united ages amounted to
6,512 years, being an average of 65 years each. The oldest
lady present was attired in Quaker costume, and gave her age
as 92. She said she remembered the declaration of peace with
France, and very much enjoyed herself at the rejoicings on the
occasion of George III.'s Jubilee. The oldest gentleman was
81. After the tables had been cleared, a number of loyal and
facetious speeches were delivered, interspersed with appropriate
glees and recitations. The cheering and singing of the old
people, though feeble, was hearty, and a most enjoyable evening was brought to a close with a resolution of congratulation
to Her Majesty, proposed by Mr. Cadman, and seconded by Mr.
Lean, the terms of which were telegraphed to the Queen as
follows :—" The aged people of Ackworth respectfully tender
their sincere congratulations to Her Gracious Majesty on the
auspicious completion of the 50th year of her glorious reign."
Shortly afterwards the following reply was received by the
Chairman (Canon Falloon):—" The Queen thanks the senders
of your telegram for their good wishes.—PONSONBY." Tuesday,
the 21st, was observed as a general holiday. At eleven o'clock,
a special thanksgiving service was held in the Parish Church,
and it was a goodly sight to see Christian brethren of different
denominations worshipping together in unity. The prayers
were read by the Rev. J. L. Saywell, Curate, and the sermon
was preached by the Rev. Canon Falloon, Rector, from the
words "God save the King ! * let us rejoice and give thanks."
At one o'clock the children mustered at their respective schools,
where Jubilee medals were distributed, after which they proces-
sioned the village, headed by the Wragby Brass Band, gaily
decorated waggons, containing the infants, heading their
respective schools. Prizes were given for the best turn out of
waggons and horses, and were awarded as follows: (1) British
School; (2) Church School; (3) Howard's School. After a

substantial tea had been enjoyed by the youngsters, a field kindly lent for the occasion by Mr. Easton, was thrown open to the public, and a scene of hearty merriment ensued. Dancing, grotesque sports, and other amusements were kept up until dusk, by which time the field had been prettily illuminated. The bursting forth of the lurid flames of Upton Beacon was the signal for a grand display of fireworks, which lasted nearly two hours, the finale piece being a magnificent portrait of Her Majesty.

     Long may she reign!

APPENDIX.

ACKWORTH COWPASTURE.

The following document is both interesting and worthy of preservation—

Quodcunque facitis in nomine Jesu Christi facite.

Be it known unto all Christian people now present and for to come, to whom this present indented composition of confirmation shall be read, heard, or understood, that in the time of King Henry the 8th, there was a stock of cows raised within the parish of Ackworth by the donation of divers and sundry persons, some of them now being departed, some are yet living, and part of the names, both of them that be departed and that be living, are as follow, that is to say, Thomas Hartyndon, priest and parson of Ackworth, John Thompson, priest there, John Hambleton the elder, Thomas Raynold, Lionel Pearey, Isabel his wife, and Isabel his daughter, Jane Monitha Rawcliff, John Huntingdon the elder, John Brook, Richard Harrison, Richard Pickering the elder, Robert Padget, Roger Jackson, John Austwicke, George Austwicke, John Horner, John Wormald, John Hill, Thomas Brook, William Bradley, Robert Bell, John Ranold, George Wormald, John Whitely, Henry Holder, Wm. Ellis, James Huntingdon, Edmond * Thomas Campanet, George, Hewitt, Richard Cliff, Henry Cliff, John Jenkinson, alias Green, Thomas Smith, Lionel Smith aliter Robinson, Percival Reynolds, Thomas Greenfield, Robert Milner aliter Biggleskirk, William Anthony, with many others all too long here to be rehearsed and written, whose names God grant may be written in the Book of Life. These, with others, the donors of the said stock, with the consent of the whole inhabitants of the parish of Ackworth, did make one composition wherein were expressed certain ordinances, to be continually observed and kept without alteration in manner and form following; that is to say, first it was ordained by the wills of the donors and by the consent of the whole body of the parish of Ackworth, that there should be four honest men chosen every year new by the consent of the parson or curate there for the time being, and the whole body of the said parish which four men should govern the stock and have authority to let and set the cows to the use and performance of these present ordinances, and to receive the rent for them, and to make their accompts to the said parson or curate, and to the whole body of the said parish yearly at their year's end; and this ordinance to be kept continually, and observed without alteration. Also it was ordained by the wills of the donors, and consent of the said parish, that these cows, nor any one of them, nor any part of the said stock, should never at any time hereafter be let to or for any time (?) of usury, that is to say, that none that took any of them should be bound to uphold the stock, nor any money that should be taken for the rent, revenues, or profits of them should be let to usury, that is to say, that no money should be given for the lending the same money, or any part thereof; nevertheless it may be lawful for the Governors of the said stock, to take good assurance for the well meating and using of the cows committed to their charge, and for the yearly rent due to be paid for the same cows; and this ordinance likewise to be observed and kept without alteration. And it was ordained by the wills of the donors, and consent of the said parish, that the cows of the said stock, nor any one of them, should be let for any more yearly rent than two shillings and eightpence, and that those honest poor men that dwelled in the said parish, should have the cows in farm before any other dwelling without the said parish, making good assurance to the Governors of the said stock, for the yearly rent paying, and for the well using and meating of the said cows. And this ordinance likewise to be continually observed and kept without alteration. Also it was ordained by the wills of the donors, and consent of the said parish, that there should no penny be taken of the yearly rent and profit of the said stock unto the yearly profit thereof, and amount to the value of three pounds *de claro* over and above all charges and reprises, and when it came to this clear value, then twenty shillings to be taken out of the said profit and to be paid yearly to the Clark towards his wages, and the rest to go forward to the maintenance upholding and increasing of the said stock; and when the profit of the said stock amounted to the yearly value of four pounds *de claro*, then forty shillings to be taken yearly of that sum, and to be paid towards the Clark's wages; and when the yearly profit of the said stock shall amount to the yearly value of eight pounds *de claro*, then three pounds thereof to be paid towards the Clark's wages; and when the yearly rent and profit of the said stock shall amount to the yearly value of ten pounds *de claro*, then four pounds thereof to be paid for the Clark's wages yearly, and there to stay, and the rest of the yearly profits over and above the four pounds aforesaid, to go forward to the maintenance upholding and increasing of the said stock. And this ordinance likewise to be observed and kept without alteration. And it was ordained by the wills of the donors, and consent of the said parish, that if it fortune the said stock of cows should be diminished by the death of the said cows, so that the yearly value of the said cows shall not amount to the yearly value of three pounds *de claro* over and above all charges and reprises, then the money which was due to the Clark, and every part and parcel thereof to stay, and not to be paid until the said stock shall increase, so that the yearly profits of the said stock do amount to the yearly value of three pounds *de claro* over and above all charges and reprises, and when it doth amount to the yearly value of three pounds aforesaid, then the said twenty shillings to be paid again towards the Clark's wages, and the said Clark's wages to increase and diminish as the yearly profits

of the said stock do increase and diminish orderly as is afore
declared. And this ordinance likewise to be continually
observed, and kept without alteration. Also it was ordained
by the wills of the donors, and consent of the said parish, that all
all the stock of cows shall be burned (branded), and so kept burned
from time to time with one burn, and the said burn (brand) to
be in the keeping of the Governors of the said stock yearly for
their time being, and this ordinance likewise to be continually
observed, and kept without alteration. Therefore be it known
further, the said composition wherein these present ordinances
were plainly expressed, being lost, that we, Thomas Huntingdon,
priest and parson of Ackworth, John Hambleton the elder,
William Thorp, John Standeven, John Huntingdon the elder,
Richard Pickering the son of Richard deceased, John Brook,
George Austwick, Edward Rusby, Anthony Walker, Henry
Huntingdon the son of James deceased, William Wormal the
son of John deceased, John Bradley the son of William deceased,
Thomas Austwick the son of John deceased, John Bell the son
of Robert deceased, Thomas Horner the son of the aforesaid
John Horner, John Howitt the son of George deceased, Robert
Brook, William Symson aliter Manser, Thomas the son of
Thomas deceased, aliter Green, Lionel Wormall the son of
George deceased, Lionel Greenfield the son of Thomas deceased,
Richard Ranold the son of John deceased, Thomas Jackson,
the son of Roger deceased, Robert Biggleskirk aliter Milner,
having full notice and perfect knowledge of these present
ordinances, by the consent, assent, and full agreement of the
whole parish aforesaid, do confirm, ratify, and grant by this
our indented composition of confirmation, that all these ordinances afore rehearsed shall be continually observed, and kept
from time to time without any alteration according to the wills
and ordinances of the donors heretofore declared at large. In
witness whereof all we last before named by the consent, assent,
and full agreement of all the whole body of the said parish to
this our indented composition of confirmation, have set to our
hands and seals the 2nd day of February, being the day of

A.D. 1568. the Purification of the blessed Mary, Christ's blessed mother, and in the year of our Lord one thousand five hundred and sixty eight.

There is also a Memorandum accompanying the above which directs that one part of the above composition should remain in the possession of the parson of Ackworth, and the other part with the Governors of the Stock, the latter to be kept under lock in the Parish Church of Ackworth, with the Inventory of Cows, and other papers. The Clerk is also directed to read the composition, or cause it to be read audibly twice a year, at the account meeting, and the meeting for the appointment of Governors.

Under the head of "Advice of the Writer," the following curious entry appears:—"Stand constantly, firmly, and perseverantly to this your foundation without alteration, least covetcousness with and dissimilation do bring your stock to destruction."

Then follow three "Articles for the better preservation of the Stock of Kine," drawn up and confirmed by the inhabitants of Ackworth on "May 5th, 1581, being Ascension Day." All payments are due to the parson and cowmaster on or before the feast of John the Baptist, and in default, to be proceeded against by law; and a footnote says that all documents and papers relative to the above "belongeth to the keeping of the parson or curate of Ackworth, as hath been the custom without (*sic*) the memory of man."

In case of an outbreak of "contagious distemper," another memorandum directs certain rules and regulations to be observed, and then follow the signatures of nineteen persons who assembled at a parish meeting held on the 18th April, 1749, to confirm the foregoing Articles of Agreement.

The whole concludes with an extenso list of the "Proprietors of Beast Gates in Ackworth Pasture in ye year 1686," "Proprietors of Cow Gates and to whom let if any in 1749, when ye Distemper was raging," and "Proprietors of Ackworth Cowgates in 1769-70."

ACKWORTH TERRIERS.

A particular account of all the lands belonging to the Rectory of Ackworth.*

	Acrs.	Rds.

Imprimis. In a field called Parkinleyes two roods lying between the lands of Philip Austwick east and west, other two roods lying between the lands of Leonard Pinder west, and Richard Twigg's close, east 1 0

In Houstead field two acres lying between the lands of Mr. George Abbott north, and Mr. William Shillitoe south; three roods Mr. John Lambe close, lying north, and the lands of John Ellis south 2 3

In Burial field† two acres lying between the field called Bennitings, north, and Sandygate Quarry south; other two acres lying between the lands of John Ash east, and Mr. John Lambe west; one acre lying between the lands of Mr. Robert Hewitt north, and John Ellis south; two roods lying between the lands of Matthew Pearson east, and Mr. Lambe west. One acre between the lands of Philip Austwicke north, and Mr. Hewitt south; one acre Burial Gate, lying on the south side, and the lands of Philip Austwicke north 7 2

In Little Castle Syke, two roods between John Huntingdon's close east, and the lands of Mr. William Shillitoe west 0 2

In Great Castle Syke, two roods between the lands of Thomas Pickering east, and Mr. Robert Hewitt west; one acre between the lands of Philip Austwicke and Mr. Robert Hewitt east; two roods between the lane east, and Thomas Pickering west 2 0

In the Middle Field, one acre between the Stony Pits north, Mr. George Abbot's land south; one acre and two roods lying between Mr. Pickering north and

---

* There is no date to this document, but by the signatures at the foot, the approximate date would be 1680.
† The scene of the skirmish referred to on pp. 56-7.

south; one acre between the lands of Henry Cawood west, and John Huntington east; two roods between Arthur Chambers south, and Mr. Pickering north ... 4 0

In old Taile Field, two roods lying between the lands of Robert Cawood north, and Anthony Crowhey south; other two roods lying between the lands of Matt. Pearson south, and Robert Hewitt north ... 1 0

In Lambcroft, one rood lying between the lands of Samuel Lambe to the north and south 0 1

In Colehill Field, four acres between the lands of Ralph Lowther, Esq., on the north, and Mr. Hewitt south; two roods Mr. Hewitt south, and Thomas Hewitt north; one acre Mr. Lowther north, and Mrs. Austwicke south; two roods Mr. Lambe Lawning north; one acre Mr. Bradley north and Philip Austwicke south; one acre Mr. Lambe's close called Wentlands west, and the land of Mr. Pickering east; one rood and a half between the lands of Matt. Pearson north, and John Huntingdon south 8 3

One other rood and a half more in Burial, one acre in close called Hollin Knowl, now in the Park field, one rood more in Hundhill Syke, three roods of meadows 2 0

In enclosure, one close called Stanbecks close, four acres; one close called Meardyke close, containing four acres; one close called Barley close, containing five acres; one close called Church croft, containing two acres; one close called Kirkecroft, containing two and a half acres; one close called Stone Steel acre; one close called Tentering, containing one acre; one close called Pond Garth, with the orchard and garden, one acre... ... ... 20 2

Belonging in all to the Rectory of Ackworth, fifty acres and one rood, with one dwellinghouse, two barnes, one stable, and another outhouse. And as for all the Tyth's of corn, hay, and other privy Tyth's, we suppose them to be worth two hundred pounds per annum.

JOHN ASH,
ROBERT CAWOOD.

Ackworth Com Ebor West Riding.

ACKWORTH TERRIER, 1716.

A true and just account of all the houses, edifices, orchards, gardens, glebe lands, tyths, augmentations, pensions, salaries, stipendarys, payments, offerings, and all other ecclesiastical dues belonging to the Rectory of Ackworth in the diocese of York.

Imprimis. One dwellinghouse, being 19 yards 1 foot in length, and 6 yards in breadth. One corn barn, with a swine coat at the end of it, 24 yards in length, and 6 yards in breadth. One other barn, 16 yards long and 6 yards broad. One cowhouse and fodder-room, 8¾ yards in length, and 4 yards in breadth new built. One stable, being a square building, containing 5½ yards each way. One privy or house of office, 3¾ yards in length, and 2 yards in breadth. One flower garden, 19 yards in length, and 9½ in breadth. One kitchen garden, 27 yards in length, and 20 yards 1 foot in breadth. One other kitchen garden, 44 yards in length, and 13 yards 1 foot in breadth. One orchard, 44 yards in length, and 17½ yards in breadth.

FIELD LAND.

Acrs. Rds.

Imprimis. In a field called Parkin Lee's, two roods between the lands of Richard Austwicke east and west; other two roods lying between the land of Leonard Pinder west, and John Heptinstall east 1 0

[The remainder of the above consists of extracts from the first inventory which has already been given in extenso.]

Total Field Land ... 27 0

IN INCLOSURES.

Imprimis. One close called Barley Close containing ... ... 5 acres.
Item. One close called Stanbecks, containing ... 4 acres.
Item. One close called Meardyke, containing ... 4 acres.
Item. One close called Wentcroft, containing ... 2 acres.

Item. One close called Kirkcroft, containing ... 2½ acres.
Item. One close called Stonestyle, containing ... 1 acre.
Item. One close called Tenter Ing, containing ... 1 acre.
Item. One close called Potwells, containing ... 2 acres.
Item. One close called Hollin Knowl, containing... 1 acre.
Item. One close called Pond Garth, containing with the Fouldstead and backside ... ... 3 roods.

Total Inclosures, 21 acres 1 rood.

TYTHE OF CORN.

Tythe Corn in this parish is paid in kind by the owner of the corn; the manner of tything is after the owner has proportioned it into equal parts, and upon sufficient warning to the minister or his servant appointed for that business, is to take the tenth stack, kiver or sheaf, and if there remain any odd shares, and the owner has more of the same grain in another place, then to count to that other till the whole be tythed. There is one part of our parish called Ryddings, now in the tenure of Sir Rowland Winn, Bart., that pays only six shillings per year for all tyths of corn, hay, and pasture, but if pastured with sheep or other goods, and those sheep, etc., are turned to the common, then they pay half tythe, or proportionally for the time they have so been pastured. If the houses be inhabited, the inhabitants pay Easter dues* as the other part of the parish do, and at the same time. John Symmons, of the Lodge, (Parol de Himsworth) pays for another part of the Riddings now in his tenure, and only for the hay and herbage thereof, one shilling and eight pence per year. Another part of the Ryddings, now in the tenure of Joseph Walker, tenant to John Bright, of Badsworth, Esq., pays five shillings for the hay and herbage of the same. One other part of the Ryddings now in the tenure and occupation of Christopher Heptinstall, commonly known by the name of Berry's Land, pays for the hay and herbage thereof, eight pence per annum. One Moiety

---

* These Easter dues are now either extinct, or absorbed into the Rectorial tithes.

of the Walton Royds, now in the tenure of Michael Mitton, tenant to Frances Mason, widow, for the hay and herbage pays one shilling yearly. Another moiety of the said Walton Royds, belonging to Henry Cawood, of Lanes, (Parol de Himsworth) pays also for the hay and herbage thereof one shilling yearly. A little piece of ground called Warren, belonging to Sir Rowd. Winn, Bart., pays yearly for the hay and herbage thereof, 6d.; being this year (1716) in the tenure of Henry Taylor, (Parol de Wragby). Sir John Wentworth, of Elmeshall, in the parish of South Kirkby, Bart., or his tenants, for Burling Houses hay and herbage, pays yearly the sum of one pound seventeen shillings for the hay and herbage of the said Burling Houses. Note that the above mentioned custom ground (excepting Sir Rowland Winn's moiety of the Ryddings, [and Quere if that ought not]) pays tythe of corn as the other parts of the parish do ; and the usual custom for the hay and herbage thereof, and of all and every part and parcel of the above-named custom ground is usually paid and discharged upon or before the 29th day of September yearly, and altho' it be corn. And further note that if any part or parcel of custom ground be sown with hemp, flax, rape, or turnips, it shall pay as the law directs for the two first, and for the third according to the use of the County, if not the tenth part, and for the last, four shillings per acre, according to the old custom established in this parish. The Ryddings and Walton Royds are full south from the Church, Burling Houses east, and the Warren west. There are several crofts or garths pay custom for hay and herbage, some more and some less, in considerable sums for the most part, an account of which is hereunto annexed.

TYTHE HAY.

Hay pays ten pence per acre thro'out this whole parish, excepting where there is a modus or prescription to the contrary, and excepting in a field or meadow called Hundell Syke, in which field or meadow every acre of hay pays two shillings per acre ; but those acres are what they call computation acres, which generally are two good acres or more each.

EASTER DUES.

Every person above the age of sixteen years, being inhabitant of this parish, pays two pence obtacon, and every master or mistress of a family pays one penny halfpenny for his or her house, five pence for his or her hen (!) whether any or none, one penny for his or her plough, one penny halfpenny for every cow and calf, one penny for every stript milk cow, one penny for every foal, and one penny for every swarm of bees. Note that the custom for the Garths is usually paid at Easter.

WOOL AND LAMB.

These are tythable in kind, the owner to choose two, and then the tyther a third at ten; if they fall short at ten, then the number to be considered, and if there are but five, then the one of the parties is to take or give one penny halfpenny except it be a fat one, then more according to discretion. If under five, then the owner is to pay the minister for every one, a penny, if above five the minister pays two pence a piece to ten, and takes the lamb.

Wool (as was said before,) is paid in kind, upon the sheet or clipping day by the tenth fleece, or by weight, as both parties concerned shall agree. The custom ground afore mentioned pays neither wool nor lamb, without the sheep have been summered or wintered upon the common, or at least have pastured there some time, and then but half tythe of either kind. Lamb is usually paid at Lammas, when it may be supposed to live as well without the dam as with her.

An Account of the Custom Garths with their respective sums, varying from 3d. to 2/2d., are next given, amounting in all to 9/6d., which it is stated " are, or should be paid at Easter, when the inhabitants pay their other Easter dues.

AUGMENTATIONS, ETC.

We have no augmentations, pensions, salaries, or stipendiary payments, belonging to this Rectory.

MORTUARIES, ETC.

Mortuaries are paid according to the statute the 21st of Henry the Eight, chapter the 6th.

EASTER OFFERINGS as mentioned before.

MARRIAGES.

Every person married by license pays ten shillings; by Banns publishing, eighteen pence.

CHRISTENINGS pay nothing at all, Sacraments being free.

Every woman churched pays eightpence to the Minister.

Every burial in the Churchyard pays one shilling.

Every burial in the body of the Church pays five shillings; if in the Chancell then more or less as the parties concerned can agree with the Incumbent.

WITNESS our hands, this 28th day of June, Anno Domini, 1716.

MATTHEW PEARSON,
RICHARD MASON,
THOMAS CALVERLEY.

PHILIP HOLLINS, Rector.
RICHD. J. BROOK,
THOMAS PEARSON, } Churchwardens.

Another Terrier was made in 1727, and a third in 1743, the former during the incumbency of Philip Hollins, and the latter during that of Dr. Timothy Lee. They are, with few exceptions, similar to the first.

ACKWORTH MANOR.

In common with many surrounding Manors, the Manor of Ackworth is of Saxon origin, and consisted of nearly the whole of the parish of Ackworth, including the Church, Park, and Manor House. As has already been intimated, Erdulf and Osulf were the first Saxon proprietors of Ackworth. It is mentioned in the Domesday Survey, from which it will be seen that at the Conquest, the Manor of Ackworth became part of the possessions of the great Lacy family, as Lords of the Honour of Pontefract. The following is a transcript of the record:—

"Man: in Acewrde, Edulf et Osulf habuerunt vi carucat: terræ "ad Geldum, ubi possuit esse v. caruca. Nunc habet Humfri-

"dus de Ilberto. Ipse ibi et Car: et dimid: et xiiii. villanos et
"ii. Bordarios cum vi. Car: Ibi Ecclesia et Presbyter, 2 Molen-
"dina xvi. Denar: T. R. E. Valebat iiii. libras modo iii. libras.
"D. B. 107. Terra Ilberti de Lacy"—i.e. "One Manor in
"Ackworth, Erdulf and Osulf, had six Carucates of land to be
"taxed, where there might be five ploughs. Humphrey now
"holds it of Ilbert. (Humphrey) himself (has) there one plough
"and a half, and fourteen villains (i.e. persons of servile
"condition), and two boors (i.e., persons who were allowed a
"cottage and a small piece of land, on condition that they should
"supply the lord with poultry and eggs for his board or table).
"There is a Church there, and a priest, one mill of sixteen
"pence, value in King Edward's time, four pounds, now three
"pounds. Domesday Book, 107. The land of Ilbert de Lacy."*

After this, the Manor of Ackworth is not mentioned in any public record until the fourth year of Edward II. (1311), in which year it reverted from the Lacys to the House of Lancaster, and so remained until the execution of Thomas, Earl of Lancaster, when it was forfeited to the Crown. On the accession of Edward III., it went back to the House of Lancaster. In the early part of this reign, the King's Park is mentioned in a list of the Honour of Pontefract in the Duchy Office, and is said to embrace a circuit of two miles, with a keeper for the King and a lodge. In the extent per contra, taken in the fifteenth year of Edward III., the Manor House is called a

* Vide sub datum, 1810.

capital Messuage, with a garden adjacent, and one hundred and four acres of land. By an original Extent, remaining in the Duchy Office, the park is said to be two leagues in circumference, with a keeper, on wages. Afterwards, when Henry (brother of Thomas, who was beheaded), Duke of Lancaster, became Henry IV. (1327), it passed again to the Crown. It continued in the ownership of the Crown until in 1603, when the Lordship of Ackworth, as parcel of the Honour of Pontefract, was granted by James I. to his Queen, with power to grant Leases for twenty one years, reserving the old rents, etc. The Queen died in 1619. In 1628 Charles I. sold the Lordship of Ackworth to Commissioners for the City of London, by whom the Park was sold to Mark Pickering, and the Manor and Manor House to T. Harlaken and others.. The latter afterwards came by purchase or marriage into the possession of — Lambe, from whom it was purchased in 1690, by Robert Lowther. From this time the Manor and Park became historically separate, and the subsequent fortunes of the Manor alone will now be traced. When Mr. Robert Lowther made this purchase, he took the conveyance from — Lambe as heir of the survivor of the four original grantees of the City of London. It was sold about 1673 by the heirs of Mr. Robert Lowther, to Dr. Edward Watkinson. By a Deed of 1770, it appears that the ancient gateway of the Manor House was then standing. After the decease of Dr. Watkinson, it became the property of Mr. Joseph Sykes, by whom it was pulled down and the materials converted into cottages. In the course of demolition, Benjamin Sykes, son of the said Joseph, who was employed as mason to do the work, is said to have found under an ancient brick oven a considerable treasure in silver coins, though, from his concealment of the matter, neither their date nor value were ever correctly ascertained. From Sykes, the site of the Manor House passed to Mr. Turton, who pulled down the cottages above named, and built upon it the house, now, or lately in the occupation of Mr. Richard Lee. The house was subsequently purchased by Henry Hill, Esq., and thus it will be seen by the continued history of the Park which follows, the Manor House and the Park Hall, after a period of some two hundred and thirty years, become united for the second time under one proprietor. The interests of the Manor itself, which consist chiefly of the village of Ackworth, are now watched by four gentlemen, who constitute and call themselves Lords of the Manor. Whether they perform their arduous (?) duties with complete satisfaction to themselves and the people of Ackworth, is another matter, and a question which perhaps had better be left open.

It would seem from one of the Parish books, that the Lords of the Manor, assembled in Court Leet and Baron, formerly possessed considerable powers in the infliction of fines and penalties. On the 21st October 1686, fines of various amounts were enacted and levied upon certain persons for neglecting to erect gates and fences round their fields; for lodging or harbouring wandering people without consent of the constable; for neglecting to ring their swine; upon the old constable, for not making up his accounts before Midsummer day; for not setting up stiles;* for neglecting to serve on Juries when summoned; for encroachments on common or waste grounds; for leaving hedges unswitched; for removing stones from the highway; on the constable for failing to erect a pinfold;† for not repairing bridges, banks, and dykes; for not cleaning sewers, and roads, etc.

At a Court Leet and Baron held on the 26th October, 1726, no less than thirty persons were presented and fined in sums varying from fourpence to ten shillings, for "Encroachments upon the Waste." Among those presented, we find the names of Turnill, Pindar, Heptinstall, Crosland, Baumbrough, Cattey, Oates, Mangle, Shillitoe, Lamb, Stanfield, Earnshaw, Wood, Winn, Sharp, Booth, Seaton, Nelstrap, Walker, Harrison, Scatchard, Balgie, Addy, and Burgess. The names of those

* Ackworth abounds in stiles.
† This still exists in good condition, and adjoins the parish hearse-house.

by whom the presentments were made are Mitton, Heptonstall, Kiplin, Norton, Calverley, Waller, Nelstrop, Walker, Atkinson, Howitt, Waller, Wager, and Wilson. By this presentment it does not appear in whose names the Court was held. The following minute also appears amongst the Court papers:

"Ackworth, the 24th of June, 1766.

"We whose names are hereunder set Do on the behalf of ourselves and others duly authorized agree to meet at the Sign of the Blue Bell in this Town on Monday the 15th day of September next at two o'clock in the afternoon to fix a time for keeping a Court Baron for the Manor of Ackworth aforesaid also upon the person in whose name such Court shall be kept in order to remove and prevent encroachments within the said Manor and concerning other matters prejudicial to the Rights and privileges of the several Freeholders on the Wastes and Commons within the Royalty of Ackworth.

T. Lee* for self, Anthy. Surtees, Esq., & Mr. Joseph White.
W. Sykes for his Brother Frs. Sykes, by virtue of a Warrt. of Attorney.

R. Hargreaves for self & James Beetham.

John North.	Henry Mitton.
Thos. Hirst.	Wm. Earnshaw.
James Townend.	Matthew Burton.

Edward Oates, a Devisee in trust in Mr. Richard Pickering's Will.
Robert Calverley.

John Collett.	Thos. Austwick.
Benjamin Turton.	Wm. Scatcher.
Thomas Pearson.	Thomas Wager.

Sufficient has now been quoted from Court papers of the Manor of Ackworth, to show how the affairs of the Manor and Court Leet were conducted in the "good old days," compared with the modern method.

* Dr. Lee, the then Rector of Ackworth.

ACKWORTH PARK.

Up to 1628, when the Park was sold by the City Commissioners of London to Mark Pickering, Ackworth Manor and Park continued in the possession of the same proprietors; after which the Park was again sold by Michael Pickering, the son of the above Mark, to the Trustees of William Rokeby. In this Deed "The Hall" is so called, as lately rebuilt from "The Lodg." About 1650 this portion of the estate was purchased by Elizabeth, widow of Wooley Leigh, Esq., of Adlington, in the County of Chester. She was the daughter of Sir John Hare, of Norfolk, Baronet. In 1650 she married Sir John Lowther, of Lowther Hall, Westmoreland, by whom she had Ralph and Robert Lowther, both of whom resided at Ackworth Park. She died in 1699, and was buried in Ackworth Church.*
William Rokeby, Esq., resided at Ackworth Park in 1671, but this could only have been as tenant. About the period of their mother's death, the Hall became the residence of Ralph and Robert Lowther. Robert died unmarried in 1720; and on the death of Ralph in 1724, it became the inheritance of his son John (M.P. for Pontefract in 1722), who died in 1729 without issue, leaving the whole estate to his sister, Mary Lowther, who inhabited the house till her death in 1753. This Mary Lowther endowed the School and Hospital at Ackworth. The estate was now inherited by Margaret, the daughter of William Norton, of Sawley, Esq. This William Norton had married Margaret, the sister of the above-named John and Mary Lowther. Their mother was Mary, the daughter of Godfrey Lawson, of Leeds, Esq. Margaret Norton married, 1st, John Bright, of Badsworth, Esq., and 2ndly, Sir John Ramsden, of Byram, Bart., by whom in 1763, the estate was sold to Francis Sykes, Esq. In 1803, Mr. Sykes or his representatives disposed of the Hall, and part of the Estate, to Grosvenor Perfect, of Pontefract, Esq. In 1804, it was purchased by Frances, widow of — Solly, Esq., of London. Mrs. Solly afterwards married J. H. Jessop, Esq., and

---

* Vide Monumental Epitaphs.

in 1810 the estate was sold to John Petyt, Esq., of London. In 1831, it was purchased by Mr. Gully, who was said to have given £21,500 for it, exclusive of the land in Purston. About twenty years later, the Park became the property of Henry Hill, Esq., whose family are the present proprietors.

Institutions.

I.—ACKWORTH COLLEGE.

This large and handsome building, commonly known as the Flounders' Institute, was established by the late Benjamin Flounders, Esq., J.P., of Yarm, with an endowment of £40,000, for training young men to be teachers in the Society of Friends. The building was opened for students in the summer of 1848. The instruction, according to the trust deed, includes ancient and modern languages, mathematics, and philosophy in all its parts; to which have been added other subjects to meet recent requirements of education, or having more immediate reference to the Society. The Institution is intended to accommodate twelve pupils.*

I am indebted to William S. Lean, Esq., M.A., for the following additional information :—

"It appears that Mr. Flounders was very much influenced in his decision to place £40,000 Three per cent. Consols, in the hands of Trustees, for certain educational purposes in the Society of Friends, by the known wishes of his uncle, Gideon Bickerdyke, Esq., from whom he had inherited a considerable portion of his property, including a landed estate at Culmington, near Ludlow, in Shropshire. This estate was sold during Benjamin Flounders' lifetime, and the deed of trust directing the mode in which the £40,000 above mentioned was to be applied, was signed by himself on November 25th, 1845. Mr.

* Bank's Walks about Yorkshire, pp. 299-300.

Flounders died April 4th, 1846, and the Institute was opened with nine students August 28th, 1848. Mr. Bickerdyke's views, expressed to his nephew in a letter dated as far back as 1807, but particularly stated to be in no way binding upon Mr. Flounders, appear to have included the founding of a larger establishment than the present, to include boys as well as young men, and also a larger staff of instructors. Ackworth is specially named in the same letter as a suitable locality for the new institution. No doubt the fact of the then comparatively recent establishment (the Friends' Public School,) influenced Mr. Flounders, as well as his uncle, in concluding that students under training for teaching would be likely to profit by living in its neighbourhood, even if they should not find opportunities for pursuing their studies within its walls."

"The Deed of Trust leaves it to the discretion of the Trustees (generally from eight to ten in number,) to determine on the number of students to be admitted to the Institute; also to provide, either wholly or partially, the expense of their education, board, books, etc. The appointment of the Principal and his assistants is in their hands, and the determination of the course of study to be pursued, also rests ultimately with them."

"From the opening of the Institute in August, 1848, to the present time, 216 students have passed through it."

"Five acres of land on which 'the College' stands were purchased by two or three gentlemen from the 'Ackworth School Estate,' and presented to the Trustees, about two years before the date of opening. Most of the stone used in the building was quarried from this land."

"The name of the first Principal, Mr. Isaac Brown, will always be associated with the work of laying out the plantations, etc., on the recreation grounds, and with the zeal which he showed in encouraging the first students."

"Another acre of land on which a dwellinghouse has since been erected, was added in 1864."

"The Institute possesses a spacious astronomical observatory, furnished with a four and a quarter inch refracting telescope by Cooke, equatorially mounted."

"Mr. Isaac Brown held the office of Principal from 1848 to 1870, when he was succeeded by Mr. William S. Lean, M.A. (Lond.), who still retains the office, and regularly shares his duties with one or two tutors."

"With the exception of a few hours a week devoted to outlying subjects, the curriculum is now arranged with special reference to the requirements of the London B.A. degree, but the limited staff of instructors militates necessarily against the prosecution of any beyond elementary studies in Science."

II.—FRIENDS' SCHOOL.

Next to the College, this school (commonly known as the Quaker School,) is entitled to the highest place amongst the institutions of Ackworth, both socially and structurally. "It is," says a member of the Society of Friends, "dear to the memories of most Friends, and is one of the eight original public boarding schools provided by the Society for the education of Quaker children in England, between the years 1779 and 1842." The building was originally a branch of the London Foundling Hospital, and to Dr. John Fothergill, a London physician, is due its conversion to its present use. It was opened for the "education, maintenance, and clothing of children whose parents are not in affluence," on Oct. 18, 1779; the first scholars being "Barton and Ann Gates, of Poole, Dorset," and since that time, scholars have come from all parts of the country to Ackworth. In the lists are to be found some names that are well known. In the year 1822, we find a "John Bright, of Rochdale," was entered; also a "James Wilson," in neither of which names, could any indication be found of the then future prefix, "Right Honourable." Generations of Howitts, too, have gone to Ackworth, from the old home at Heanor, in Derbyshire. A description of the building, inside and out, will here be both interesting and useful. Entering the gates from the road, the School itself is in front, on the right is the Meeting-house, and on the left, offices for the shoemaker, tailor, carpenter, and others. A colonnade of severely plain pillars forms the façade, and from this the entrance hall leads into the "Great Passage." From this, right and left, are dining rooms, library, lecture-room, store-rooms, kitchens, housekeeper's rooms, etc. At each end of the passage, stairs of stone lead to the bed-rooms above, and to bath-rooms, etc. The class rooms, in common with all the rooms, are lofty, well ventilated and warmed, scrupulously clean and plain, and are fitted up with abundance of maps, diagrams, designs, aquaria, cabinets of shells, ores, clocks, galvanic-batteries and other apparatus. Play has its sheds, courts, and cricket-field, with all the necessary appliances. Each scholar has a little plot of ground, for the practical study of botany and horticulture. For the sick there are nurseries, and for the convalescent, reading rooms. A house not far distant is utilised and fitted up as a Sanatorium. There are spacious swimming baths, gas-works, steam-laundries, and other appliances; the whole being surrounded by vast gardens, farm yard, and macadamised play ground.* The School possesses its own Temperance Hotel. The discipline is firm, but kind. There is no corporal punishment. The management of the School is vested in a Committee appointed at the General Annual Meeting in June, at which time, Friends from all parts of the country visit the dear old spot, to renew the associations, and revive the recollections of their happy school-days. Periodical examinations are made by the Committee, and by examiners from the Universities. By gift and subscription, the School has accumulated in land, buildings, etc., a surplus

* The "flags" is a footpath dividing the boys' from the girls' playground. Here brothers and sisters, and cousins of both sexes, are privileged to meet, and converse, having of course first obtained permission.

capital of nearly £40,000, which enables it to give to the little
Friends a good, and comparatively cheap, education. The
payments made for each child vary according to the position
and means of the parents or guardian, but the balance may be
considered as the Society's contribution to the education of the
poorer of its members' children.* The full number which may
be accomodated is 290. Since the establishment of this School,
eleven others in different parts of the kingdom have been
opened, the first in 1785, and the last in 1842.† The following
additional information has been extracted from Mr. William
Smith's "Old Yorkshire,"‡ and Mr. Thompson's "History of
Ackworth School." "The whole property covers an area of
270 acres, and originally cost about £12,000. In the Report
for 1884, it is estimated to be worth £40,000. In July, 1773,
the Institution was closed, and remained empty for some years,
part of the estate was sold, and the turret clock and bells
disposed of to the Marquis of Rockingham. Tradition says
that the grounds were allowed to become a wilderness, the foxes
roaming freely through the deserted halls. Amongst those
who took a great interest in the Foundling Hospital were Dr.
Lee, Rector of Ackworth, who planned the central building,
Sir Rowland Winn, of Nostell Priory, and Sir Charles Whitworth, of London. The following is a description of the dress
of the children in 1781, two years after the School was opened:
'In the early days of the School, its juvenile groups might
have reminded us of the pictures of olden time, when the cocked
hat, the long-tailed coat, the leather breeches, and the buckled
shoes, were the dress even of boys. The girls figured in white
caps, the hair turned back over them, or combed straight down
on the forehead, checked aprons with bibs, and white neck
handkerchiefs folded neatly over their stuff gowns in front.

* Vide "Quiver," March, 1885. Much, however, of the foregoing information has been obtained by the compiler after a personal inspection.
† Bank's Walks about Yorkshire, p. 300.
‡ Vide "Yorkshire Educational Establishments," pp. 164-73.
  Published in 1879.

Their walking costume was a kind of hat, the pattern of which we are unable to indicate, and a long cloth coat, with coloured mits reaching to the elbows.'* In 1816, the visit of Joseph John Gurney gave such an impetus to Biblical study at Ackworth School, that 'they took their Bibles to bed with them, read them by the early morning light, pored over them at leisure hours during the day, and especially on First Day,' so that twelve months afterwards 'the whole aspect of affairs was changed.'" A tabulated list of Masters will be found at the end of this volume. The following men and women of renown were educated at Ackworth School:—The Right Hon. John Bright, M.P.; The Right Hon. James Wilson, M.P., of the "*Economist*;" Henry Ashworth; J. F. B. Firth, M.P.; William Allen Miller, author of the "Elements of Chemistry," formerly Professor of Chemistry in University College, London; Dr. George S. Brady, F.G.S., Sunderland; Henry Bowman Brady, F.R.S., Newcastle; John Gilbert Baker, F.R.S., F.L.S., of Kew, an eminent botanist; Sarah Ellis, née Stickney, authoress of "Women of England," etc.; Jeremiah H. Wiffen, F.R.S.L., poet and translator; Benj. B. Wiffen; William Howitt, author of "Homes and Haunts of British Poets," etc.; Henry Thompson, author of "History of Ackworth School." The following additional particulars have been extracted from "A sketch of the History of Ackworth School," by John S. Rowntree, published in the "Proceedings of the Centenary Celebration" in 1879. "The earliest notices of the School are very favourable. Sir Rowland Winn, of Nostell Priory, is said to have been affected to tears when he saw the healthy happy faces, and recurred to the unhappy experience of the foundlings who before occupied the building." Offenders, it appears, were punished at meal times, by being placed at a table which was called "the table of disgrace," and which was distinguished from the rest, by having no cloth upon it. It is said that Robert Whitaker once entered the dining room, and finding two

* Vide Pumphrey's Diary, written at Ackworth School.

monitors sitting at this table, he lifted up his arms, and his voice, exclaiming "Fallen! fallen!" Speaking of ancient customs, Mr. Rowntree says "the Committee Friends" at one time "closed the day's labour over glasses of spirits and water, whilst fragrant fumes sped upwards from their long clay tobacco pipes!" Amidst the grave debates of the Committee many quaint or ludicrous passages occurred. For example, when the wooden trenchers were abolished, a venerable Friend, with much emphasis, expressed a hope that they would be carefully preserved, as he was assured that they would at no distant date be again wanted for use! "Ackworth School," says William Howitt in his work, entitled,"The Boy's Country Book,"* "differs remarkably from all other public schools, in the complete isolation of the children. They have ample and airy playgrounds, but they are as perfectly separate from the world as if they were not in it. * * It is impossible that evil communications from without can corrupt their good manners: and within, they are free from the distinctions of wealth and rank which torment the world, and excite many keen heart-burnings in public schools." At Ackworth School "not a sense of them exists. The utmost equality, the most cordial harmony prevail. One child is distinguished from another only by the difference of person, talents, disposition, and proficiency in learning. Happy estate! admirable foundation for a noble and erect carriage; for establishing in the mind a habit of valuing men, not by wealth and artificial rank, but by the everlasting distinctions of virtue and talent."

CHURCH SCHOOLS.

These very commodious school-rooms were erected in 1846, and conveyed to Trustees for the education of the children of the poor. The estate was purchased for £200, and at the cost of about £100 more, the buildings thereon were renovated and converted into schools and class-rooms. Since then, however,

* Vide Chapter xvi., pp. 260-1.

they have been considerably enlarged and improved, in accordance with the requirements of the Education Department. The Trustees are the Rectors of Ackworth and Badsworth, and the Vicar of Featherstone, for the time being; the sole management of the school being reserved to the Rector of Ackworth. It is a mixed school. The Title-Deed is in possession of the Rector of Ackworth for the time being.

MRS. HOWARD'S SCHOOL.

This School is situate at Low Ackworth, and consists of two rooms, the one for girls, and the other for infants, and a mistress's house, neatly built, bearing the following inscription: "Rachael Howard bought this ground, and built thereon a school-room and tenement for a mistress, 1833. She died in the Lord, 24th Sept., 1837, aged 33.—Rev. vii., 13, 17; xiv., 13." The following extracts from the published correspondence of the late Mrs. Howard, respecting the building of the school, are historically valuable. Writing to a friend on January 25th, 1833, she says,—"The estimate for T. Rickman's plan for a cottage school-room, amounted to very nearly £500; much of which, he assured me, was bestowed in mere ornament and finish. These two considerations have brought me to the conclusion, to build a smaller and plainer school-room, and I have given directions to the Wakefield builder accordingly; but he is not to have anything to do with the contract. I expect the reduced plans and specifications home in a few days." On the 8th of April following, she writes,—"This has been a very busy day with me, and as I have now made all needful arrangements with B., I transmit the particulars." [Here follow the amounts of her several contracts with mason, slater, plasterer, joiner, plumber, and painter; the total being £362 6s. 3d.] "When I tell thee that the rejected estimates taken together, would have amounted to the sum of £456 10s. 6d., I think thou wilt agree with me, that the difference is sufficient to repay a good deal of trouble." On the 5th December, she writes to her sister-in-law R. R. H., saying, "What to call my school I really cannot tell. It is not, certainly, a Lancasterian or British School; for we exhibit pictures, and teach natural history, and a little geography and singing. Nor can it be called an Infants' School; for in the gallery a stranger might happen to see a top row of girls almost as tall as women. Some of them are new scholars, and contrast rather awkwardly in the classes with the little ones who scarcely reach their shoulders. Poor things! I really feel an affection for them, they show so much zeal, coming from West-Hardwick and Purston, in a little troop, for the sake of the superior instruction they, or their parents expect at the 'new school.' About twenty scholars, out of the fifty who are on the list, are from the adjacent villages.—Ackworth does not yet shew its sense of the advantage offered." Miss Sarah Grice was the first mistress, and was succeeded, at her resignation, by Miss Moore.* The School has recently been transferred to a Church of England Board of Management and control, subject to certain conditions, and is now under Government Inspection. For particulars respecting the little Burial Ground adjoining the School, see under date 1848.

THE WESLEYAN CHAPEL.

"The rise of Methodism in Ackworth is somewhat obscure. Originally this village formed part of the Wakefield Circuit, and became part of the Pontefract Circuit, when the division took place in 1796. The first Chapel was built in 1791, and opened by John Nelson: it had at first a front gallery, which was subsequently extended along the sides of the chapel, and contained 90 sittings in the gallery, four pews in the body, and about 100 free seats. In 1791, Mr. Robert Ranson, of Ackworth, conveyed a plot of ground containing 433 square yards with the Methodist Chapel thereon for the amount of £22, to the following trustees:—Messrs. William Nelstrop, and P. Thwaites,

* Miss Moore was succeeded by Miss Moseley, who resigned in 1866. Miss Moseley was succeeded by Miss Spink, who resigned in 1869. Miss Spink was succeeded by Miss Murray, of Archingoule, near Huntley, in Aberdeenshire, who has held the position ever since. Miss Murray has invariably succeeded in obtaining the excellent merit grant.—J. L. S.

of Ackworth; John Elwell, Joseph Holdsworth, and John Newhouse, of Wakefield; John Ranson, of Warmfield; Thomas Bamford, of Cudworth; William Nicholson, of Carleton; and William Scott, of Wakefield. In 1821 the chapel was re-conveyed to the following:—Messrs. James Ranson, Thomas Legg, Richard Smith, and Joseph Wilson, of Ackworth; and Messrs. Wm. Moxon, James Robinson, Joseph Watson, William Dawson, and John Brice, of Pontefract. Over the door of the Chapel, a stone, two feet by one and a half, was placed by Mrs. Nelstrop, which bore the following words:—

> 'Sinners obey the Gospel word,
> Haste to the Supper of my Lord ;
> Be wise to know your gracious day,
> All things are ready, come away.'
> 1790.

Upon the building of the new chapel, this stone was placed in the back wall of the vestry where it may still be seen. * * The foundation stone of the present beautiful Chapel was laid on Good Friday, April 2nd, 1858, by William Peel, Esq., of Ackworth Park. There was a large company present on the occasion. * * The Architect was Mr. Wilson, of Bath ; and the builders were Messrs. Simpson and Wilson, of Ackworth. The Chapel with the schools attached, cost about £1,500. Mr. Peel headed the subscription list with £300, and presented the Organ. * * The following inscription was placed in a bottle under the stone :—'The foundation stone of this Wesleyan Methodist Chapel was laid by W. Peel, Esq., of Ackworth Park, on Good Friday, April 2nd, 1858.' " * The scroll also bore the names of the President of the Wesleyan Conference (Rev. F. A. West), the Secretary of the Conference (Dr. Hannah), four ministers of the Pontefract Circuit, the Circuit Stewards, and the Trustees of the Chapel. " The Chapel was opened in the following year, when eminent ministers conducted the services." Notices of these will be found under the head of " Annals." The Chapel has been recently renovated at a cost of over a hundred pounds.*

* Vide " Wesleyan Methodist Circuit Record," August, 1882.

THE PRIMITIVE METHODIST CHAPEL & SCHOOLS.

These buildings owe their existence to the munificence of Mr. Field, an American gentleman, who temporarily resided here. The population of Ackworth had so rapidly increased at the Moor-Top, that it was deemed absolutely necessary that a place of worship, with schools attached, should be erected to supply the spiritual needs of the people. It is well known that an attempt to do this was first made by the Rector of Ackworth, but the difficulties in the way of procuring a suitable site, etc., were found to be so great, that the attempt was temporarily abandoned until a more convenient opportunity presented itself. Mr. Fields then stepped in and enabled the Primitive Methodists to erect the present commodious chapel and schools, which have admirably served their purpose up to the present time. The foundation stone was laid by Mr. William Fields, son of the above, and the chapel was formally opened for public worship on May 10th, 1863. The school was opened in October, 1877, and in December, 1878, there were 62 infant children on the books. The following extract is from the examiner's Report on his visit to the School in June, 1878:—
"The School which has been very recently set on foot, already gives excellent promise of future usefulness. The children are taught in a kindly and sympathetic manner, which evidently wins their confidence, and quiets their attention." Miss Fanny Jones, of Ackworth, was the first mistress appointed by the Trustees, and she held the position until her marriage in 1885. The Government Grant earned by this school in 1878, was £18 8s. 8d.

Antiquities.

I.—CASTLE SYKE.

The name "Castle Syke" certainly indicates the existence of a Castle at Ackworth at some remote period, and the natural [position and surroundings of Castle Syke Farm, would seem to favour the supposition. The farm itself stands high, the ground undulating towards the west, and culminating in what has evidently been a dyke or moat of considerable dimensions. This dyke is now a lane, and might probably be worth excavating. The name and moat however, are all that remain of byegone times. The Castle would most likely be the residence of the first Saxon lords of Ackworth, as indicated by the Saxon word *Syke* or fountain; and it is not at all improbable that the building was levelled to the ground when William, the Norman Conqueror, laid waste these parts of Yorkshire.

II.—LADY-WELL.

This very ancient well is one of the several public wells, which has in recent years somehow become enclosed. From what it derived its name is not known, but from the fact of its being the oldest, it is not unlikely that it was originally set apart by some religious service, and dedicated to "Our Lady" for the use of the inhabitants of the village. In pre-reformation times this custom was common, some wells having miraculous powers ascribed to their waters by the superstitious, like the well of St. Keyne, and in modern times, the "Holy Wells" in Ireland; but nothing of the sort attaches to the well of "Our Lady" at Ackworth. As the population increased it was found necessary to sink other wells. One in the centre of the village, near the "Brown Cow Inn," was constructed in 1791, but the approach to it was so dangerous, that, after a child had been drowned in it, it was altered into a pump. There is an old well at Brackenhill.

III.—THE VILLAGE ELM.

Of the great tree on the village green we have no certain particulars. We may, however, easily draw for ourselves the picture of its being planted and nurtured from generation to generation, until it became the pride, not only of Ackworth, but of the surrounding neighbourhood! But the ravages of time, fire, wind, tempest, and barbarous usage, have ruthlessly deprived the old trunk of many of its largest branches, and now it stands in mournful majesty like a dethroned monarch weeping over the past. It is described by Thompson* as a "grand old giant elm, with its iron-bound cavernous trunk, its great naked arms telling of generations of seasons and storms, yet interspersed with luxuriant foliage, testifying to the yet unquenchable vigour of its constitution." Mrs. Harriet Beecher Stowe's word picture of an aged elm is so fine, that its insertion here will be at once appropriate, and descriptive of the elm at Ackworth. It is "a great rugged elm, with all its lacings and archings of boughs and twigs, which has stood cold and frozen against the metallic blue of winter sky, forgetful of leaves, and patient in its bareness, calmly content in its naked strength, and crystalline definiteness of outline. But in April, there is a rising and stirring within the grand old monster,—a whispering of knotted buds, a mounting of sap, coursing ethereally from bough to bough with a warm and gentle life; and though the old elm knows it not, a new creation is at hand."† It is said that, within the recollection of some still living, a pair of venerable owls took up their abode in one of the great hollow fissures of the tree, but their appearance was greeted with so many superstitious head-shakings, that they were soon dislodged from their retreat by the pungent fumes of burning cotton and cayenne pepper, a proceeding, however, which might have proved disastrous to the tree itself. The elm has frequently been struck by lightning, as its many zinc patches testify. There it has stood and still stands like a mighty sentinel drawing down, as it were, by its faithful stability, the indignation of the elements upon its devoted head. Under its branches many a village may-queen has been enthroned; many an open-mouthed rustic beguiled by the village politician; village tittle-tattle retailed; village synods, for the discussion of great national events, convened and held; and village scenes of all shades and descriptions, both sombre and gay, enacted;

---

* Vide " History of Ackworth School."
† Vide " Literature of all Countries," Vol. xvii., p. 53.

in short, if the venerable old monarch could only have been endowed with the faculty of speech for a single day, what an incalculable service it might have rendered to the compiler of the "Parochial History of Ackworth!"

IV.—THE VILLAGE CROSS.

Tradition says that this cross was erected to commemorate a plague which carried off great numbers of the inhabitants.* The date of this sickness has not been preserved, but that it occurred before the Reformation is certain from the cause of it, which has also been handed down by the same channel. Previous to the Reformation, there was in the Chapel of St. Mary, in the Church of Ackworth, a Chantry, of our Lady, founded by Isabel de Castleford. There is no reason to suppose that this Chantry was supplied from the Priory of Nostel, as some have thought, but we may naturally conclude that the existence of the Chantry would cause frequent communication between the two places; nor is it unlikely that some of the Brethren of Nostel might occasionally minister at Ackworth, during the absence of the Chantry Priest. Assuming this to have been so, the tradition as to the origin of the plague in question is much strengthened. It is said that a Monk of Nostel, who, probably from the cause just suggested, was held in affectionate remembrance by the people of Ackworth, dying abroad, his body was brought back to be interred at Nostel. As it passed through Ackworth, the people wished the procession to halt, and the corpse to be uncovered. This being done, the infectious complaint which was the cause of death, a kind of putrid fever, was communicated to the bystanders. The Cross is said to have been erected on the exact spot where the body rested, to commemorate at once that event, and also the dire consequences which were permitted by God to flow from it. The date of its mutilation, the removal of the Cross, and the substitution of a ball, (the emblem of the world,) is generally ascribed to the time of the Great Rebellion.

* Thompson says "three or four hundred."

V.—THE GROTTO.

This is a modern name given to a small ruin at the north east corner of the Rectory garden. In 1852, the outer walls only were standing, but soon afterwards, it was roofed and made water-tight with some of the refuse material left from the Church restoration. What it has been, it is difficult to say, as there is no record of its history. Some say it is a pre-Reformation Oratory; and others, the Sanctum of the Chantry Priest. Of its antiquity there can be no doubt, for the three old yew trees which surround the ruin, are at least three centuries old. The adjacent pond also confirms this theory. It is not a modern pond, as its enormous lilies testify. The piece of land upon which the ruin stands is triangular in shape, and belongs, in reality, to no one in particular. All that is known about it is that, previous to 1777, it was part and parcel of the Ackworth Park Estate, and was bought by the then Rector (Dr. Timothy Lee), and (according to the terms of his will,) presented by him to the "Rector of Ackworth for the time being and his successors for ever." Dr. Lee's will is dated March 30, 1777, and the terms of the bequest run as follows:—"I give and devise unto Anthony Surtees, of Ackworth, Esq., and his heirs all that small parcel of land as it is now fenced off from the hempyards in Ackworth aforesaid wherein the Grotto stands not now belonging to the Rectory, but I request that the said Anthony Surtees and his heirs |will for ever hereafter permit the Rector of Ackworth for the time being to enjoy and occupy the said parcel of ground without paying anything for the same. And I also request that the said Anthony Surtees or his heirs will do any lawful act for conveying and assigning the same parcel of ground to my successors the Rectors of Ackworth for ever."

VI.—THE OLD HALL.

At the west end of the parish, "looking across the valley of the infant Went," stands an interesting old building called the "Old Hall." Tradition says it was one of the places of concealment selected by John William Nevison, the great robber and highwayman of Yorkshire, better known in history as the confederate of the celebrated "Dick Turpin." The story runs thus:—Towards the close of the year 1683, a gang of masked ruffians commenced a series of depredations in the neighbourhood of Ackworth and Pontefract, and for some time remained unmolested and unrecognized. Suspicion, however, fell upon Nevison, a native of Pontefract, who, it was known, had "taken to the road" as a profession, and who, it was supposed, was leader of the band. About Christmastide in the year 1684, their nocturnal visits became so frequent and daring, that the district was alarmed, and a number of parish constables, watchmen, and beadles were induced to pursue, and if possible, capture the robbers. For a long time the miscreants eluded their pursuers, Nevison actually hiding himself in a small compartment over the front door of Ackworth Hall in Purston Lane, access into which he gained by a secret trap door, and there he remained undiscovered, whilst the officers who had seen him enter the house, were busily engaged in searching every corner of the building. The trap door and compartment which is now known as "Nevison's room," are still shewn to the visitor. In the following year Nevison gave his persecutors a chance, and a hot pursuit resulted in his capture by Captain Hardcastle,[*] in a public house called the "Magpie," at Sandal, and one of the then three Inns known as "Magna Sandal Three Houses," between Pontefract and Ferrybridge. A steep declivity near Sandal is pointed out and known as "Nevison's leap." He was subsequently tried, and executed on the Tyburn gallows, outside Micklegate Bar, at York, May 4th, 1685. Nevison was born at Pontefract in 1639, and educated there.[†] "Dick Turpin's" ride from London to York in 16 hours, is ascribed by Lord Macaulay to Nevison.[‡] "The Old Hall has"

[*] In reality, a valiant tailor who went by the sobriquet of "Captain Hardcastle."
[†] Vide Johnson's "Life of Nevison."
[‡] Mr. Harrison Ainsworth's graphic description of Turpin's ride is therefore fabulous.

says Thompson, the historian of Ackworth School, " long been haunted, but I have not been able to trace the existence of this superstition in the village; probably the extensive improvements which have recently been made in and around the building, have banished, for a time, all ghostly spectres, both from the scene, and memory of the villagers." In 1879, "this once handsome Tudor dwelling, with its lines of mullioned windows, and its elegant gables, some of the latter toppling to their fall, its roof in holes, and its accessory buildings a heap of ruins, had just reached that hoary quality and suggestive wierdness, which would have rejoiced the author of the 'Castle of Otranto.' In its old crumbling walls, the white and the brown owl reared their broods, and furnished appropriate music in the gloaming."* But thanks to the care of Lord St. Oswald, this monument of antiquity has been substantially and judiciously restored, and is now in a condition to weather the storms of at least another century.

VIII.—THE PLAGUE STONE.

Thompson, in his "History of Ackworth School," makes this interesting relic contemporary with the Village Cross, but it is more probable that it dates from a second and more recent epidemic of the Plague which occurred in 1645. He is correct, however, in saying that it was " for many months the only point of contact between the people of Ackworth and the outer world;" and that upon it " the Ackworth purchaser dropped his money into a vessel of water,† for which, a few hours after, he found his return in merchandise." A careful observer will still perceive a trough-like construction upon the inside of the stone. It is most desirable that the stone, or what little remains of it, should be removed to a place of security ere it entirely disappears, for it is certainly worthy of preservation as a relic of antiquity.

* Vide " History of Ackworth School," p. 304.
† A very wise precaution under the circumstances.

OLD CHALYBEATE BATH.

The site of this old bath is still pointed out at Ackworth Moor-Top, about a quarter of a mile north of Ackworth School, the pupils of which, before the new swimming baths were constructed, made a practice of bathing at six o'clock in the morning, and often when the ground was covered with hoar frost! The water of this bath was a strong Chalybeate, and excessively cold. In 1861, the old bath-house was changed into a dwelling. An engraving of the bath, as it then appeared, is given in Thompson's "History of Ackworth School," published in 1879.

OBELISKS.

There are two fine obelisks in the village, both of them large, but comparatively modern. To a stranger, they possess a commemorative or memorial appearance, but in reality, they were erected by the Lords of the Manor, as combination guide and distance stones. 1.—At the junction of the Ackworth and Pontefract roads. Erected in 1827. Hexagonal shaft, triangular cap, surmounted by a globe. Height about ten feet. From this point, East Hardwick is distant 2½ miles, Darrington 3, Pontefract 2½, York 27, Sheffield 13, and Barnsley 10. 2.— Opposite the Friend's School. Erected in 1805. Its height and description are the same as the foregoing, which was evidently copied from this one. Pontefract is distant from it 3 miles, Hemsworth 3, Snaith 15, Wentbridge 3, and Doncaster 13. A lamp surmounts the globe.

Charities.

Scarcely any parish in England is endowed with so many Charities as Ackworth, indeed it is *pauperised* by them. The original deeds are quoted where available.

WORMALL'S CHARITY.

By Deed, dated 18th May, 1660. This Indenture, made the 18th May, in the year of our Lord 1660, between William Child, of Sutton, in the Parish of Campsall, and County of York, yeoman, and Dorothy his wife, on the one part, and Thomas Hewitt, of Ackworth, in the county aforesaid, yeoman, on the other part, witnesseth that the said William Child, and Dorothy, his wife, for divers good causes and considerations them thereunto moving, and more especially for and in consideration of the sum of sixty pounds of good and lawful money of England, to them or the one of them in hand paid by the said Thomas Hewitt, at and before the sealing and delivery thereof, the receipt whereof they, the said William Child and Dorothy, his wife, do hereby acknowledge and confess themselves therewith fully content, satisfied, and paid, and thereof and of every part and parcel thereof do clearly acquit, exonerate, and discharge the said Thomas Hewitt, his heirs, executors, administrators, and assigns, and every of them, for ever by these presents, have given, granted, bargained, aliend, sold, enfeoffed, and confirmed, and by these presents do from them, their heirs and assigns, fully, clearly, and absolutely give, grant, bargain, alien, enfeoffe, and confirm unto the said Thomas Hewitt his heirs and assigns for ever, all those three acres of arable land (by estimation, be the same more or less) lying and being in a certain field called Berriall Field, in twelve selions (? sections), commonly called Cock Platte, between a Baulk on the east and the Fur shot adjoining to Berrial Balke west, abbutting on the Hobheadland, north, and two acres of arable land (by estimation more or less) lying and being in a certain field called Middlefield, near the High Ashes, the one of them whereof lyeth between lands of William Lambe, gentleman, north, and Phillip Austwick, south. And also, one other half acre of arable land (by estimation more or less) lying and being in the said Middlefield, on a Fur Shot called Long Longlands between the lands of Thomas Huntington, north, and Matthew Lambe, south, with all ways, easements, profits, commons, commodities, advantages, and appurtenances, whatsoever, to the same belonging, or in anywise appertaining. All which said lands are lying and being within the precinct, liberties, and territories of Ackworth aforesaid, in the said County of York, and are now in the tenure and occupation of the said William Child, his assignee, or assignees, to have and to hold the said five acres and a half of arable land and all other the before granted premises with all and of them, by these presents, that he the said Thomas Hewitt, his heirs, and assigns, and every of them, shall and may by force and virtue of these presents, from time to time, and at all times hereafter for ever, lawfully, peaceably, and quietly, have, hold, use, and occupy, possess, and enjoy the said five acres and a half of arable land and all and singular the before granted premises, with their and every of their rights, members, and appurtenances, and have, receive, and take, the rents, issues and profits thereof to his and their own proper use and behoof for ever, without any lawful let, suit, trouble, denial, interruption, molestation, or disturbance of them, the said William Child and Dorothy, his wife, their heirs, or assigns, or any of them, or of Nathaniel Baine, his executors, administrators, or assigns, or any of them, or of any other person or persons whatsoever, lawfully claiming the same by, from, or under them, or any of them. And that free and clear, and freely and clearly acquitted, exonerated, and discharged, or otherwise from time to time and at all times hereafter well and sufficiently saved and kept harmless and indemnified by the said William Child and Dorothy, his wife, their heirs, executors, administrators, or some of them, of and from all and all manner of former and other bargains, sales, gifts, grants, leases, mortgages, jointures, dowers, titles of dower, statutes, merchant, and of the staple recognizances, extents, judgments, executions, uses, entails, rents, arrearages of rents, forfeitures, fines, issues, and amerciaments, and of and from all and singular other titles, troubles, charges, and incumbrances whatsoever, had, made, committed,

suffered, omitted, or done by the said William Child and Dorothy,
his wife, or either of them, their heirs, or assigns, or George
Child, father of the said William Child, his heirs, or assigns, or
the said Nathaniel Baine, his executors, administrators, or
assigns, or by any other person or persons whatsoever lawfully
claiming the same from or under them, or by from or under
their or any of their means, acts, title, consent, interest, privity,
or procurement (the said yearly rent of two shillings and ninepence and one rent charge of *twenty-eight shillings* of lawful
money of England due and payable to *John Wormall, his heirs
and assigns and the Minister and Churchwardens of the
Parish of Ackworth aforesaid for the use of the said parish*
only excepted and foreprized.

And further, the said William Child and Dorothy, his wife,
do, for themselves, their heirs, executors, and administrators,
and every of them, covenant, promise, and grant to and with the
said Thomas Hewitt, his heirs and assigns, and to and with all
and every of them singular their and every of their appurtenances, and every part and parcel thereof, unto the said Thomas
Hewitt, his heirs and assignees for ever. To be holden of our
Sovereign Lord the King, his heirs and successors, in fee favour
as of His Highness Manor of Enfield, in the County of
Middlesex, in fee and common socage and not in capite nor by
knight service, yielding and paying yearly to the hands of the
receiver or receivers of the Fee Farm Rent thereof for the time
being, the yearly rent of two shillings and ninepence of lawful
money of England, at such days and times as the same is
appointed and accustomedly paid. And the said William Child
and Dorothy Child, his wife, for themselves, their heirs, executors,
and administrators, and every of them, do covenant, promise,
and grant to and with the said Thomas Hewitt, his heirs and
assigns, and to and with all and every by these presents, that
they, the said William Child and Dorothy, his wife, their heirs,
and assigns, and all and every other person or persons, and
their heirs, lawfully having or claiming, or rightfully pretending

to have or claim any estate, right, title, interest, or demand, in to or out of the said premises or any part or parcel of them, shall and will, from time to time, and at all times hereafter upon the reasonable request and at the costs and charges in the law of the said Thomas Hewitt his heirs or assigns make, do, perform, acknowledge, levy, execute and suffer or cause to be made, done, performed, acknowledged, levied, executed, and suffered all and every such further lawful and reasonable act, thing and things devise or devises in the law assurance and conveyances whatsover for the further, better, and more peaceful and perfect assuring and conveying of all and singular the before hereby granted premises, with their and every of their rights, members, appurtenances, unto the said Thomas Hewitt, his heirs, and assigns, for ever. Be it by fine or fines, feoffment or feoffments, deed or deeds, enrolled or not enrolled, the enrolment of these presents, recovery or recoveries, with the single or double voucher or vouchers, release or confirmation, or by all and every or any the ways and means aforesaid, or by any other ways or lawful means whatsoever as by the said Thomas Hewitt, his heirs, or assigns, or his or their Counsel, learned in the laws of this nation, shall be reasonably devised, advised, or required, so as the said William Child, and Dorothy, his wife, their heirs, and assigns, or such other person or persons who shall be required to make such further assurance be not compelled to travaile forth of the County of York, nor farther than the City of York, for the doing and executing thereof. And further it is covenanted, concluded, condescended unto and fully agreed upon by and between the said parties to these presents, that all fines, feoffments, recoveries, and assurances in the law whatsoever so had made, acknowledged, levied, suffered, or done by or between the said parties or any of them after touching or concerning the said land, and all and singular the before hereby granted premises, with their and every of their rights, members and appurtenances, and every and any part thereof shall be and inure, and shall be construed, esteemed, adjudged, and taken to be and inure to the only purpose and behoof of the said Thomas Hewitt, his heirs, and assigns, for ever, and to no other use and purpose whatsoever. In witness whereof the parties above named to these present indentures interchangably have set their hands and seals the day and year above written (1660).

WILLIAM CHILD   (Seal.)
DOROTHY CHILD   (Seal.)

Sealed and delivered and also full and peaceable possession. Liverie and seizin was given and delivered the day and year within written by the within named William Child, and Dorothy, his wife, to the within named Thomas Hewitt, in their proper persons, of, in, and upon the half acre of land within mentioned lying on Long Longland, in the name of all the lands and premises within granted, with the appurtenances to the use within specified according to the tenor, effect, and true meaning of these presents, in the presence of us, Robert Hewitt, Thomas Thwaites, Philip Austwicke, Matthew Lambe, Richard Pickeringe.

Dr. Lee says that the original Deed was in possession of Mr. Vaux, but where it is now, no one knows.

Upon the list of Charities painted up in the Parish Church, this charity is described as follows:—

	£	s.	d.
John Wormald to the Poor..................	0	8	0
And for putting out poor children.........	1	0	0

but there is no evidence remaining to show how this sum of £1 8s. comes to be thus apportioned. Reference is made to it in the above quoted deed of May, 1660, wherein certain lands in Ackworth are conveyed by William Child and his wife to Thomas Hewitt; this sum of £1 8s. being reserved as payable to the Minister and Churchwardens of Ackworth, for the use of the poor.

THE POOR'S ESTATE, ACKWORTH.

This estate, originally called the Paddock, and containing five acres and sixteen perches, was purchased in 1763, for the poor of Ackworth. It was the property of Mr. Barwell, Gentleman, and was conveyed, in trust for the benefit of the poor of Ackworth, to Sir Rowland Winn, of Nostel, Bart., the Rev. Timothy Lee, Rector of Ackworth, and Doctor in Divinity, and Francis Sykes, of Ackworth Park, Esq., in whose representatives the legal estate is, of course, still vested. The title deeds of the estate are in the parish chest, in the custody of the Rector. The price was £400. Of this sum £300 was derived from the following benefactions:—

	£	s.	d.
1692.—Elizabeth, Relict of Sir John Lowther, Baronet	20	0	0
1703.—Robert Mason, Gentleman	10	0	0
Ann, Relict of the Rev. J. Bolton	10	0	0
Cash from a Stock of Cows	20	0	0
1717.—Robert Lowther, of Ackworth, Esq.	50	0	0
1718.—Margaret, wife of William Norton, of Sawley, Esq.	20	0	0
1722.—Ralph Lowther, of Ackworth Park, Esq.	20	0	0
1724.—Ann, daughter of Ralph Lowther, Esq.	50	0	0
1724.—Elizabeth, daughter of Lawson Trotter, of Skelton Castle, Esq.	10	0	0
1729.—John Lowther, of Ackworth Park, Esq.	50	0	0
1739.—Thomas Bright, of Badsworth, Esq.	20	0	0
1764.—The Rev. Wm. Key	20	0	0
	£300	0	0

To this sum of £300, £40 was added, either by accumulation of interest, or from some donations, the particulars of which are not now known. The amount, therefore, available for the purchase was £340. The remaining £60 had to be borrowed. Some difficulty occurring as to the security of this latter sum,

Dr. Lee got over it by advancing to the parish the amount required, in consideration of a lease of the estate being granted to him for 99 years, at a reserved annual rent of £12. To the original quantity of land, viz., 5a. 16p., the Enclosure Commissioners, in 1774, allotted 2a. 2r. 28p., making the whole estate 7a. 3r. 4p. Dr. Lee's lease expired in February, 1863. The rent of £12 per annum, is regularly paid to the Rector, Churchwardens, and Overseers of the Poor, and is distributed by them on St. Thomas's Day.

The following is a copy of the conveyance from Sir John Ramsden, Bart., and his Lady, to Sir Rowland Winn, Bart.:—

THIS INDENTURE, made the 20th day of October, in the year of our Lord one thousand seven hundred and sixty-three, between Sir John Ramsden, of Byram, in the County of York, Baronet, and Dame Margaret his wife, one of the nieces of Mary Lowther, late of Ackworth Park, in the said county, Spinster, deceased, the devisee of all her real estate not specifically devised by her last Will and Testament, on the one part, and Sir Rowland Winn, of Nostell, in the said county, Baronet, the Reverend Timothy Lee, Rector of Ackworth, in the said county, and Doctor in Divinity, and Francis Sykes, of Ackworth Park aforesaid, Esquire, on the other part.

Whereas, Robert Lowther, late of Pontefract, in the said county, deceased, by his last Will and Testament in writing, bearing date on or about the 10th day of August, which was in the year of our Lord 1717, did, amongst other things therein contained, give to the Poor of Ackworth Fifty Pounds, to be laid out in the purchase of land, and the rents thereof to be distributed yearly by the Minister and Overseers of the Poor of Ackworth for the time being.

And whereas, Ralph Lowther, late of Ackworth Park, aforesaid, Esquire, by his last Will in writing, bearing date on or about the 11th day of June, in the year of our Lord 1722, did, amongst many other things therein contained, give to the Poor of the Parish of Ackworth Twenty Pounds, to be laid out in lands, and the produce thereof to be distributed yearly by the Ministers and Churchwardens of the said Parish.

And whereas, John Lowther, late of Ackworth Park aforesaid, Esquire, did, by his last Will and Testament, bearing date on or about the 3rd day of February, in the year of our Lord 1728, amongst other things therein specified, give to the Poor of the said Parish of Ackworth, the sum of Fifty Pounds, and did direct that the same should be laid out in the purchase of lands, and that the rents thereof should be annually distributed by the Minister and Churchwardens of the said Parish to such Poor within their said Parish as they, in their discretion, should think proper objects of the said charity, as in and by the said recited Wills, reference being thereto had, may more fully appear. And whereas, the said Sir John Ramsden and Dame Margaret his wife, as the legal representatives of the said Robert Lowther, and John Lowther, have in their hands the said two several legacies of Fifty Pounds each and Twenty Pounds, making together the said sum of One Hundred and Twenty Pounds, and have duly paid the interest thereof to the Minister and Churchwardens of the said Parish for the time being, at Christmas yearly. And whereas, divers other persons [*see Parochial Magazine, March, 1859,*] have at many different times left divers legacies and sums of money to the Poor of the said Parish, the whole of which amounts to Two Hundred and Twenty Pounds, and which said Two Hundred and Twenty Pounds is now in the hands of the said Timothy Lee, as Rector of the said Parish, and for which he hath duly paid the interest, and the same has been distributed yearly, at Christmas, amongst the Poor of the said Parish, by the Minister and Churchwardens there.

And whereas, the said Sir John Ramsden, and Dame Margaret, his wife, are now seized in fee simple of the Messuage, Closes, and Hereditaments hereinafter mentioned to be hereby granted, which are of the full value of Four Hundred Pounds, and they are desirous that the said One Hundred and Twenty Pounds should be laid out in the purchase of lands for the benefit of the said Poor, according to the intention of the said several Testators, and the said Timothy Lee is also desirous that the said Two Hundred and Twenty Pounds in his hands should be laid out in the purchase of lands for the benefit of the said Poor. And therefore, at a Public Vestry Meeting of the inhabitants of the said Parish lately had, after due notice was given for that purpose, it was unanimously agreed that application should be made to the said John Ramsden to purchase of him the said Messuage and Premises for the sum of Four Hundred Pounds, out of which the said sum of One Hundred and Twenty Pounds so given by the said Robert Lowther, Ralph Lowther, and John Lowther, as aforesaid, should be deemed as part of the said purchase-money. And the said Sir John Ramsden upon such application hath agreed to sell the said Messuage and Premises for the said sum of Four Hundred Pounds, for the benefit of the said Poor, and that the said sum of One Hundred and Twenty Pounds so given as aforesaid, shall be in part thereof, in order to satisfy and discharge the said three several Legacies, so that he will have to receive only the sum of Two Hundred and Eighty Pounds, the residue of the said purchase-money, and towards payment thereof the said Two Hundred and Twenty Pounds now in the hands of the said Timothy Lee, is to be paid and applied. And in regard there will be a deficiency of Sixty Pounds towards completing the said purchase, the said Sir Rowland Winn, Timothy Lee, and Francis Sykes, having agreed to advance and lend the same for the benefit of the said Poor, until they can be repaid the same out of the said Hereditaments and Premises, in such manner as is hereinafter specified.

Now, therefore, this Indenture witnesseth, that in pursuance of the said recited agreements, and in consideration of the said One Hundred and Twenty Pounds so given by the said Robert Lowther, Ralph Lowther, and John Lowther, as aforesaid, and in satisfaction and discharge of the same, and to the intent that the said One Hundred and Twenty Pounds may be vested in land for the use of the said Poor of Ackworth for ever, according to the intentions of the said three several Donors, and that the rents and profits of the said lands may be distributed, yearly, for ever, by the Minister, Churchwardens, and Overseers of the Poor of the said parish, to and amongst such of the said Poor, and in such manner as they, in their discretion, shall think fit and proper. Also, in consideration of the said sum of Two Hundred and Twenty Pounds in the hands of the said Timothy Lee, belonging to the Poor of the said Parish, and by him paid to the said Sir John Ramsden, at or before the executing hereof. And also in consideration of the said sum of Sixty Pounds by the said Sir Rowland Winn, Timothy Lee, and Francis Sykes, now advanced and lent, and by them paid to the said Sir John Ramsden, at or before the executing hereof, the receipt of which said several sums of Two Hundred and Twenty Pounds and Sixty Pounds, making together the said Two Hundred and Eighty Pounds, the said Sir John Ramsden doth hereby acknowledge, and thereof, and of every part thereof, doth hereby acquit and discharge the said Sir Rowland Winn, Timothy Lee, and Francis Sykes, severally and respectively, their several Heirs, Executors, and Administrators; and which said sums of One Hundred and Twenty Pounds, Two Hundred and Twenty Pounds, and Sixty Pounds, make together the said sum of Four Hundred Pounds, the purchase-money agreed to be paid and allowed for the said Hereditaments and Premises.

They, the said Sir John Ramsden and Dame Margaret his wife, have bargained, sold, released, and confirmed, and by these presents do grant, bargain, release, and confirm, unto the said Sir Rowland Winn and Francis Sykes (in their actual possession now being by virtue of a bargain and sale to them thereof made by the said Sir John Ramsden and Dame Margaret, his wife, for one whole year by Indenture, bearing date the day next before the day of the date hereof, and by force of the Statute made for transferring of uses into possession) and to the Heirs and Assigns of the said Sir Rowland Winn and Francis Sykes for ever, all that Messuage or Tenement, situate and being in Ackworth aforesaid, wherein Nathaniel Barwell, Gentleman, now deceased, formerly dwelt, and all the Barns, Stables, and other Outbuildings, Court yards, Foldsteads, Gardens, Orchards, Hereditaments, and Appurtenances thereto belonging. And also all those three Closes of Meadow and Pasture Ground thereto adjoining and belonging, commonly called or known by the names of the Lower Croft, the Upper Croft, and Barn Croft, or by what other name or names soever the same are now called or known; and also two Cow Gates, or Pasture for two Beasts in Ackworth Common Pasture, and which said Messuage, Closes, and Premises were late the Estate of the said Mary Lowther, and are now in the tenures or occupations of John Aneley and Jonathan Thompson, and are all situate and being in Ackworth aforesaid, together with all Ways, Waters, Watercourses, Privileges, Advantages, Commons, Common of Pasture, Hereditaments, and Appurtenances, whatsoever to the said Messuage, Closes, and Premises belonging, or in any wise appertaining, *except* the Pew in Ackworth Church, lately enjoyed by Mrs. Barwell deceased, and the reversion and reversions, remainder and remainders, rents, issues, and profits of the said Messuage, Hereditaments, and Premises, and every of them. And also all the Estate, right, title, and interest of them the said Sir John Ramsden and Dame Margaret, his wife, and of either of them, into and out of the said Messuage, Hereditaments, and Premises, and every part thereof, together with all deeds, writings, and evidences whatsoever, touching or concerning the said hereditaments and premises, or any of them, and now in the custody or power of the said Sir John Ramsden, and which he can come at without suit at law or in equity.

To have and to hold the said Messuage, Closes, Hereditaments, and Premises above mentioned, to be hereby granted and released, with their Appurtenances, unto the said Sir Rowland Winn and Francis Sykes, and their Heirs, to the only use and behoof of them and their Heirs for ever. *In Trust*, nevertheless, for the Poor of the Parish of Ackworth aforesaid, for the time being for ever, and to the intent that the rents, issues, and profits of the said Messuage, Closes, and Premises may at all times hereafter be had, received, and taken by the Minister, Churchwardens, and Overseers of the Poor of the said Parish of Ackworth, for the time being, or may be paid over into their hands or distributed by them at Christmas and Whitsuntide yearly for ever, to and amongst the said Poor, in such manner as the said Minister, Churchwardens, and Overseers of the Poor for the time being shall, in their discretion, think fit and proper, and to no other use, and upon no other Trust whatsoever, but subject, nevertheless, to the proviso hereinafter mentioned.

And the said Sir John Ramsden hereby for himself, his Heirs, Executors, and Aministrators covenant and agree with the said Sir Rowland Winn and Francis Sykes, their Heirs and Assigns, that he, the said Sir John Ramsden, and the said Dame Margaret his wife, and their respective Heirs, shall, and will at any time hereafter, upon the request and at the cost and charge of the said Sir Rowland Winn and Francis Sykes, their Heirs or Assigns, acknowledge and levy in his Majesty's Court of Common Pleas, at Westminster, in due form of law, unto the said Sir Rowland Winn and Francis Sykes, and to the Heirs of one of them, one fine sur conuzance de droit come coe, &c., with proclamations to be thereupon had, according to the form of the Statute in that case made and provided, of the said Messuage, Closes, and Premises above-mentioned, to be hereby granted and released, with their appurtenances, by such names and descriptions as shall be thought requisite to describe and ascertain the same, which said fine so or in any other manner to be levied; and all and every other fine and fines heretofore or hereafter to be levied, of the said Hereditaments and Premises above-mentioned or any of them, by or between the said parties hereto or any of them, or whereunto they or any of them are, is, or shall or may be a party or parties, shall be and enure, and is and are hereby agreed and declared to be and enure to the said only use and behoof of the said Sir Rowland Winn and Francis Sykes, their Heirs and Assigns for ever, and to no other use whatsoever. And the said Sir John Ramsden doth hereby also for himself, his Heirs, Executors, Administrators, and Assigns, further covenant and agree with the said Sir Rowland Winn and Francis Sykes, and their Heirs in manner following, that is to say, that for and notwithstanding any act, matter, or thing whatsoever by them, the said Sir John Ramsden and Dame Margaret his wife, or either of them, or by the said Mary Lowther, made, done, committed, or suffered to the contrary, they, the said Sir John Ramsden and Dame Margaret, his wife, now at the executing of these presents are and stand or one of them is and standeth, lawfully and absolutely seized of the said Messuage, Closes, and Premises above-mentioned, of a good, sure, absolute, and indefeasible Estate of Inheritance in fee simple, without any manner of trust, condition, power of revocation, or any other restraint, matter or thing to alter, change, charge, incumber, or make void the same Estate. And also, that for and notwithstanding any such act, matter, or thing as aforesaid, they, the said Sir John Ramsden and Dame Margaret his wife now have in themselves good rightful power and absolute authority to grant, release, and convey the said Messuage, Closes, and Premises, and every of them to the said Sir Rowland Winn and Francis Sykes, their Heirs and Assigns, in manner aforesaid.

And further, that the said Messuage, Closes, and Premises are, and every of them are, clear and free, and for ever hereafter shall be clearly and freely acquitted and discharged of and from all incumbrances whatsoever, in title, charge, estate, or otherwise, howsoever committed, done, or suffered by them, the said Sir John Ramsden and Margaret his wife, and Mary Lowther, or any of them. And *moreover*, that they the said

Sir John Ramsden and Dame Margaret his wife and their respective Heirs, and all persons whatsoever, having, or lawfully claiming any Estate, right, title, or interest into or out of the said Messuage, Hereditaments, and Premises above-mentioned, or any of them, by, from, or under the said Sir John Ramsden and Dame Margaret his wife, or either of them; or by, from, or under the said Mary Lowther, shall, and will from time to time, and at all times hereafter, within the space of ten years now next ensuing, upon the request and at the cost and charge of the said Sir Rowland Winn and Francis Sykes, their Heirs or Assigns well and truly make, do, and execute any further or other lawful and reasonable act, deed, conveyance, and assurance in the law whatsoever, for the better and more perfect conveying and assuring of the said Messuage, Closes, and Premises, or any of them, unto the said Sir Rowland Winn and Francis Sykes, their Heirs and Assigns for ever. So as such further or other assurance contain or imply no further or other warranty or covenants than against the respective acts of the party or parties who shall make the same; and so as such party or parties be not compellable to go from his, her, or their respective abode for or about the doing and executing the same. Provided always, nevertheless, and it is hereby agreed and declared that it shall and may be lawful for the said Sir Rowland Winn and Francis Sykes, their Heirs and Assigns, at any time hereafter to levy or raise by mortgage of a competent part of the said Premises the said sum of Sixty Pounds so advanced and lent by them, the said Sir Rowland Winn, Timothy Lee, and Francis Sykes, as aforesaid, and in the meantime to deduct and retain out of the rents or profits of the said Hereditaments and Premises interest for the said Sixty Pounds at the rate of Four Pounds per centum per annum. And also that in case the said Sir Rowland Winn and Francis Sykes, their Heirs or Assigns, shall think fit and proper at any time hereafter to raise the said Sixty Pounds so lent by them, and the said Timothy Lee as aforesaid, by taking any fine or foregift for the making of any lease or demise of the said Hereditaments and Premises above-mentioned, for any term of years as is hereinafter mentioned, that then it shall and may be lawful to and for them the said Sir Rowland Winn and Francis Sykes, their Heirs or Assigns, to demise the said Messuage, Closes, and Premises, to any person or persons whatsoever for any term or number of years not exceeding ninety-nine years, and to take any fine or foregift for the making of any such demise or lease, so as such fine or foregift be not less than the said sum of Sixty Pounds, and so as the rent to be thereby reserved be made payable at Whitsuntide and Christmas yearly, and be not less than the annual sum or rent of Twelve Pounds over and above all taxes, charges, assessments, and other out-payments whatsoever affecting the said Messuage, Closes, and Premises, during the said term. To the intent that the income and produce to arise from the several charities and donations above-mentioned may not be lessened, and may be certain and permanent so far as the nature of such things will admit of, and according to the true intent and meaning of the parties to these presents. In witness whereof the parties to these presents interchangeably have set their hands and seals the day and year first above written.

JOHN *(Seal)* RAMSDEN.   MARGARET *(Seal)* RAMSDEN.

Sealed and delivered in the presence of us, the several erasures being first made, and the said Timothy being first interlined.

THOS. RAMSDEN.   R. WILKINSON (Sworn).

Received the day and year first within written, of the said Timothy Lee, the sum of Two Hundred and Twenty Pounds in full discharge of the consideration money within mentioned, to be paid by him to me. I say, received the same by me,

JOHN RAMSDEN.

Witnesses: THOS. RAMSDEN. RICHD. WILKINSON. £220.

A similar receipt to Dr. Lee and Francis Sykes for Sixty Pounds, witnessed by the same.

A memorial of the within-written Deed was registered at Wakefield, the Tenth day of December, Seventeen hundred and sixty-three, at eleven in the forenoon, in Book A Y, page 725, and number 896.

JONATH. WARD, Depy. Regr.

Counterpart of Lease from Sir Rowland Winn, and Mr. Sykes to Dr. Lee, of the Estate belonging to the Poor of Ackworth.

This Indenture, made the twenty-fourth day of November, in the year of Our Lord one thousand seven hundred and sixty-three, between Sir Rowland Winn, of Nostel, in the County of York, Baronet, and Francis Sykes of Ackworth Park, in the Parish of Ackworth, in the said County, Esquire, on the one part, and the Rev. Timothy Lee, Rector of Ackworth, aforesaid, and Doctor in Divinity, on the other part.

Whereas by Indenture of lease and release bearing date respectively the nineteenth and twentieth days of October last, the lease made between Sir John Ramsden, of Byram, in the said County, Baronet, and Dame Margaret, his wife, with such addition and description as is therein mentioned on the one part, and the said Sir Rowland Winn, and Francis Sykes on the other part. And the release made between the said Sir John Ramsden and Dame Margaret, his wife, on the one part, and the said Sir Rowland Winn, Timothy Lee, and Francis Sykes on the other part, after divers recitals therein contained, and for the considerations therein mentioned, the said Sir John Ramsden and Dame Margaret, his wife, did grant, release, and convey unto the said Sir Rowland Winn, and Francis Sykes, and their heirs, all that Messuage or Tenement, situate and being in Ackworth aforesaid, wherein Nathaniel Barwell, gentleman, deceased, formerly dwelt, and all the barns, stables, and other out-buildings, courtyards, foulsteads, gardens, orchards, hereditaments and appurtenances thereunto belonging. And, also, all those Three Closes of Meadow and Pasture Ground thereto adjoining and belonging, commonly called or known by the names of the Lower Croft, the Upper Croft, and Barn Croft, or by what other name or names soever the same were then called or known. And, also, two Cowgates, or Pasture for Two Beasts in Ackworth Common Pasture, and which said messuage, closes, and premises were late the Estate of Mary Lowther, spinster, deceased, and are now in the tenures or occupations of John Aneley and Jonathan Thompson, and are all situate and being in Ackworth aforesaid, together with all ways, hereditaments and appurtenances to the said premises belonging, except the pew in Ackworth Church, lately enjoyed by Mrs. Barwell, deceased.

To Hold the said messuages, closes, hereditaments, and premises unto the said Sir Rowland Winn and Francis Sykes, and their heirs, to the use of them and their heirs.

In Trust, nevertheless for the poor of the said Parish of Ackworth, for the time being for ever, and to the intent that the rents, issues, and profits, might at all times thereafter, be had, received, and taken by the minister, churchwardens, and overseers of the poor of the said Parish of Ackworth, for the time being, or might be paid over into their hands, and distributed by them at Christmas and Whitsuntide, yearly, for ever, to and amongst the said poor in such manner as the said minister, churchwardens, and overseers for the time being should in their discretion think fit and proper. But subject, nevertheless, to a proviso thereinafter mentioned. And it is therein provided, agreed, and declared that it should and might be lawful for the said Sir Rowland Winn and Francis Sykes, their heirs and assigns, at any time thereafter to levy or raise, by mortgage of a competent part of the said premises, the sum of sixty pounds therein specified to be advanced and lent to them by the said Timothy Lee, towards purchasing the said hereditaments and premises of the said Sir John Ramsden and Dame Margaret, his wife, and in the meantime to deduct and retain out of the rents and profits of the said hereditament premises interest for the said sixty pounds, at the rate of four pounds per centum per annum.

And, also, that in case the said Sir Rowland Winn and Francis Sykes, their heirs and assigns, should think fit and proper, at any time, to raise the said sixty pounds so lent by them and the said Timothy Lee aforesaid, by taking any fine or foregift for the making of any lease or demise of the said hereditaments and premises for any term of years, as is therein after mentioned, that then it should and might be lawful to and for them, the said Sir Rowland Winn and Francis Sykes, their heirs or assigns, to demise the said messuages, closes, and premises to any person or persons whatsoever for any term or number of years not exceeding ninety-nine years, and to take any fine or foregift for the making of any such demise or lease so as such fine or foregift be not less than the said sixty pounds, and so as the rent thereby to be reserved be made payable at Whitsuntide and Christmas yearly, and be not less than the annual sum or rent of twelve pounds over and above all taxes, charges, assessments, and other out-payments whatsoever, affecting the said messuage, closes, and premises during the said term, as in and by the said in part recited Indentures, reference being thereto had, may more fully appear.

And Whereas the said Sir Rowland Winn and Francis Sykes think it will not be for the benefit and advantage of the said poor to raise the said sum of sixty pounds by mortgage of any part of the said premises, but that it will be the best for them for the said sixty pounds to be raised by making a lease of the said premises and taking a fine or foregift of sixty pounds for the making thereof, according to the power given to them, the said Sir Rowland Winn, and Francis Sykes, in and by the said Indenture of Release. *And, therefore,* they have agreed to take the said foregift of sixty pounds of the said Timothy Lee, and to demise to him the said hereditaments and premises in such manner as is hereinafter mentioned. *Now this Indenture*

Witnesseth that in consideration of the said sum of sixty pounds of lawful money of Great Britian by the said Timothy Lee to the said Sir Rowland Winn and Francis Sykes, in hand, paid at or before the executing hereof, as a fine or foregift for the making of this present demise, and which said sixty pounds they, the said Sir Rowland Winn and Francis Sykes, have thought fit and proper to raise in full payment and satisfaction, and discharge of the said sixty pounds so advanced and lent by them and the said Timothy Lee, towards purchasing of the said premises as aforesaid, the receipt of which said sixty pounds they do hereby acknowledge; *and, also*, in consideration of the yearly rent of the covenants and agreements, hereinafter mentioned, to be paid and performed by the said Timothy Lee, his executors, administrators, and assigns, they, the said Sir Rowland Winn and Francis Sykes, have demised, leased, and to farm, let unto the said Timothy Lee, his executors, administrator, and assigns, *all* the said messuages, closes, hereditaments, and premises above mentioned and recited, to have been granted and conveyed to the said Sir Rowland Winn and Francis Sykes, and their heirs as aforesaid. *To have* and *to hold* the same unto the said Timothy Lee, his executors, administrators, and assigns, from the thirteenth day of February next, for, during, and until the full end and term of 99 years from thence next ensuing, and fully to be complete and ended. Yielding and paying, therefore, yearly and every year during the said term, unto the said Sir Rowland Winn and Francis Sykes, their heirs or assigns, the sum of twelve pounds of lawful money of Great Britain, at the feasts of Whitsuntide and Christmas in every year during the said term by even and equal portions, over and above all taxes, charges, assessments, and other out-payments whatsoever, affecting the said premises during the said term, and without any deduction whatsoever. *In trust* for the said poor of the said Parish of Ackworth, and according to the true intent and meaning of the said recited Indentures. *Provided* always nevertheless that if the said yearly rent or sum of twelve pounds or any part thereof shall be behind and unpaid by the space of twenty days next after the same or any part thereof shall become due as aforesaid, that then it shall and may be lawful to and for the said Sir Rowland Winn and Francis Sykes, their heirs or assigns, into the said demised premises, or any part thereof in the name of the whole, to re-enter and the same to have again, re-possess, and enjoy as in their or any of their former estate, anything herein contained to the contrary notwithstanding. *And* the said Timothy Lee doth hereby, for himself, his executors, and administrators, covenant and agree with the said Sir Rowland Winn and Francis Sykes, their heirs and assigns, in manner following (that is to say), that he, the said Timothy Lee, his executors and administrators, shall and will well and truly pay unto the said Sir Rowland Winn and Francis Sykes, their heirs or assigns, the said yearly rent or sum of twelve pounds, at the days and times, and in the manner above mentioned for payment thereof, over and above all taxes, charges, assessments, and other outpayments whatsoever, affecting the said premises during the said term, and without any deduction whatsoever. *And,* also, shall and will, from time to time, and at all times hereafter, during the said term, pay and discharge all lays, taxes, and assessments whatsoever, which are, shall, or may be laid, taxed, or assessed upon, or for, or in respect of the said demised premises, or any part thereof. *And,* also, shall and will, from time to time, during the said term, when and so often as need shall require, well and sufficiently amend, repair, and keep the said messuage, and buildings with all needful and proper reparations and amendments whatsoever. *And, also,* well and sufficiently amend repair, scour, and cleanse the hedges, fences, ditches, gates, styles, and watercourses belonging the said premises, and shall and will, at the expiration of the said term, leave and yield up to the said Sir Rowland Winn and Francis Sykes, their heirs or assigns, the said messuage and buildings, and, also, all the gates, styles, hedges, ditches, and fences, belonging to the said premises, in good and sufficient repair and order. And, also, that he, the said Timothy Lee, his executors, administrators, or assigns, or any of them, shall not, nor will, within the last seven years of the said term, dig or plough up any part of the said closes of ground hereby demised (except such part thereof as shall be then used as garden ground), without the license and consent of the said Sir Rowland Winn and Francis Sykes, their heirs or assigns, in writing first had and obtained. And the said Sir Rowland Winn and Francis Sykes, for themselves and their heirs, covenant and agree with the said Timothy Lee, his executors, administrators, and assigns, that he and they, paying the said yearly rent, and performing the covenants and agreements above written, shall and may peaceably and quietly have, hold, use, occupy, possess, and enjoy the said messuage, closes, and premises above mentioned, to be hereby demised, without any molestation, hindrance, or disturbance of or by them, the said Sir Rowland Winn and Francis Sykes, their heirs or assigns, or any of them.

In witness whereof the parties to these presents interchangeably have set their hands and seals the day and year first above written.

Signed, T. LEE.

Sealed and delivered in the presence of us, John Watson, R. Wilkinson. Sworn.

A Memorial of the within-written deed was registered at Wakefield the twenty-second day of March 1764, at Eleven in the Forenoon, in Book A Z, page 274, and number 36.

JONATHAN WARD, Deputy Registrar.

N.B.—In the iron chest belonging to the parish, but in the custody of the Rector, there are the purchase deeds of the above house and crofts, with the fine annexed. They are dated 6th and 7th March, 1733, and are thereby conveyed by Mr. Barwell to Mrs. Mary Lowther.

There is, also, a Lease for a year from Sir John and Lady Ramsden to Sir Rowland Winn and Francis Sykes, dated 19th October, 1763. It is registered at Wakefield, in Book A Y, page 725, and number 896.

There is, also, a counterpart of a Mortgage upon Mr. Barwell's Estate, dated 30th April, 1681.

EXTRACT FROM THE AWARD, 1774.

No. V. of the Stinted Pasture, allotted to Dr. Lee for the term of his lease, which expires in February, one thousand eight hundred and sixty-three, and then to the poor.

T. Lee, Lessee of the Trustees for Poor Allotment in the Stinted Pasture.
No. V.
A. R. P.
2 2 28

And we do also assign, set out, allot, and award unto the said Timothy Lee, to be held in severalty by him, his heirs, and assigns, during the continuance of his lease, and from immediately after the determination thereof, to be held in severalty by the said Sir Rowland Winn and Francis Sykes, and their successors, Trustees for the time being of the Poor of Ackworth aforesaid, one parcel of land, being part of the said Stinted Pasture, within the Parish of Ackworth aforesaid, marked in the said map hereunto annexed with the No. v., containing two acres, two roods, and twenty-eight perches, statute measure. An allotment, No. iv., herein made to Ann Hattersley, being on the east, the Rector's allotment, No. vi., on the west, a private road and the Rectors' allotment, No. xxviii., in Parkin Leys Field on the north, and the River Went on the south, and do order and award that the owner and proprietor of the said last mentioned allotment, No. v., for the time being shall make and for ever maintain a good and sufficient fence and ditch on the west side or boundary thereof.

At the expiration of Colonel Anthony Surtee's lease in 1863, the house and land were sold to the late J. M. Hepworth, Esq., for £2316, which was subsequently invested in the 3 per cent. Consols. the interest of which, amounting to £12, is given away in the shape of casual relief and dole.

LAMBE'S CHARITY.

This small charity is secured by deed dated 18th August, 14th Charles I., by which thirty square yards of land was granted to William Lambe, for erecting a windmill upon Ackworth Moor, at the rent of five shillings yearly, payable to the Lords of the Manor for the use of the poor of Ackworth, and upon the feast days of the Annunciation of the Blessed Mary the Virgin, and St. Michael the Archangel, by even and equal portions for ever. A copy of the original deed is in possession of the Rector. In 1859, Mr. Rishworth was the owner of the land charged by the above deed. The original deed is supposed to be lost, but perhaps it is in the hands of the Lords of the Manor, who, in number, remind one of the seven wise men of Greece; but who, in their management of the parish property, act more like the wise men of Gotham, who went to sea in a bowl, and of whom the old rhyme says:—

"If the bowl had been stronger,
My story had been longer."

Copy of the Deed by which thirty yards square of land is granted to William Lambe for erecting a Windmill upon Ackworth Moor, at the rent of Five Shillings yearly, payable for the use of the Poor of Ackworth. Dated 14th Charles I.

"This Indenture made the Eighteenth daie of August in the year of the raigne of our Soveraigne Lord Charles by the Grace of God of England, Scotland, France and Ireland King Defender of the Faith, &c., the fourteenth . . . . .
Between Samuel Carter of Ackworth . . . Rober Abbott of Ackworth . . . . Henry Bannister of Ackworth aforesaid gent . . . John Huntington of Ackworth . . . Richard Adams of East Ardwicke in the County of . .
Witnesseth that the said Samuel Carter Robert Abbott Henry Huntington . . . . . for and in consideration of five shillings . . . granted bargained sould released and con-

firmed and by these p'sents doe grant bargain sell release and confirm unto the said William his heirs & assigns for ever all the estate right title interest property claim and demand whatsoever of the said Samuel Carter Robert Abbott Henry Huntington . . . . Adams Thomas Horncastle John Goodyeare Henry Wilkinson and John Wright their heirs and assigns of and in all that . . . piece of grounde . . . . one Windmill of . . . . the Mannor of Ackworth aforesaid .

. . . .

To have and to hold the said piece of square Ground containing thirtie yards with the appurtenances to the said William Lambe his heirs and assigns for ever to the sole and proper use and behoofe of the said William Lambe his heirs and assigns for ever Yielding and Paying therefor yearly and every year for ever unto the said Samuel Carter Robert Abbott Henry Bannister John Huntington Edward (or Richarde) Adams Thomas Horncastle John Goodyeare William Wilkinson John Wright and their Heirs and successors Lords of the said Mannor of Ackworth the sum of five shillings of lawful money of England for the use and bereft of the Poor of the Parish of Ackworth and upon the Feast Days of the Annuncieon of the Blessed Mary the Virgin and St. Michael the Archangel by even and equal porcons for ever.

In Witness whereof the parties first above-named to this p'sent Indenture interchangeably have put their hands and seals.

Signed and Delivered in the presence of us—

HASTINGS RASBY
JOHN KILLINGBECKE.

A true Copy of the Original."

The original Mill was erected of wood, and being burnt down, the land was not built on for a considerable time. It eventually came into the possession of Sir John Ramsden, of Byram, Bart., through his marriage with Margaret, the widow

of John Bright, of Badsworth, Esq., whose maiden name was
Norton. This Margaret Norton was the niece of Mrs. Mary
Lowther, of Ackworth Park. In February, 1758, Sir John
Ramsden, and Margaret, his wife, leased and released the site
of the above Windmill, then lately standing, together with a
Water-mill, to John Pearson. In November, 1765, John Pear-
son leased and re-leased the property to Joseph White. Joseph
White, by will bearing date November, 1799, bequeathed it to
Samuel Thorp, his son-in-law. Samuel Thorp, by an agreement
of bargain and sale, dated March, 1808, assigned it over to
Thomas Rishworth; and it was afterwards conveyed to him,
probably about 10th October, 1808. The Rishworths were
owners of the property in 1859.

CALVERLEY'S DOLE.

This consists of ten shillings per annum to the poor of
Ackworth, charged on a portion of the estate of the late Mr.
Hill. The money is regularly paid and distributed to the poor
on St. Thomas' Day. The following is a copy of the will of
Ann Calverley, the donor.

*Copies of Ann Calverley's Will and of the Deed by which, in
1777, the original security was transferred to other lands.*

ANN CALVERLEY'S WILL.

"In the name of God, Amen. In the eleventh year of the
reign of our Sovereign Lord William the Third, over England,
&c., Defender of the Faith, and in the year of our Lord 1699.
I, Anne Calverley, of Ackworth, in the County of York, widow,
being weak in body but in good and perfect memory, praised
be God, do make and ordain this my last will and testament in
manner and form following: First, I give and bequeath my
soul into the hands of Almighty God, my Maker, hoping
through the merits and satisfaction of Jesus Christ, my Saviour,
to receive full remission and forgivenesss of my sins, with a
joyful resurrection of the blessed, and my body to the ground
from whence it came, to be buried at the discretion, decently,
of my executor hereafter named.

"As for that worldly estate Almighty God hath endowed me with, my will is to dispose of it in manner and form following, that is to say ;—I give unto John Petty one pound; I give unto William Petty one pound; I give unto Elizabeth Abbott one pound; and as for wearing clothes, I give unto my sisters Ann Petty and Elizabeth Abbott.

"I give unto the poor of Ackworth ten shilling every year for ever, to be paid upon Good Friday. And as for security thereof, I appoint one acre of land which lyeth in Colehill, in two places, which is three roods and one rood; that if any default be in payment hereof, according to the day abovenamed, then to enter to the three roods and one rood above mentioned. I give unto the poor twenty shillings to be disposed of at my burial. I make my beloved son, Thomas Calverley, sole executor of this my last will and testament. Witness my hand and seal the 29th day of September, Anno Domini 1699.

"ANNE CALVERLEY,
"Signed and sealed in the presence of us—   her + mark.
"Jane Bradley,
"Savile Bradley,
"Fra. Bradley."

DEED BY WHICH SECURITY WAS TRANSFERRED TO OTHER LANDS.

"*Mr. John Thistlewood to the Rev. Dr. Lee.* This Indenture, made the fourth day of August, in the tenth year of the reign of our Sovereign Lord George the Third, by the Grace of God, of Great Britain, France, and Ireland, King, Defender of the Faith, and so forth ; and in the year of our Lord one thousand seven hundred and seventy, between John Thistlewood, of Tupholm, in the County of Lincoln, grazier, on the one part, and Timothy Lee, of Ackworth, in the County of York, Doctor in Divinity, Rector of Ackworth, on the other part. Whereas Anne Calverley, formerly of Ackworth aforesaid, widow, did, in and by her last will and testament, in writing, bearing date the

29th day of September, in the year of our Lord one thousand six hundred and ninety-nine, give unto the poor of Ackworth, ten shillings every year for ever, to be paid upon every Good Friday, and for security thereof, the said testatrix appointed one acre of land, which lieth in Colchill, in two places, which is three roods and one rood that, if any default be in payment thereof, according to the day above-named, then to enter to the three roods and one rood above-mentioned, as in and by the said Will, reference being thereto had, will more fully appear. And whereas the said John Thistlewood is now become entitled to the said lands and premises, out of which the said sum of ten shillings, above mentioned, is secured to be paid, and hath lately contracted and agreed to sell and convey the same, together with other lands and hereditaments freed and discharged of and from the said yearly payment, the said John Thistlewood did thereupon consent and agree to charge the tenements and hereditaments, hereinafter mentioned, for ever hereafter with the due payment thereof. Now, this Indenture witnesseth that the said John Thistlewood, in consideration of the premises and to the intent that the said yearly sum of ten shillings may be continued to be paid to the poor of Ackworth aforesaid, in pursuance of the said, in part recited, Will, doth hereby for himself and his heirs, covenant and agree, to and with the said Timothy Lee and his successors, as Rectors of Ackworth for the time being, that all that messuage or tenement, situate, standing, and being in Ackworth aforesaid, late in the possession of Mr. Joseph Haddon, with the malt-kiln, malt-house, barns, stables, foldstead, and garden thereto belonging, and also all that close of meadow or pasture ground adjoining, on the back side of the said messuage, called by the name of the Home Close, containing by estimation three acres, more or less, now belonging to him, the said John Thistlewood, with their appurtenances, shall from time to time for ever hereafter be subject to and chargeable with the due payment of the said sum of ten shillings yearly, to the poor of Ackworth aforesaid, on Good Friday, according to the purport, true intent, and meaning of the said recited will. And also that he, the said John Thistlewood, his heirs, executors, and administrators, shall and will, for ever hereafter, save harmless and indemnify the purchaser of the said lands and premises so charged by the said Anne Calverley with the payment of the said annual sum of ten shillings, and also the said lands and premises of and from the payment of the same and every part thereof, and also of and from all costs, charges, and expenses which shall or may be had or occasioned by non-payment thereof. In witness the parties to these presents interchangeably have set their hands and seals the day and year first above written.

"John Thistlewood. +

"Sealed and delivered in the presence of us—

"R. Wilkinson, } Sworn.
"Wm. Sugden, }

" A memorial of the within-written deed was registered at Wakefield, the seventh day of August seventeen hundred and seventy, near eleven in the forenoon, in Book B. L. page 556, and number 799.

"Tim Topham, Dep. Regr."

A comparison of the above Deeds with the Table of Benefactions, set up in the Church, will lead us to the conclusion that the Table is not to be depended on. It is there stated that Ann Calverley's gift to the poor is ten pounds, and this error alone fully justifies the remark of the late W. R. Hay, that "the Table was painted and put up in the Church very unadvisedly, and it is in many respects inaccurate."

Calverley's Dole is regularly paid by Henry Hill, Esq., the present owner of the estate charged by the Deed of 1777, and is distributed to the poor on St. Thomas's Day. It may also be remarked that the lands originally charged, as well as those to which the charge was transferred by the Deed of 1777, are again, as in Thistlewood's time, united under one proprietor.

The originals, both of Anne Calverley's Will, and the Deed of 1777, are in the parish chest and in excellent preservation.

LAMBE'S DOLE.

This also consists of ten shillings per annum. It was left by Matthew Lambe in the 14th year of Charles I., and was charged on certain lands now belonging to Joseph Nelstrop, Esq. The following is an extract from the title deeds:—

"Matthew Lamb, of Ackworth, on the 5th September 1680, did give and bequeath unto the poor of the Parish of Ackworth yearly to be paid upon St. Thomas's Day, being the 21st December, the sum of Ten Shillings, which should be paid unto the Minister and Overseers of the Poor by the hands of Samuel Leake, his heirs and assigns for ever, out of the yearly value or profit of one acre of arable land, lying in a field called Berrial, between the lands of George Abbott, Gent., North, and the lands of William Austwick, South, which said acre he then purchased of Ellen Wright. For want of such true yearly payment of 10 shillings, it was his will and desire that the said Minister and Overseers of the Poor should enter and have power to let the said acre for the use of the poor of the parish of Ackworth, so long as the world should continue."

MITTON'S CHARITY.

Henry Mitton, of Ackworth, in the County of York, Yeoman, by his will dated 10th October, 1809, and proved at York, 16th February, 1810, ordered and directed his Trustees and Executors, after the decease of his wife, to pay Twenty Pounds into the hands of the Churchwardens and Overseers of the Poor of Ackworth, aforesaid, in order that they place the same out at interest, upon good security, and apply the interest thereof to twenty poor widows, or so many as may attend, belonging to Ackworth, on New Year's Day, for ever, after it became due. This was reduced by the legacy duty to £18, which is invested on the note of hand of the Trustees of the Public Rooms in Ackworth, and the interest regularly distributed according to the donors' wishes. Also on the decease of his wife, Henry Mitton ordered and directed his said Trustees to lay out £20 in the construction of a Hearse, for the conveyance of corpses from the outside of the Parish to inter at Ackworth Church ; to be under the management and direction of the Churchwardens of Ackworth aforesaid.

RISHWORTH'S CHARITY.

The Board of benefactions says :—

" John Rishworth to the poor, £1."

It should have been " £1 per annum." This sum was given by John Rishworth, by will dated 22nd October, 1660. The original is preserved in the parish chest. It is scarcely legible in the inside, but is endorsed : " Deed by which a piece or parcel of ground, called the 'Outgangs,' is granted for payment of 20s. yearly to the poor of Ackworth for ever, payable 5th December yearly, and to be distributed by the Rector, Churchwardens, and Overseers of the Poor on St. Thomas's Day, in the sight and at the discretion of the inhabiters of the Park Hall, George Abbott's House, at Hundhill, and T. Calverley's House, in Ackworth." The following is a copy of the original Deed :—

"To all good people to whom this present writing shall come to, be read, seen, or heard, John Rishworth, of Visit, in the Parish of Hemsworth and County of York, Yeoman, sendeth greeting in our Lord God Everlasting.

Know ye, that the said John Rishworth, for the continuing and perpetuating of the Yearly Rent hereafter expressed due and issuing out of the lands and premises hereafter mentioned unto the Poor in the Parish of Ackworth in the said County of York, that the same may hereafter be duly paid and distributed amongst the most needful Poor of the said Parish of Ackworth as is hereafter mentioned, and for divers other causes and valuable considerations, him, the said John Rishworth, hereunto especially moving, hath given, granted, and confirmed, and by these presents doth fully and absolutely give, grant, and confirm unto Thomas Birkbecke, Clerk, the present

Rector of the Rectory of Ackworth aforesaid, Thomas Wilkinson and Robert Lamb, the present Churchwardens, and Robert Hewitt and Leonard Pinder, the present Overseers of the Poor of the said Parish of Ackworth, and the successive Minister, Churchwardens, and Overseers of the said Parish of Ackworth for the time being for ever, one annuity or Yearly Rent Charge of Twenty Shillings of lawful money of England yearly to be had, taken, provided, and received to be issuing and going out and in all that parcel of ground or waste commonly called the Outgang, containing by estimation fifteen Acres more or less lying and being within the Manor of Ackworth aforesaid, to be paid to the Minister, Churchwardens, and Overseers, and their successors for ever at or upon every fifth day of December yearly. To *have* and to *hold*, receive, preserve, and enjoy the Annuity or Yearly Rent Charge of Twenty Shillings aforesaid unto the said Thomas Birkbecke and the said Churchwardens and Overseers of the Poor of the said Parish of Ackworth and their successors, Minister, Churchwardens, and Overseers of the Poor of the Parish of Ackworth, for the time being and for ever in manner and form before declared. To the end that the said Twenty Shillings may yearly and every year upon St. Thomas's Day next following after the receipt thereof at the sight, judgment, and discretion of the several Inhabitants, Possessors, and Occupiers of the several Mansions and now Dwellinghouse of William Rokeley, Esq., of Ackworth Park, George Abbott, of Hundell, in the parish of Ackworth, aforesaid, gentlemen, Richard Pickering, of Ackworth, aforesaid, yeoman, and Thomas Calverley, of Ackworth, to be disbursed, distributed, and disposed of to the most needful Poor and impotent people of the said Parish of Ackworth. And if it happen the said Annuity or yearly Rent Charge of Twenty Shillings be behind or..............................* by the space of six days after the time of payment thereof aforesaid, in which it is by those presents appointed to be paid, that then

---

* So faded as not to be legible.

and so often as any such default shall be made at any time or times hereafter, it shall and may be lawful to and for the said Thomas Birkbecke, and the Churchwardens, and Overseers of the Poor of the said Parish of Ackworth, or any of them and their successors, Ministers, Churchwardens, and Overseers of the Poor of the said Parish for the time being, or any of them at his or their pleasure to enter into and upon the said parcel of Ground or Waste, called the Outgang, or into such part or parcel thereof as they shall think meet and there to distrain for all the Arrearages of the said Annuity or Yearly Rent of twenty shillings then behind and unpaid, and the distress or distresses there so had and taken lawfully, to bear, lead, drive, carry away, impound, and retain, and keep without restraint or replevin for the space of four days, and if the said Arrearages of the said Annuity shall not within the space of four days be paid to the said Minister, Churchwardens, and Overseers of the said Parish of Ackworth for the time being, or unto some of them according to the intent of these presents then at his or their pleasure, to bargain or sell the corn, goods, and chattels so taken by way of distress at such price or prices as they or any of them may or can get, and with the money coming of the sale thereof, to satisfy, pay and allow themselves not only all Arrearages of the said Annuity or Yearly Rent being behind and unpaid, but also his and their reasonable costs, charges, and disbursements sustained in that behalf. And the residue of the same (if any be) to render and pay unto the said John Rishworth, his Heirs, and Assigns, and that from time to time as often as any such distress or distresses shall be so had or taken. But if no sufficient distress can be found in and upon the said parcel of ground called the Outgang whereupon to distrain, that then it shall and may be lawful to and for the said Thomas Birkbecke, and the said Churchwardens, and Overseers of the Poor of the Parish of Ackworth and their successors for the time being, or any of them into the said parcel of Ground or Waste, called the Outgang with the appurtenances, to enter and the same to enjoy without let, trouble, or hindrance of the said John Rishworth, his Heirs, or Assigns, and the issues and profits thereof to receive and take. To the end that the said sum of Twenty Shillings may be disposed of in manner and form above said without any account thereof to be made unto him the said John Rishworth, his Heirs, or Assigns. And the said John Rishworth hath put the aforesaid Thomas Birkbecke, and the said Churchwardens, and Overseers of the said Parish of Ackworth, in full possession of the said Annuity or Yearly Rent of Twenty Shillings in form as aforesaid (to be had, received, and taken) by the delivery and payment of the sum of Twelve-pence, which the said John Rishworth hath at the sealing and delivery of these presents given and delivered unto the said Thomas Birkbecke, and the Churchwardens, and Overseers aforesaid in the name of possession of the said Annuity.

In witness whereof, the said John Rishworth hath hereunto set his hand and seal the two and twentieth day of October, in the twelfth year of the reign of our Sovereign lord Charles II., by the grace of God king of England, Scotland, France, and Ireland, Defender of the Faith, and so forth. (1660.)

JOHN RISHWORTH. ×

Sealed and delivered, and also twelve-pence given by the within-named John Rishworth, in the name of a possession and seizin of the annuity within-mentioned, according to the tenor, effect, and true meaning of these presents, in the presence of us,

James Wood, Michael Pickering,
George Abbott, John Biamount,
Thomas Birkett, Richard Pickering."

CAWOOD'S CHARITY.

By an indenture, dated 9th January, 1653, Stephen Cawood* gave an estate consisting of 69 acres of land in East Hardwicke, in the Parish of Pontefract, for the erection and endowment of

* Entry in Pontefract Church Books: Feb. 19th, 1653 (4). "Stephen Cawood, of East Hardwick, within this parish, yeoman, departed this life, and his corps was interred in his owne ground in East Hardwick, aforesaid, the twentieth day

a Chapel and Free School in East Hardwick. The Minister was to have "£20 per annum in respect of his preaching the Word of God on every Lord's Day, and keeping a Free School there for all such children whomsoever as shall desire to be taught there." The sum of 20s. per annum was to be paid to the poor of Ackworth, 10s. per annum to the poor of East Hardwick, and 10s. per annum to the repair of Housestead Lane. This estate has been, from time to time, let at an increased rent, the annual payments to the several charities being proportionately increased. The charity is managed by six feoffees, three of whom are chosen from Ackworth, and three from East Hardwick. The trustees of this charity are the patrons of the Vicarage of East Hardwick. In 1871, when the chapelry was constituted a separate benefice, the offices of Minister and Schoolmaster† were divided, the sum of £40 a year being allotted to the former, and £50 to the latter; the advowson to be sold, and the profits invested in augmentation of the school endowment.‡ The sum now annually paid by the Trustees of this Charity is to the Incumbent, £70 (which has since been increased by the interest of invested subscriptions, and grant from the Ecclesiastical Commissioners, to £140); to the Poor of Ackworth, £4 10s.; to the Poor of East Hardwick, £2 5s.; and towards the repair of Housestead Lane, £2 5s. Scholars are sent from Ackworth to the Free School at East Hardwick, which, however, is not now free, the uniform charge per head for all children being two pence.

of the same moneth." It will be seen that Cawood died only a little more than a month after he had executed his deed of gift. The words "*in his own ground,*" are supposed to mean his own private burial ground, (probably a family mausoleum in his own grounds,) and it is also very likely from the entry, that the Chapel provided for in the deed was not built at the time of Mr. Cawood's death, but soon afterwards, "October 26th, 1667, Mr. Lawrence Addam was buried in ye Church of East Hardwicke." The building was never consecrated, at least, there is no record of it.

† Of the order of "Preaching Schoolmasters." The Rev. Anthony Sigismund Teutschel, Ph.D., was the last of these, and the first Incumbent of East Hardwick.

‡ Vide *Pontefract Telegraph*, June 10th, 1871. For further particulars concerning the Church and Parish, see brochure published by Holmes, Pontefract, 1871.

SEATON'S BEQUEST.

Jervas Seaton, of East Hardwick, left, for the use of the poor of Ackworth, 6s. 8d. per annum, for ever, charged on an acre of land in Thorpleys. It is received by the Overseers of the Poor, but there are no documents to show whence the payment arises.

THE TOWNSLEY ESTATE.

In 1803, Sarah and Francis Townsley died intestate, and in possession of a house, maltkiln, and seven acres of land adjoining the Rectory, on the east, and four acres of land, called "Pudding Bush." This estate, for want of heirs, went to the Trustees of the Manor of Ackworth (to whom, in the reign of Charles I, the Duchy of Lancaster had granted away the Manor of Ackworth with all its privileges), for the benefit of the freeholders. The rents and profits of this estate, which now rents for £40, are paid to the Trustees of the Manor.

LINDSAY'S LEGACY.

In 1873, David Lindsay, an Ackworth man, who had amassed considerable wealth in commercial transactions, died at Leeds, and left by his will, £150 to be invested for the benefit of the Lowther's Hospital, at Ackworth. The benefaction is duly recorded upon the Charity board in the Parish Church, and the interest of the money, which is invested in the 3 per cent. Consols, is regularly distributed by the Churchwardens for the time being.

GRANT TO JOHN TOPHAM.

"John Topham, for one acre of land on the Common, 4s. 8d." There can be no doubt that this was a grant from the Parish of a portion of the Common, or Ackworth Moor, at this reserved rent. The acre of land in question is set out in the map attached to the award of 1774, and is the eastern portion of the field which forms one of the angles where the Barnsley Road and the Turnpike Road cross each other at the Moor-Top.

It measures 1a. 0r. 4p. In 1859, the payment had been withheld for many years, and I am informed that it is lapsed, and cannot now be recovered by law.*

LOWTHER'S CHARITY.

In 1741, Mrs. Mary Lowther endowed an Hospital for six poor women of Parishes of Ackworth, Badsworth, and Featherstone; and a school for twenty children of the parish of Ackworth. The income of this charity, which is variable, in 1885, was £81 11s. 5d., arising from money invested in the Funds, in the names of the Charity Commissioners, and from £700 invested on mortgage of the Tolls of the Doncaster and Tadcaster Turnpike Road. The master receives from the Trust £16 per annum, and each of the poor women about £7 15s. The funds of Mrs. Lowther's Charity have twice sustained pecuniary loss to the extent of £700, once, by the failure of its bankers in 1809, and again, in 1843, to the amount of £50, through the mismanagement of its accountant. The following inscription appears above the doorway of the Lowther School :—

"1741.

"MARY LOWTHER
ERECTED AND ENDOWED THIS HOSPITAL FOR A SCHOOLMASTER AND SIX POOR WOMEN."

The Governors of the Hospital are the Rectors of Ackworth, Badsworth, and the Vicar of Featherstone for the time being. The Master receives his £16 per year, on the understanding that twenty poor children are taught by him free of expense; but for some cause or other, although the money is still received, the children are not now taught in accordance with the conditions of the Trust. The same remark applies to East Hardwick School, the master of which, for the time being, receives a specified sum, according to the terms of the trust deed for the free education of ten boys of the parish of Ackworth. The ten boys, however, are neither received nor educated.

* The total annual income from five of the principal charities at Ackworth, in 1885, was £83 7s. 10d.

WATKINSON'S HOSPITAL.

The following is the Report of the Charity Commissioners of 1826, on this Hospital:—

"Edward Watkinson, M.D., by will dated 17th April, 1765, after bequeathing several legacies, gave to Samuel Saltonstall, whom he appointed his executor, all the residue of his personal estate upon trust, to pay to the testator's wife the annual produce thereof, and after her death to pay the said residue and the produce thereof to such persons as should for the time being be the Rector of Ackworth, the Rector of Hemsworth, the Vicar of Pontefract, and the Mayor, Recorder, and two Senior Aldermen of the Borough of Pontefract, or the major part of them, in trust that the said Samuel Saltonstall and such persons for the time being as aforesaid, or the major part of them, should place at interest or otherwise dispose of the money they should receive, and apply the interest and dividends thereof for the benefit of the persons therein named and subject thereto, for the maintenance of nine poor unmarried persons of the Protestant Religion to be elected in the manner therein mentioned; and the testator directed that the said Trustees or the major part of them should, after the death of his wife, meet in the Moot Hall, at Pontefract, and choose two poor men and two poor women, who should then live in Ackworth, and two poor men and two poor women who should then live in Pontefract, as eight of the said nine persons; and also one woman, who should live in either of the said townships, to be the servant of the said eight poor persons, and to wait and attend on them as such; and that such eight persons and their servant should have the same interest and dividends paid equally amongst them at such times and in such manner as the Trustees should think proper; and he thereby willed and declared that no married person should be capable of being elected one of the nine persons; and that if any of the nine persons should after election marry, such person should cease to have any share of the said interest or dividends and be displaced from having any benefit under the will. And he directed that the Trustees or the major part of them might from time to time displace any of the persons for immorality or bad behaviour according to the discretion and judgment of the Trustees or the major part of them. And that whenever there should be any vacancy of any of the eight persons by death or removal, the Trustees or the major part of them should choose in the Moot Hall other poor persons, so as always to make up two poor men and two poor women, belonging to Ackworth, and two poor men and two poor women, belonging to Pontefract; and that when the maid servant should die or be displaced, another proper person living in Ackworth or Pontefract, should be nominated by the Trustees, or the major part of them, in her place. And he directed that a book should be kept for making entries touching the trust estate and the income and application thereof, and all elections and orders relative to the trust and the execution thereof, and that the Trustees might appoint a proper person to be their Clerk for making all entries and orders, and keeping all accounts relating to the trust, and allow him yearly a sum of money not exceeding £5 for his trouble."

Like Dr. Fothergill,* Dr. Watkinson reserved a life interest for his wife in the property he was about to give in charity. His will, which being in full in Fox's History, renders it unnecessary that it should be here reproduced, is dated 17th April, 1765, but did not become operative till after the death of his wife in 1778.

On 9th Feb., 1778, the Trustees, the Rectors of Ackworth and Hemsworth, the Vicar of Pontefract, the two senior Aldermen, and Ald. Samuel Saltonstall, Dr. Watkinson's executor, held their first meeting under the presidency of Mr. Lawrence Fox, Mayor, and the week following purchased a plot in Northgate for their building. The Mayor died during his year of office, and Mr. Saltonstall succeeding for the remainder of

* Vide "Pontefract Charities," p. 132.

his year, had the gratification of seeing the buildings progress. It was, however, not till 25th October, 1779, that the first appointments were made.

"The residue of the testator's estate applicable to the purposes of the Charity amounted to £1803 16s. 8d., and by an order of the Trustees, made in 1778, it was ordered that such sum of money should be laid out in the purchase of lands for the benefit of the Trust, and that the sum of £200, being the amount of savings which had accumulated from the yearly income of the testator's estate, should be applied for or towards the expense of building an Hospital.

"By a further order of the Trustees in October, 1779, it was ordered that the sum of £80 should be retained by Samuel Saltonstall, the executor, as the purchase money of land in Northgate, upon part of which the hospital was then built, and that such land should be conveyed to the Trustees for the term of 999 years, at the yearly rent of 1s., which was done accordingly by indenture of demise, dated 31st October, 1779.

"The clear residue of the testator's estate after payment of all expenses relating to the building of the Hospital, etc., received previous to 1778, being £1,590, was laid out in the purchase of £2,650 South Sea Annuities, and in 1783 a further sum of £205 being received as the purchase money arising from the sale of a house, which had belonged to the testator, the sum of £180, part thereof, was laid out in the purchase of the further sum of £274 6s., South Sea Annuities, the residue being carried to the General Account of the Charity. And the property held in trust for the support of the Hospital consists of £2,924 6s., Old South Sea Annuities, being the amount of the Stock purchased as aforesaid, producing an annual dividend of £87 14s. 6d.

"The Hospital contains apartments for eight poor persons and the servant, and there is a small garden and forecourt used by the poor persons. The Almspeople are chosen according to the directions of the will from the parishes of Ackworth and Pontefract, and they and the maid servant receive each of them a monthly stipend, which varies according to the state of the income remaining after the payment of the expenses of the repairs of the hospital, and amounts in general to about 15s. a piece.

"The other expenses of the trust, besides that of repairs, consist of the salary of the Clerk, £5 per annum, and the postage and charges attending the receipt of the dividends, amounting in general to 15s. or thereabouts.

"The accounts are kept by the Clerk and Treasurer and made up yearly. In 1819 there was a balance of £51 4s. 8d. in the hands of the late Treasurer, and, to enforce payment thereof, an action was brought by the Trustees in 1823, but the defendant in the action having gone to prison and taken the benefit of the Insolvent Act, the money was lost."

The mode of investment was changed about twenty-five years ago, and the property of the Charity now consists of £3,086 10s. 4d. in Consols, producing £91 12s. 8d., which allows of an income of 15s. each per month to the nine inmates; the salary of the Clerk being £5 as before.

It will be seen that the Commissioners of 1826 made no complaint as to the accounts of the Charity, but in 1854 the the Corporation Committee alleged that they could get no accounts except for the previous twelve years.

In 1865, a subscription was raised in the town to give a slight entertainment to the inmates, under the impression, nurtured by a tablet on the face of the building, that the Hospital was established in 1765; but as shown above, the real centenary was on 25th October, 1879, the first inmates being elected on 25th October, 1779. The year 1865 was only the year in which the will had been signed.

BRADLEY'S ALMSHOUSES.

There are in Ackworth, two tenements built by Dr. Bradley in 1666, "for two poor ancient widows, and two others that might assist them in washing, making their beds, etc." On the front wall outside are Dr. Bradley's Coat of Arms, and an inscription nearly obliterated. The inmates are put in by the Rector, though the Overseers of the Poor have occasionally repaired the houses. Before the restoration of the Church, the following epitaph might have been seen upon a monumental slab inside the Church:—

"Here resteth the Body of Doctor Thomas Bradley,
Rector of this Parish.
E. T. R.
His Almeshouse built here shews in part his Goodness
to the poor, his pious Books
And Learned Works in print will tell you more, by which
He being dead yet Speaketh.
Obiit October 10, An. D., 1673.

Celebrities of Ackworth.

I.—JOHN FOTHERGILL, M.D., F.R.S.

The name of John Fothergill will always be cherished by the Friends of Ackworth. He was a London Physician, and an ardent member of the Society of Friends. He was the founder, or rather originator of the Ackworth Quaker School, and is mentioned by Mr. J. G. Baker, F.L.S., of the Royal Herbarium, Kew, in his presidential address at Barnsley, in 1884, as one of "The fathers of Yorkshire Botany."

The following particulars concerning him have been extracted from a biographical sketch written by James Hack Tuke, and read by him at the Ackworth Centenary Commemoration:—

"For three or four centuries," says Mr. Tuke, "families of this name (Fothergill) have resided in the wild and secluded valleys of Ravenstonedale and Mallerstang, in Westmoreland, which adjoin upon 'Sedber and Wensleydale.' Sufficient for us, * is the fact, that a John Fothergill migrated thence to Counterset, in Wensleydale, and afterwards to Carr End, soon after the year 1600. * * On the banks of the small and quiet lake of 'Semer Water,' there dwelt Alexander and Ann Fothergill, who were probably convinced by George Fox (about the year 1652), as 'he passed up the Dales, warning people to fear God, and preaching the everlasting Gospel to them.'* Here, in 1676, John Fothergill the elder was born, and, after the death of his father in 1695, he inherited the little estate at Carr End. A year after his father's death, when about twenty-five years of age, he began his ministerial work, and gave up housekeeping, the house at Carr End, and, soon afterwards, even the land, in order to be more 'completely at liberty' for his journeys in the ministry. * * When about thirty-four, he married Margaret Hough, of Sutton, in Cheshire, a woman likeminded with himself, and settled down for some years in the old family house at Carr End. Here seven children were born to him, brought up with a 'zealous concern that they might have an inward experience of a holy living principle operating in their hearts' in order to 'lead them from error and unrighteousness into all truth and the practice of every Christian virtue.' Two of these children— the second son, John Fothergill, the future doctor, who was born on the 8th of March, 1712,† and Samuel Fothergill, the sixth son, the most distinguished Quaker preacher of the middle of the last century,—were striking instances of the value of this teaching." After leaving the elementary day

* Vide George Fox's Journal, folio, p. 72.

† A small pocket Bible belonging to Dr. Fothergill, was exhibited at Ackworth during the Centenary. It belonged to his mother before her marriage. On the last fly-leaf is the following inscription:—" Margaret Hough, Her Book, and she was born ye 30th day of ye 3rd Month, 1679. On the first page of the New Testament:—" John Fothergill was born the 8th of 1st mo. (o.s.), 1712. Joseph Fothergill was born 16th of 12th mo., 1712-13.

school at Frodsham, in Cheshire, he was sent (at twelve) to the old-established Grammar School at Sedbergh, where he remained for four years, leaving in 1728, to be apprenticed for seven years to Benjamin Bartlett, an eminent apothecary at Bradford, and a Minister in the Society of Friends known to young Fothergill's father, with whom he travelled extensively.*

* It was probably as some recognition of the fidelity of these services that he was liberated before the expiration of his term of apprenticeship, to pursue his medical studies in Edinburgh. * In 1736, young Fothergill wrote his Latin Thesis; took his degree of M.D., and left Edinburgh, proceeding to London, where he entered himself as a pupil in St. Thomas's Hospital. Four years later he took a house in White Hart Court, Gracechurch Street, and fairly established himself in practice. Here he laboured unremittingly for forty years, attaining to the highest rank in his profession, and numbering among his patients some of the most worthy and distinguished characters of the century. * * In 1754, Dr. Fothergill was elected a Fellow of the College of Physicians of Edinburgh, and during this time John Wesley was one of his patients, but, ill as he was, his earnest spirit did not allow him to carry out the Doctor's advice to rest and repair to the Hot Wells at Bristol for change. Probably, like his comrade Whitfield, he thought 'that *perpetual preaching* was a better remedy than a perpetual blister.'

In 1760, the year in which George III. came to the throne, Dr. Fothergill wrote the address of congratulation sent by the Society of Friends to the King on his accession to the Crown, and shortly afterwards presented a report of a Committee of the Friends' Meeting for Sufferings, to the Yearly Meeting on Education.

His leisure moments were occupied in the study of chemistry, conchology, entomology, corallines, and especially botany; and

* Vide "Memoirs of the Life and a view of the Character of the late Dr. John Fothergill," by Gilbert Thompson, M.D., 1782.

in 1762 he purchased the gardens at Upton, so well known in after days as the hospital residence and grounds of the late Samuel Gurney. Here he employed no less than fifteen gardeners; and so well known were his grounds, that foreigners of all ranks came to visit it. Several plants perpetuate his memory. The French botanist, Aublet, named a genus "Fothergilla," after him, now called *Miconia Fothergilli*, and the younger Linæus, an American shrub. Three other plants are named after him, viz :—" Fothergill's Lily " *(Nerine Fothergilli)*; the *Calceolaria Fothergilli;* and the *Pelargonium Fothergilli*. The Doctor also took a great interest in the artistic working of North American and Cornish clays, and often corresponded with Josiah Wedgewood. The black bust (an engraving of which is here given), from a model taken by Flaxman, after the death of Dr. Fothergill, is of Wedgewood ware. The munificent assistance which he rendered to Anthony Purver, in the translation and publication of his version of the Old and New Testaments must not be overlooked. Not only did he give the translator pecuniary assistance to the extent of two thousand pounds, but, it is said, revised the whole of the sheets as they passed through the press.

But the most eventful year in the Doctor's life, so far as Ackworth is concerned, is the year 1777, in which year Ackworth School was established, and which Luke Howard styled "The Era of a Reformation in our Religious Society."* A full account of the preliminary proceedings, and final transactions connected with the purchase of Ackworth School, will be found in the "Centenary Proceedings" of 1879.

"Dr. Fothergill paid three visits to Ackworth, and died on the 26th of December, 1780, at the age of sixty eight." Thus ended the eventful career of "Ackworth's Benefactor," and truly it was a magnificent sunset. His remains were interred in the burial ground of Winchmore Hill, about seven miles

---

* Vide " The Yorkshireman," by Luke Howard.

from London, where, side by side, may be seen two small headstones which record the names of a devoted brother and sister, "J. and A. Fothergill."

Dr. Fothergill was a prolific writer, especially on medical subjects. His "Key to the New Testament" is still in use at Ackworth School.

"The following graphic description of him, as he probably appeared at the time of his last visit to York, written by a great-nephew, cannot fail to be of interest:—

"Dr. Fothergill was pious, generous, and benevolent, rather above the middle age; very delicate and slender, of a sanguine temperament; his forehead finely proportioned; his eyes light-coloured, brilliant, acute, and deeply penetrating; his nose rather aquiline; his mouth betokened delicacy of feeling; his whole countenance expressed liability to irritation, great sensibility, clear understanding, and exalted virtue."*

Besides the very beautiful black basalt bust, Wedgewood also executed one or more very fine cameo portraits in white-ware, and from one of these the portrait here inserted is copied. There are also many paintings and engraved likenesses extant, the most valuable of which is a portrait in oils, painted by Hogarth in 1764, now in the possession of the Royal College of Physicians, London.

Dr. Fothergill contributed the following papers to the Philosophical Transactions of the Royal Society:—

1744.—Upon the origin of Amber, xliii, 20.
1744.—Observations on the Manna Persicum, xliii, 86.
1745.—Observations on a case published in the last volume of the "Medical Essays," of recovering a man dead in appearance, by distending the lungs with air; printed at Edinburgh, 1774. By John Fothergill, Licen. Col. Med., London, xliii, 275.

* Vide "Records of John Fothergill," York, 1793.

1746.—De Diaphragmate sisso et mutatis quorundum viscerum sedibus, in Cadavere Puella decem mensium observatus, Epistola xliv, 11.*

II.—SIR ROGER HOPTON.

Sir Roger Hopton, of Armley, near Leeds, had a lease of the manor and demesnes of Ackworth, and probably resided there. He had served in the wars in France, where he was knighted. He married Annie, daughter of — Savile, by whom he had two daughters; one, married to — Kiddal, and the other to — Usleet. He died in 1506 (21st Henry VII.), and, with his wife, was buried in the south aisle of Ackworth Church.†

III.—REV. THOMAS BRADLEY, D.D.

Dr. Bradley was presented to the livings of Castleford and Ackworth, 5th March, 1831, and was at that time also Prebendary of North Newbald, in York Minster. He was driven thence by the troubles of the Civil Wars, and so remained until 1660, when, with the return of the King (Charles II.), whose Chaplain he subsequently became, he returned to the living again. From Walker's "Sufferings of the Clergy," we gather the following particulars concerning Dr. Bradley:—

"He was first Chaplain to the old Duke of Buckingham, and went with him to the Isle of Rhea, and the siege of Rochelle. After his return, he was made Chaplain to King Charles I., and had the livings of Castleford and Ackworth given him (both in the King's gift), and was made Prebendary of York. On the 5th March, 1631, he married Frances, the youngest daughter of the Right Hon. John Lord Savile, Baron of Pontefract, by whom he had several children. In the year 1642, he writes himself—'*Sacræ Theologiæ Professor et serenissimo Regi Carolo a Sacris.*' He was a person of most

---

* "Old Yorkshire," Vol. I., p. 47.

† Vide Monumental Inscriptions.

incomparable parts and learning, an excellent preacher, a ready and acute wit, and of a generous and genteel temper. He was sequestered of his living of Ackworth, and thrust out by one Mr. Burbeck, a stiff-rumped Presbyterian. He was sequestered of Castleford also, which living was usurped by Mr. H. Moorhouse, an army chaplain. Dr. Bradley was a very great sufferer. Twice sequestered, and plundered of all that he had, his lady and all his children turned out of doors, to seek their bread in desolate places; and that which most of all he complained of, was the perfidiousness of one John Lake, of Castleford, with whom he trusted his library, who betrayed it into the hands of his enemies. I heard a gentleman say, he once went to see Dr. Bradley, and that he was so poor that he was forced to eat puddings made of boar's blood, and he found him with this diet."*

It is generally supposed that Dr. Bradley attended Charles I. to the scaffold.† In one of the Parish Registers (1663), the Doctor records that on the following Candlemas Day, Lady Frances, his wife, who had died 30th January, at the "very same hour (as neere as may be conjectured) wherein his [late] Majesty suffered," was "honourably inter'd." In all probability, therefore, the Dr. would not accompany Charles Stuart on the scaffold, but, as is more natural to suppose, was at his proper place by the deathbed of his wife. He remained faithful to the house of Stuart until his death,‡ and was a man of mark in his time. "He published," says Walker, "some sermons, in the dedication of which, as I am informed, is to be found more of his sufferings; but I have not yet seen it." An oil portrait of Dr. Bradley, in good condition, is preserved at Ackworth Rectory.

IV.—WILLIAM BUCHAN, M.D.

In the west cloister of Westminster Abbey lie the remains of one who was considered a man of mark in his day. He

* Vide Walker's "Sufferings of the Clergy," II., p. 85.
† Only a tradition.
‡ Vide sub datum, 1642.

was born at Ancrum, near Jedburgh, in Scotland, in 1729. Dr. Buchan was educated at Edinburgh, and first began to practise his profession as Physician to the Foundling Hospital at Ackworth. Afterwards he practised at Sheffield, but, eventually, returned to Edinburgh, became a Fellow of the Royal College of Physicians, and remained there for some years, having married a lady named Miss Peter. Ultimately, he removed to London, where he enjoyed a lucrative practice. He died, according to the journals of the day, at his son's house in Percy Street, Rathbone Place, Feb. 25th, 1805, aged 76. His will, dated 30th January, 1805, was not proved until 7th August, 1806. To his son, Dr. Alexander Peter Buchan, he bequeathed all his literary property and M.S.S., and the residue of his estate equally to him and his sister, Helen Buchan, spinster, both of whom proved the will. Dr. Buchan is best known as the author of "Domestic Medicine, or, The Family Physician," which was first published in 1769.* From "Bellchamber's Biographical Dictionary," we get some additional information, as follows:—"This popular medical writer was born in 1729, at Ancrum, in Roxburghshire. Being destined by his friends for the Church, he repaired to Edinburgh to study divinity. At the University he spent nine years, studying anything rather than theology. At this period of his life, mathematics and botany were among his favourite pursuits. Finally, he devoted himself wholly to medicine. He enjoyed, at this time, the friendship of the illustrious Gregory, whose liberal maxims are believed to have had a great influence over his future life. Before taking his degree, he was induced by the invitation of a fellow student, to settle in practice for some time in Yorkshire. While established in that district, he became physician to the Ackworth Foundling Hospital, in which situation he laid the foundation of that knowledge of the diseases of children, which afterwards appeared so conspicious in his writings. He subsequently

---

* Vide "Old Yorkshire," vol. iii., p. 88; Chester's "Westminster Abbey Registers;" and Dean Stanley's "Memorials of Westminster Abbey."

removed to Sheffield, where he appears to have spent the years between 1762 and 1766. He then commenced practice at Edinburgh, and for several years was very well employed, though it was allowed that he might have enjoyed much more success, if his convivial habits had not distracted so much of his attention. Having for a considerable time directed his attention to a digest of popular medical knowledge, he published, in 1769, his work, entitled, "Domestic Medicine, or the Family Physician; being an attempt to render the Medical Art more generally useful, by showing people what is in their own power, both with respect to the prevention and cure of certain diseases; chiefly calculated to recommend a proper attention to regimen and simple medicines." He died in 1805 ✕

V.—LUKE HOWARD, F.R.S.,

was born in London, Novr. 28th, 1772. He was the son of Robert Howard, and of Elizabeth Leatham, of Pontefract. He was educated at Burford, near Oxford, at a school kept by a member of the Society of Friends, to which body his parents belonged. Here he received a good classical education, especially in Latin. During his apprenticeship, he diligently pursued his studies, Chemistry, Natural History, and Meteorology, specially occupying his attention. He traced his interest in the latter science to the extraordinary fog, and northern lights of 1783. From quite a schoolboy he was a great observer of nature, and about the year 1820, he published the result of his researches in a book, entitled, "The Climate of London," in two volumes. His nomenclature of the clouds (which was adopted by scientific men,) led to a correspondence with the celebrated German poet Göethe, and in a letter addressed to him in February, 1822, Luke Howard writes, that after leaving school he studied "French, Chemistry, etc. The works of Labaisiere and his fellow labourers" he adds "produced an effect upon many of us like that of the rising sun after morning moonlight."

In 1796, Luke Howard married Mariabella Eliot, a lady of a remarkably benevolent disposition and superior judgment, who aided him materially in carrying out his plans and efforts, especially those of a benevolent character. The education of the poor was to Mrs. Howard and her two daughters, a deeply interesting object. In 1823, Mr. Howard purchased the estate of Ackworth Villa, which, from that time, became the family home for the greater part of the year. Finding there the need of education, the two Miss Howards commenced a school for the farmers' daughters in the neighbourhood, this being held in a room on the premises, and taught by the ladies themselves on three mornings in the week. The Boys' British School in the village was also set on foot by Mr. and Mrs. Howard. The school was a great blessing, but soon became too large for the arrangement; and the younger sister planned and built the neat school-room and mistress's house, opposite the Villa gates. Her name, Rachel Howard, is engraved over the front entrance. Her father partially endowed the school, which is still carried on with much satisfaction.

For many years Luke Howard successfully carried on the business of a manufacturing chemist at Stratford, in Essex. In this he was succeeded by his two sons, Robert and John Eliot, and the firm still continues under the name of Howard and Sons.

The latter years of his life were very much spent at Tottenham, where, under the roof of his eldest son, he enjoyed all the care and comfort that could be bestowed on an honoured old age. He died in 1864, at the advanced age of ninety-two, in the true faith and trust of the Saviour whom he had loved and served. Since his death, the family have not resided at Ackworth, though the estate remains in their possession. It is now the residence of Captain Armytage, known as "The Court." In 1823, he invited a number of them to drink tea with him, at the "Villa," and in 1829, he most "kindly rendered assistance in the 'Apothecary's shop' in dispensing medicine," during a visitation of fever, "acquiring thereby, from one of the nurses, the designation of 'the old Potecary.'" The following anecdote is told of him:—"I recollect" says Thomas Hunton, "on one occasion, Luke Howard, with his characteristic disregard of conventionalities, breaking up the week-day meeting after about half-an-hour, remarking, much in unison with our feelings, that, under the present circumstances, he thought the children ought to have shorter meetings and a more generous diet." He was an author of some repute, and was deeply read in the science of meteorology.

VI.—REV. TIMOTHY LEE, D.D.

This worthy divine was the revered Rector of Ackworth from 1744 to 1777. A faithful biographer would not shrink from recording the vices as well as the virtues of his subject, but in this instance, nothing but good is left upon record. Dr. Lee was a model pastor from whichever direction he is viewed, one over which even Herbert himself would have waxed warm with enthusiasm. That he was a charitable man may be gathered from his will. In one of the parish books Dr. Lee is called "Rector and benefactor of Ackworth." In Mr. Thompson's "Centenary History of Ackworth School," it is said that "the Architect was a Mr. Watson, though Dr. Timothy Lee, the Vicar (sic) of Ackworth, planned the centre." St. Cuthbert's Cottage, near the Church, was built by Dr. Lee for the use of his wife in case she survived him; but the Rector survived, Mrs. Lee dying before the building was finished, and which was afterwards occupied by two maiden ladies named Walker, sisters of George Clark Walker, Esq., of Doncaster, who was three times Mayor of that town.

Copy of Clause in the Will of the Rev. Timothy Lee, D.D., Rector of Ackworth, dated 30th March, 1777.

"I give and devise unto Anthony Surtees, of Ackworth, Esquire, and his heirs, all that small parcel of land as it is now fenced off from the Hempyards, in Ackworth aforesaid, wherein the grotto stands not now belonging to the Rectory; but I request that the said Anthony Surtees and his heirs will for ever hereafter permit the Rector of Ackworth for the time being to enjoy and occupy the said parcel of ground, without paying anything for the same. And I also request that the said Anthony Surtees, or his heirs, will do any lawful act for conveying and assuring the same parcel of ground to my successors, Rectors of Ackworth, aforesaid, for ever."

Exception of the piece of land in the Hempyards, above referred to, out of the conveyance from Dr. Lee to the Trustees of Mr. Francis Sykes.

"By Indenture bearing date the 29th day of May, 1765, made between the Rev. Timothy Lee, Doctor in Divinity, of the one part, and William Sykes and William Willock, in trust for Francis Sykes, Esq., of the other part, for the considerations therein mentioned, the said Timothy Lee hath conveyed, from and after his decease, unto the said William Sykes and William Willock, amongst other lands and tenements, all that parcel of land called the Hempyard, in Ackworth, except one part of the said Hempyard, about the middle of the west side thereof, then and for a long time used and occupied with the plantation, or Brick-kiln Croft, belonging to the Rectory of Ackworth, upon part of which is built a grotto and the rest is a plantation, and is now separated from the said Hempyard by a stone wall; and which piece of ground is 23 yards, or thereabouts, from east to west, and 35 yards, or upwards, from north to south."

There is an oil portrait of Dr. Lee at the Rectory, which is well worth the inspection of connoiseurs. On the back of the picture is fastened a faded sheet of paper bearing the following inscription :—

"TIMOTHY LEE, S.T.P.,
WAS PRESENTED TO THE RECTORY OF ACKWORTH,
DECR., 1744.
HE DIED THERE APRIL 19TH, 1777, AGED 63 YEARS.
UNIVERSALLY LAMENTED,
AS BEFORE HE HAD BEEN BELOVED AND HONOURED BY HIS
PARISHIONERS.

This portrait, painted by the elder Killingbeck, of Pontefract, a few years before Dr. Lee's death, and esteemed to be a strong likeness, is presented by one of his successors (Rev. R. Hay) to the Rectors and Churchwardens of Ackworth for the time being, for the use of the Parish, in the hope that it may be allowed to remain in the Rectory House, as a mark of respect to the memory of the original."

VII.—THE EARL OF DARLINGTON.

The Bedale Hunt, now so called, originally formed part of the immense reach of country hunted by the Raby hounds, the property of the Earl of Darlington, who resided for some time at Ackworth.

William Henry, 3rd Earl of Darlington, and 1st Duke of Cleveland, hunted the Raby and Badsworth countries; he rented Belham House, near Ferrybridge, and established a hunting club there. During his Badsworth reign, a celebrated run from Howell Wood was commemorated in verse, the following stanza applying to the Master:—

"Then first in the burst, see dashing away,
Taking all in his stroke, on Ralpho the grey;
With persuaders in flank, comes Darlington's peer
With his chin sticking out, and his cap on one ear."

The horse Ralpho, here mentioned, no doubt was a great favourite, as the noble Earl was painted on him, with a few celebrated hounds. Somewhere about 1794, the Earl gave up the Badsworth country, and hunted the Raby and Bedale countries. When hunting the Bedale country, he resided at Newton House, near Bedale, now the residence of Captain Rassell, R.N., a good friend to foxes. The Earl of Darlington seems to have kept a large pack of hounds, probably seventy couple, and they are described as big, strong hounds, with remarkably short cupped ears. Failing health compelled Lord Darlington to give up the Bedale country at the end of the season 1831-32, and in 1839 he gave up the Raby country, having been Master of Hounds for fifty-three years. From old hunting diaries of the Earl of Darlington, now in possession of Captain Russell, of Newton House, it appears that the Earl hunted the most days in 1811, having been out 192 days. In 1807, he was out 106 days, and killed 103 foxes, beginning on the 3rd of October, and ending on the 16th of April. On Lord Darlington, afterwards 1st Duke of Cleveland, giving up the country, Mr. Mark Milbank, of Thorpe Penow, near Bedale, was requested to hunt the Bedale country, which he undertook in 1832, originating the Bedale Hunt, the present Master of which is Mr. Geo. Wm. Elliot, M.P. for the Richmondshire Division. William Henry, 3rd Earl of Darlington, K.G., who was born in 1766, was created Marquess of Cleveland in 1827, and elevated to the Dukedom in January, 1833, and died on January 29th, 1842, when the honours devolved on his oldest son, Henry, the 2nd Duke of Cleveland.*

VIII.—MR GULLY, M.P.

John Gully, late of Ackworth Park, and M.P. for Pontefract, and the well-known sportsman, died at Durham, on Monday, March 9th, 1863, in the 80th year of his age. In all the crowd of "characters that have ever made up the ring on a race-course, there were few more famous, and no one whose career has been so much of a romance, as that of John Gully. He was indeed essentially one of the men of his time, and the tyro or stranger would crave for a look at him long before his hero-worship would centre on the jockey-lord, etc." And yet Mr. Gully was by no means a remarkable man in his appearance, or, rather, in no way noticeable for the mere emphasis of his tone or the quaint cut of his coat. With a mien singularly quiet and almost subdued, he associated the air and presence of a gentleman, while his fine frame and commanding figure gave an innate dignity to his deportment that none who knew him would care to question. In fact, as your gaze rested on him, it was almost impossible to identify the man with the earlier stages of his history,—the butcher's boy, the prize-fighter, the

---

* I am indebted to the Rev. R. V. Taylor, B.A., for this and the following sketch.—J.L.S.

public-house landlord, or the outside betting man. It was easier far to recognise him as a country squire of good estate, the owner of a long string of racehorses, or the honourable member of a reformed Parliament. In a new country like America or Australia, we can readily imagine that the fighting butcher might in due time develop into the stately Senator; but here, in Old England, Mr. Gully's success was unparalleled. And he owed this, not merely to his great wealth, but far more to his keen judgment, his good sense, and a certain straightforward respectability about everything he did." The gentlemen of the turf from the very first, took kindly to Gully, for they felt they could do so without any of the danger or disgust but too often resulting from the society of a self-made man. Mr. Gully was born at Bristol, sometime in the year 1783. He was brought up to the trade of a butcher, but very soon evinced a handiness in taking care of himself, in sundry fistic tourneys with his comrades about home. On leaving the ring, Mr. Gully, like most successful pugilists, inclined to the public life of a Boniface, and was for many years landlord of "The Plough," in Carey Street, Lincoln's Inn Fields. But another ring found attractions for him, and he very soon devoted himself to the business of a betting man. In 1812, he had horses of his own, and in 1827 he purchased the winner of the Derby, Mameluke, from Lord Jersey, for 4000 guineas. In 1832 he, along with a partner, Mr. Ridsdale, won both the Derby and the Leger. Shortly after this, he assaulted Mr. Ridsdale in the hunting-field, and had £500 to pay as damages. He also fought a duel with Mr. Osbaldeston, who sent a ball through his hat. As Mr. Gully examined the course of the ball, he jokingly remarked, "It is better through my hat than through my head." He must have been very successful, for he purchased Upper Hare Park, near Newmarket, from Lord Rivers, where he for some time resided; but he sold this to Sir Mark Wood, and bought in 1831, for £21,000, Ackworth Park, near Pontefract; an accession which somewhat unexpectedly led to his representing that Borough in the Radical interest for some sessions in Parliament. He was twice returned, and on the first occasion without a contest. During his long sojourn there, he also figured as a good man over a country, and as one of the chief supporters of the Badsworth Foxhounds. But the turf, after all, was his ruling passion; his horses won both the Oaks and the Derby in 1846, the famous Sam Day being his jockey. Rarely has any man enjoyed more signal success in his favourite pursuit; but, as we have said before, Gully owed much of this to his fine judgment, especially in the way in which he could reckon up a race-horse, or pick out a young one. Latterly, what with increasing years and failing strength, he had gradually declined, and having sold Ackworth to Mr. Hill, had lived some years at Marwell Hall, near Winchester, though he had still property in the North, including, we believe, some coal mines and hence his death occurring at Durham. He left a family of five sons and five daughters, and his funeral took place at Ackworth Park, being attended by the Mayor and Corporation, etc. His will was proved under £70,000 personality, the executors being Mrs. Mary Gully, his relict, and Mr. Thos. Belk, of Hartlepool, his son-in-law, etc., the dispositions being confined to members of his family. Among the specific bequests is one of a piece of plate presented to the testator by the burgesses of the borough of Pontefract, which he bequeathed to his son Richard, etc. Mr. Gully was also for some time a Unitarian preacher, and kept a Chapel somewhere (on his own estate, I think), in which he himself used to officiate.

James Smith, in his "Rejected Addresses," gives the following epigrammatic reason for the election of John Gully, the pugilist, for Pontefract:—

> "You ask me the cause that made Pontefract sully,
> Her fame, by returning to Parliament Gully?
> The etymological cause, I suppose, is—
> His *breaking* the *bridges* of so many noses."

The word "Pontefract" means "broken bridge."

Mr. John Gully is said to have bought Ackworth Park, containing about 200 acres, with its large house and buildings, for £21,500, in 1831. Mr. Gully was buried in his own grounds, against the Churchyard wall; and about 1851, the property was again sold. There is an engraved portrait of him, as "Champion," with an autograph letter, signed 1833. For a portrait and memoir of him see Baily's "Magazine," etc.

The following sad memorial of a member of the Gully family appears, in the shape of a marble tablet, on the south wall of Ackworth Church:—

"SACRED TO THE MEMORY
OF
ROBERT GULLY, SON OF JOHN GULLY, ESQ.,
Of Ackworth Park,
Who, after suffering the horrors and privations of shipwreck on the Island of Formosa, in the brig *Ann*, on the night of the 10th of March, 1842, in which vessel he was a passenger, he was, together with the rest of the crew, taken prisoner by the Chinese, and suffered the greatest privations and hardships, which he bore with the most exemplary fortitude, manly and cheerful resignation, to about the 13th of August, when he, together with about 300 other British subjects, was most barbarously murdered in cold blood by the Chinese authorities, in the town of Tywan Foo, aged 28 years. He was endeared to a large circle of friends for his manly virtues and kindness of heart. This tablet is erected by a bereaved and afflicted father."

IX.—ROBERT WHITAKER,

who was a native of Rossendale, in Lancashire, was born in the year 1766, and was the only child of pious parents of the Baptist persuasion. He was considered to be a boy of superior intelligence, and he made rapid progress in the best schools which the district afforded, his studies being completed under a clergyman of the Church of England. Before he had attained the age of 21 years, he became acquainted with several members of the Society of Friends, whose intellectual tastes had great attractions for him; their religious principles he carefully examined and adopted as his own, continuing to be warmly attached to them to the close of his long life. Whilst still a young man, he took charge of a Boarding School at Llanidlass, in Montgomeryshire, established, in great measure, by the well-known Quaker philanthrophist, Richard Reynolds, for the education of children of the Society of Friends, resident in Wales. Here he remained four years, during which he became much interested in the Welsh people, whose language he learnt to speak and read with considerable facility, and, when circumstances, not entirely under his own control, induced him to leave his Cambrian home, he did so with great regret. In the year 1805 he was appointed to the superintendence of the Friends' School, in Ackworth, which proved to be a most arduous undertaking, in consequence of the finances of the Institution not then being, by any means, adequate to its requirements, so that for many years he had a constant struggle in order that expenses might be kept within the limits of income. To effect this most desirable object, he cheerfully made great personal sacrifices. Robert Whitaker's extraordinary intuitive perception of character, his strong sense of justice, and his delicate tact, secured for him the hearty co-operation of those who laboured under him, and, although his numerous duties did not allow of his spending much time in the schools, the Teachers well knew that he possessed a tolerably accurate acquaintance with what was passing in them, whilst the warm interest he took in their own private studies was an incentive to diligence in this direction, which, in not a few instances, led to very creditable results. Of the individual characters of the pupils in the School, he was able to form a singularly correct estimate, and it is scarcely too much to add that he possessed the love and respect of a large number of them, both on the boys' and the girls' sides of the house. The charge of so large a number of young people was felt by Robert Whitaker to involve great responsibility, and, as he was sensitively alive to the sufferings of his fellow creatures, it was a great distress to him when illness prevailed in the family. He studied the treatment of diseases incident to children, and was able to prescribe remedies and to devise plans which were found to be of great use, more especially so, as the Medical attendants of the Institution were then resident at a distance of three miles from it.

Though a practical agriculturist was engaged to have charge of the Farm attached to the establishment, its financial concerns were in the hands of Robert Whitaker, who also took great interest in the general management of it; and as his sympathies were by no means confined to his fellow creatures of the human family, but extended to all beings endowed with life and feeling, his concern was often manifested for the animals on the farm. He studied the diseases of cattle to some extent, and the writer of this sketch has a lively recollection of the sorrow depicted on his countenance as he stood by an invalid cow, whose sufferings he was anxious to relieve.

Very keen was his appreciation of the beauties of nature, both in its grander and softer aspects. Fine trees he greatly admired, and was very particular about the timber on the School estate, which could then boast of some splendid oaks, such indeed as are scarcely to be seen in the district now. The large garden also had a share of his attention, and with great pains he supplied it with a capital stock of fruit trees, which he lived to see produce abundant crops. Of flowers he was exceedingly fond, and would have taken great pleasure in the culture of them, could he have found leisure for it.

Whilst closely occupied by duties of a rather heterogeneous nature, he fully maintained his position as the head of an educational establishment, and he corresponded extensively with persons in various parts of the island who were interested in the subject of education. Strangers who visited the School were greatly attracted by his genial manners, and pleasing conversational powers; and if he had not leisure to mingle extensively with his fellow-residents in Ackworth and its vicinity, it was fully understood by them that the high standard of Christian character was a true guarantee that, under all circumstances, he would pursue an honourable course where their interests were concerned, and in him the poor felt they had a true friend.

In this feeling of general respect, Robert Whitaker's excellent wife, who was a true helper in his labours and cares, had a full share. She died, after a short illness, when on a journey, in the year 1833, and it was abundantly proved that the event which prostrated her husband, was a sorrow in which Friends and neighbours feelingly participated.

If Robert Whitaker was what may be termed a "strict Friend," it may truly be written of him, that he loved all, of whatsoever denomination, who loved the Lord Jesus Christ in sincerity.

This sketch will scarcely be complete without alluding to the fact that Robert Whitaker took great interest in various philanthrophic movements of the day, amongst which the British and Foreign Bible Society, and the Anti-Slavery Society may be especially mentioned.

The following letter from John Hattersley, how was equally famous as a Linguist, as a Mathematician, is inserted on account of the testimony it bears to the soundness of the elementary instruction given at Ackworth School during his superintendence of it:—

Dear and respected Friend,

I cannot but write to tell thee of the favourable completion of my studies at Cambridge, on the 22nd inst. I learnt my place in the Mathematical List,—8th Wrangler. This is a much better degree than I had ventured to hope for; it is, in all human probability, the introduction to a course of occupation of of a character the most consonant to my tastes and pursuits, the teaching of young men of a high order of intellect,—the picked men of England, I might say,—under circumstances the most favourable for success. At Ackworth School, and under thy government, I began that course of study which has issued in this success: to the sound elementary instruction I received there, I am quite sure, I have been indebted for my best habits, such as have done much to antagonize the almost inevitable evils of an after course of self-instruction. As the first Ackworth scholar, I believe, whose name has been published on the door of our

Senate House, I feel a pride and pleasure in making here acknowledgment of the benefits received from my first Alma Mater, and will not affect to doubt that the acknowledgment of it will gratify all whom I have so much reason to love and respect.

      Believe me, dear Friend,
        Most affectionately thine,
Jan. 21st, 1847.   JOHN HATTERSLEY.

X.—REV. W. R. HAY, M.A.,

thirty-fifth Rector of Ackworth, was the third and youngest son of the Hon. Edward Hay, sometime Governor of Barbadoes, by Mary, daughter of Peter Flower, merchant, of London. His father was the fourth son of George Henry, seventh Earl of Kinnoul, by Lady Abigail Harley, daughter of the Lord Treasurer Oxford; and younger brother to Robert, Lord Archbishop of York. Mr. Hay received his education at Christ Church, Oxford, where he took the degree of M.A., on Oct. 24, 1783, and during the early period of his life devoted his talents to the study and practice of the Law. He was brought into connexion with Lancashire in his capacity as a barrister on the circuit, where, in 1793, he married Mary, widow of John Astley, Esq., of Dukinfield, the beautiful and accomplished daughter of William Wagstaffe, Esq., of Manchester. In 1797, he took Holy Orders, and soon afterwards, was presented to the Rectory of Ackworth by the Chancellor of the Duchy of Lancaster. In the year 1803, he succeeded Thos. Butterworth Bayley, Esq., as Chairman of Quarter Sessions for the Hundred of Salford, which office he held till the year 1823, when he retired into private life. It is understood that the strong recommendations made in his favour to Lord Sidmouth, by the municipal authorities and other respectable inhabitants of Manchester, with regard to his conduct as a Magistrate during the riots of 1818, induced the government to ask and obtain from the Archbishop of Canterbury, his presentation to the valuable Vicarage of Rochdale, net yearly value £1730, which was conferred upon him in 1819. For several years he held both livings, ultimately resigning the Vicarage of Rochdale, and with it the Chairmanship of the Salford Hundred Quarter

Sessions, the duties of which he had performed with great ability for more than twenty years. On this occasion, he was presented with a splendid vase, as a token of his people's affection. His character and talents were greatly admired by all those who came within the sphere of his acquaintance, and cause him to be remembered by his friends with affection, and by his political enemies (for personal enemies he had none) with a feeling of deep respect. Early introduced into the most polished circles, and the best literary society of his own time, he constantly bore about him the marks of that refined sphere in which he had been nurtured, and never forgot what was due to himself or others in his intercourse with men of every class and station; of a cast of mind and frame of body almost alike herculean, he could grapple with the greatest legal difficulties, and undergo the most continued bodily exertion with a perseverance and ease which it astonished his feebler associates to contemplate. No threat of personal danger could shake a nerve of his frame; no sudden mental difficulty find his intellect unprepared; no rudeness of personal insult disturb the equanamity of his temper. His conduct as a magistrate is confessed, even by those who feel no great affection for his acknowledged opinions, to have been beyond all praise. Five minutes before the opening of the court, always found him seated in the chair; and while he occupied it, the mingled dignity and suavity of his deportment, the knowledge even of the nicest technicalities, as well as of the general principles of law which he exhibited, the unbiassed impartiality with which he formed his decisions, and, the concise, dignified, and perspicuous language with which those decisions were enunciated, all tended to vindicate the majesty of the law, and secure admiration and regard towards him who so admirably dispensed it.

It is painful to look back to the melancholy scenes which were enacted on the celebrated 16th of August, 1818. But we believe that all right-thinking men, and real patriots of whatever shade of political opinion, are now ready to confess that Manchester owed then as much to the firmness and admirable coolness and decision of Mr. Hay, as Newport has more recently done to the patriotic conduct of Sir Thomas Phillips. From the time he quitted the chair of the Quarter Sessions, Mr. Hay resigned, in a great measure, the duties of a magistrate, and devoted himself exclusively to those of his sacred profession. In that profession, he maintained the same love of order and adherence to principle, the same contempt of mere popularity at the expense of right, which distinguished his legal career. This rigid adherence to the line of strict duty brought upon him much public obloquy and personal disquiet, which a less precise line of conduct would have escaped; but he grappled with all the difficulties of such a situation with the intellect of a giant, encountered his bitterest opponents with the unvarying manners of a gentleman, and submitted to evils which he could not overcome, with the philosophy and piety of a Christian. In the intercourse of private life, the playful brilliance of his imagination, as well as the almost infantile simplicity of his fancy, his well stored fund of historical and political knowledge which from a long and accurate observation of men and things had brought, his pleasing reminiscences of great men and great events in the last generation, united with a perfect knowledge of, and unfailing interest in the men and events of the present, his kind consideration for the wants and wishes of all around him, from the highest to the lowest, his unchanging good humour, his faithful attachment, his sober and unaffected piety, will justify his personal friends in saying what has often been said before, but never with more truth: "We ne'er shall look upon his like again."

The remainder of his life at Ackworth was marked only by a faithful and earnest discharge of his ministerial duties. There are still living a few very old inhabitants of Ackworth who remember him with affection, and cherish his portrait with pride, because it was given to them by "Old Mr. Hay." He died on the 10th December, 1839, aged 78 years, and was buried N.W. of the Churchyard,* by the side of his wife. "In my early days," says Miss Whittaker, an old resident of Ackworth, "the society in the village was considered to be of a decidedly superior order, the Rector (the Rev. W. R. Hay) being a relative of the Earl of Kinnard, and his marriage with the widow of a wealthy gentleman of Dukinfield, near Manchester, named Astley, probably secured for him a good position in the district." Miss Mary Hay, his only daughter, was a lady of a peculiarly kind and genial disposition, and, like her mother, was greatly beloved by the villagers. Dr. Hay's only son (The Rev. Edward Hay) was born in 1800.

XI.—ALEXANDER PETER BUCHAN, M.D.

This "physician of no mean repute" was the only son of the celebrated Dr. William Buchan, and was born at Ackworth in 1763. He died at Weston Street, Somers Town, December 5th, 1824, aged 61, and was laid to rest "among the illustrious and the brave," by the side of his father in the west cloister of Westminster Abbey. His will, dated 3rd June, 1824, was proved 28th January, 1825. He bequeathed £70 per annum for the maintenance and education of his only child, Helen Anna Buchan, during her minority, and the residue of his estate to his wife and sister, except £100, which he gave to his cousin, Alexander Peter Buchan. In an affidavit, he was described as late of Percy Street, St. Marylebone, Doctor of Medicine.†

XII.—WILLIAM HOWITT,

Better known as the popular writer of "Books for Boys," and whose name is a "Household Word" in every home, was born at Heanor, "on the borders of the Peak of Derbyshire,"‡ Decr. 18th, 1792. and educated at Ackworth. He gives a

* Vide Monuments.
† Vide "Old Yorkshire," Vol. III., p. 89.
‡ Vide "Boys' Country Book," p. 2.

lengthy and graphic description of his school life, which extended from 1802 to 1806, in one of his works, under the chapter heads of " School-Days," and " In the School."* Under the latter, he refers to four contemporary school fellows, as follows:—" Boxall, the chanter of Homer and Ossian ; Stackhouse, the satirist, and engraver on wood ; Wiffen, the translator of Tasso ; and Sams, who has since trod the deserts of Egypt, and explored Jerusalem for ancient MSS." " One lad," says Mr. Howitt, "Jemmy Ward by name, a rough Lancashire lad, with a strong dialect," who was repeatedly convicted of pilfering, ultimately "became a butcher by trade, and was actually hanged in his native county for sheep-stealing !" Mr. Howitt was a prolific writer. Besides the " Boys' Country Book," he wrote " The Rural Life of England," " Visits to Remarkable Places," etc. His first work, a volume of poems, was published in 1808. He married in his 28th year, Miss Botham, of Uttoxeter, so well known afterwards as Mary Howitt. The "Forest Minstrel," published in 1823, was the united production of these two writers. The remainder of his works were: " The Book of Seasons," " The History of Priestcraft in all Ages," a romance entitled " Pantilla," " Student Life of Germany " (1841), " Rural and Domestic Life in Germany" (1842), "German Experiences" (1844), " Homes and Haunts of the British Poets " (1847), two novels entitled respectively, " The Hall and the Hamlet," and " Madam Donnington," " History of the Literature of Scandinavia," " History of Discovery in Australia," " Land, Labour, and Gold," " Letters on Transportation," " Illustrated History of England " (9 vols.), and many others. William Howitt died at Rome, on the 3rd of March, 1879, and was interred in the Protestant Cemetery there.

XIII.—EDWARD WATKINSON, M.D.

The late Edward Watkinson, of Ackworth, M.D., by his will dated April, 1765, gave (after payment of some small legacies) all the residue of his personal estate, after the death of his

* Ibid, xvi., xvi,, pp. 237-276.

wife, unto the Rector of Ackworth, the Rector of Hemsworth, and the Vicar of Pontefract, for the time being, the Mayor, Recorder, and two senior Aldermen of the Borough of Pontefract for the time being, upon trust that they and his friend Mr. Alderman Samuel Saltonstall should put the same out at interest, and pay and apply the produce thereof (after payment of some annuities) for the maintenance, support, and comfortable living and subsistence of nine poor unmarried persons of the Protestant religion, for ever; to be nominated, chosen, and elected as follows, viz.: the said trustees to nominate and choose two poor men and two poor women who should live in Ackworth, and two poor men and two poor women who should live in Pontefract, and also one other woman who should live in either of the said townships, to be the servant of the said eight poor persons, and to wait and attend upon them as such; and which said eight poor persons and their servant should from time to time have the said interest, produce, and dividends paid equally amongst them, share and share alike. And the said testator wills and declares that no married person shall be capable of being elected one of the said nine persons, and that if any of them do afterwards marry, that such person shall cease to have any share in the said produce and dividends, and be displaced from having any benefits or advantage. And he also gives the said trustees power to displace any of the said persons guilty of any immorality, misconduct, or bad behaviour. And also to fill up vacancies, so as there shall always be therein two poor men and two poor women, belonging to each of the said townships of Ackworth and Pontefract, and a maid servant. And he gives the said trustees a discretionary power as to the best method of perpetuating and performing the trusts of his will, and all matters and things relating thereto.

On February 9th, 1778, the trustees held their first meeting to put the said will in execution, and soon afterwards purchased a piece of ground in Northgate, and built a handsome house thereon under the directions of the said Mr. Saltonstall. On

October 25th, 1779, the said hospital being ready for the reception of its intended inhabitants, the trustees 'nominated eight poor persons and a servant to dwell therein according to the said will, and ordered them to be paid ten shillings each every calendar month.

The vacancies arising by death or otherwise have been regularly filled up from time to time, and the trustees have laid out the testator's estate in the purchase of South Sea Annuities, the dividends of which are paid monthly to the poor people of this hospital, now amounting to fifteen shillings each person ; and the trustees take care to keep their respective apartments clean and in good repair, rendering this place a desirable and comfortable retreat to old age and infirmity.

XIV.—DR. JOHN FOTHERGILL.

John Fothergill, M.D., F.R.S., and founder of Ackworth School, was born at Carr End, Semerwater, between Askrigg and Hawes, in Wensleydale, on the 8th of March, 1712. He was educated at Sedbergh School, and apprenticed to Benjamin Bartlett, an eminent apothecary at Bradford, and afterwards studied at Edinburgh and London. Here, during the succeeding forty years (from 1740,) he laboured unremittingly, attaining to the highest rank in his profession, and numbering among his patients some of the most worthy and distinguished characters of the century. But in estimating his character, it would be a great mistake to regard him simply as a great physician ; it was in its highest and widest meaning, *as a friend to man*, that he has a claim upon our regard and admiration. There is scarcely a point which affects the physical, moral, and religious interest of the race, which did not attract his attention, and receive benefit from his judicious and untiring labours.

Notwithstanding the intense pressure of his varied engagements, we find that he was an Elder, and became a member of the Yearly Meeting's Committee, appointed to visit the Meetings of Friends in the various counties of England. He was thus engaged for many weeks, chiefly in Yorkshire, Lancashire, and Westmorland, and it was whilst thus engaged that he paid his last visit to Carr End, in 1777. It may have been that these visits, and the ignorance he found in many quarters, gave additional force to his long-cherished desire to see a sound and Christian education more generally valued, and made accessible to all classes in the Society of Friends. Be this as it may, it was in this year that he succeeded in giving a practical shape to his long-cherished wish; and we now come to that point in our narrative which, extending over the three remaining years of Dr. Fothergill's life, gives the history of the establishment of Ackworth School, which was, as Luke Howard justly called it, "the Era of a Reformation in our Religious Society." Nor does it render him less entitled to have his name handed down to the latest posterity, as the founder of Ackworth School, that he did not, as has often been stated, purchase it wholly, and present it to the Society. And jointly with his name, and entitled to our gratitude and remembrance, we must not omit to mention that of his warm and devoted friend, David Barclay, of London; and in Yorkshire, those of his friends, John Hustle, of Bradford, and Wm. Tuke, of York.

In the summer of 1780 (the last of his life), Dr. Fothergill paid his second, and subsequently a third, visit to Ackworth School.

One of the most important objects of Dr. Fothergill's life was now accomplished, and we can only devote a few words to the account of its close. Before doing so, however, the following graphic description of Dr. Fothergill, as he appeared probably at the time of his last visit to York, written by a great nephew, cannot fail to be of interest:—

Extract from Records of John Fothergill, of York (1743): "Dr. Fothergill was pious, generous, and benevolent, rather above the middle size; very delicate and slender, of a sanguine temperament; his forehead finely proportioned; his eyes light-coloured, brilliant, acute, and deeply penetrating; his nose rather aquiline; his mouth betokened delicacy of feeling, his whole countenance expressed liability to initiation, great sensibility, clear understanding, and exalted virtue."

Two months after his return from his last visit to Ackworth, he was again seized with illness, which terminated his useful, busy life in about a fortnight. His death took place on the 26th of December, 1780, at the age of 68. Thus died the distinguished Yorkshireman, John Fothergill, who in life had so thoroughly exemplified his own saying, "that the great business of man as a member of Society is to be as useful to it as possible, in whatsoever department he may be stationed."

The above is chiefly an abridgement from an article on "Dr. John Fothergill, F.R.S.," by James Hack Tuke, in "Old Yorkshire," vol. iv., pp. 133-141, illustrated with a medallion portrait of Dr. Fothergill, and a fac-simile of his autograph; with engravings of Ackworth School, and Carr End, Semerwater.

For several anecdotes of Dr. Fothergill's beneficence humanity, and generosity, see "Yorkshire Anecdotes," pp. 175-179; and "Sketch of the Life of John Fothergill, M.D., F.R.S," by James H. Tuke, 1880, with a cameo-portrait of the Doctor. For an engraving of a medal of John Fothergill, M.D., see the "Gentleman's Magazine," vol. 65, p. 474, etc. His "works," consisting chiefly of medical pieces, have been printed in three volumes, 8vo., with his "Life" prefixed; also in 4to., 1785, with portraits. See the "Life of Dr. Fothergill," by Lettsom; also, a "Tribute to the Memory of Dr. Fothergill," by Dr. Hird, of Leeds; "Gentleman's Magazine," from 1780-87; Hartley Coleridge's "Northern Worthies," pp. 694-720; and Cunningham's "Lives of Illustrious Men," vol. vi., p. 113, etc. There are several portraits of this celebrated doctor.

XV.—BENJAMIN FLOUNDERS.

Benjamin Flounders, Esq., a most munificent benefactor at Yarm, in the North Riding of Yorkshire, died there about the year 1847. He also established an Institute or School at

Ackworth (since called by his name), with £40,000 for training young men to be teachers in the Society of Friends. The building was opened for students in the summer of 1848. The instruction, according to the trust deed, includes ancient and modern languages, mathematics, and natural philosophy in all its parts, to which have been added other subjects to meet recent requirements of education, or having more immediate reference to the Society. The Institution was intended to accommodate twelve pupils (see also the "History of Ackworth School," and Whellan's "North Riding," vol. ii., p. 175, etc.). He also bequeathed £500 to the Grammer School at Yarm, and £1000, in the Three Per Cents., to the Yarm National School, for which 50 children are taught free; and £500 for the founding and endowing of an Infant School there. This munificent benefactor also left £20 a year to the poor of that parish. A scheme has just been passed for establishing, on a large scale, a boarding school of the second grade, for the counties of Northumberland, Durham, and the North Riding of Yorkshire; and it affords an interesting example of the combination of the older endowed system, with the simple country school. The foundation consists of about £50,000; £10,000 the property of an old foundation, St. John's Hospital at Barnard Castle, where the School is to be situated; of about £30,000 bequeathed some thirty years ago by Benj. Flounders, of Yarm, in North Yorkshire, for the promotion of education of any class in any part of Her Majesty's dominions; and of £10,000 raised by voluntary subscriptions, for a building fund. The North-Eastern County School is said in the scheme, to be intended mainly for the sons of farmers and tradesmen, of eleven years old and upwards, whose education is supposed to terminate at sixteen; with accommodation for about 350 boarders, at £31 a year.

XVI.—JOHN BRIGHT.

Reference has been made elsewhere to this illustrious name, but the following additional information will no doubt be read with interest by those who delight to honour the memory of our departed friend John Bright.

The "Liverpool Courier" of May 24th, 1888, in one of its leaders, contributes the following testimony:—"The Bright family, John Bright in particular, have always been regarded as model Quakers. He is related to families whose names are amongst the most venerated in the history of the denomination. He is connected by marriage with the M'Larens, a name honoured in the capital of Scotland; his second wife was a sister of that scholarly eloquent Quaker, the Wakefield banker, Edward A. Leatham, and he was related to such well-known and respected Friends as Gurney, Lucas, and others. Whether it is in the secluded Quaker colony of agriculturists of Ackworth—a charming spot between Wakefield and Pontefract—where Mr. Bright received his early education, and where he was afterwards a frequent and welcome visitor to his brother-in-law at Hemsworth Hall, and at the village of Ackworth; in the great manufacturing towns of Lancashire, or in the Friends' meeting-house in this city, where he was sometimes to be seen when he came to Liverpool, Mr. Bright has always been honoured for his high personal character, and is a model member of that religious body with which he and his family have so long been prominently identified."

From the "Rock" of a more recent date, I cull the following extract:—

The Quakers' "Testimony" to John Bright is now being privately circulated. It has the quaint old phraseology adopted generations ago. It is a testimony from the Lancashire Monthly Meeting, which sends it "to the power and goodness of God as shown in the life and services of John Bright, M.P." After stating in a sentence his birth and death, it says that "Divine grace enabled our friend John Bright to be a true minister of Jesus Christ in the remarkable line of service to which he was called." It details his taste for study, his "deep sense of responsibility in the sight of God, and his intense human sympathy," his love and reverence for the Scriptures, and his simple habits, diligent attendance of Quaker meetings, and loyalty to the Society of Friends. Without flattery of the dead statesman, it testifies fully to his worth among his own people.

Another phase in John Bright's life is revealed by the "Liverpool Evening Echo," of December 1st, 1889, as follows:

"By accidental conversation in a railway compartment during a journey last June to Ackworth for the Old Scholars' Meeting, Mr. Hodgson (the author of some remarks on John Bright's schooldays, in the Ackworth Old Scholars' Magazine) learned that Joshua Sutcliffe, of Todmorden, was at Newton School with Bright, his bedfellow and close companion; and there was a damsel there, Alice Wilkinson, of Slaidburn, who attracted the fancy of both boys. Bright's love of arbitration would almost appear to have shown incipient budding even thus early, for we are told that, instead of becoming deadly rivals as per the fashion of fiction, 'so close was the friendship of the two boys, that they entered into the school-boy compact that John was to marry Alice; and Joshua, John's sister.' How this little romance worked itself out history sayeth not, but we learn that when Joshua, in due time, went to Slaidburn to propose to Alice, his bosom friend John accompanied him, and 'she was married to Joshua Sutcliffe in 1836.' By all the rules of love-telling this should terminate the tale.. But Joshua Sutcliffe died in 1873, and Alice, his widow, during the present year. Amongst her most treasured possessions, after her decease, this letter was found:—

Rochdale, January 17th, 1873.

My Dear Mrs. Sutcliffe,—I will venture to address you, although it is so many years since we met. I was grieved and shocked to hear of your great bereavement, and I wish, even at the risk of seeming intrusion at this sad time, to tell you how deep is my sympathy for you. This event carries my mind back to pleasant times, and to scenes in which you, in your girlhood, were always a pleasant picture. You know how intimate was the friendship in those days between him you have so lately lost, and me—an intimacy which, unfortunately, has not been continued, owing-mainly to the fact that our paths in life have been so very different, and our engagements have seldom brought us together. But I cannot, and do not wish to forget the past, although it is so long past. I am very sorry I can see my old schoolfellow and friend no more, and I feel much for your family in the affliction which has befallen you. Pray forgive my freedom in writing you this letter; I wish I could send you any word of comfort; but comfort in these troubles can only come from a higher source, as I doubt not you have already discovered.—Believe me always very sincerely yours, JOHN BRIGHT.

To Mrs. Sutcliffe, Fur Grove, Burnley."

From the same source I reproduce "John Bright's letter to a School-girl."

"In 1879, Miss Mabel Tangye was at school at Weston-super-Mare, and, indignant at the remarks of the 'Tory' young ladies in the school, she wrote to Mr. John Bright, telling him her troubles. Mr. Bright promptly replied:—'My dear Mabel, —May I thus address you, though I do not know you, and have never seen you? I am very much amused at your pleasant and interesting letter, which I have read over several times; and I can, in some degree, imagine the enthusiasm and the daring which led you, or induced you, to write it. You think I have endeavoured to do some good things in my public life which have been useful for our people, and especially for the poor among them, and your sympathy for them has made you think kindly of me. I like to think of this, and to think that many who are strangers to me, and whom I have never seen, and perhaps may never see, can approve of some things I have wished to do, or have done. I am glad you liked the great meeting at Birmingham. I hope it was useful to many there, and to some who were not there. If our people knew more of what is good for them, they might be much happier than they are; they would have more comfortable homes, and they would be able to secure for themselves a better government; we should have less of war, and ignorance, and poverty, and crime. I have always wished for this, and have spoken earnestly for it. When you grow up, and have more influence than you have now, I hope it will always be used in favour of justice and mercy, and goodness; and now, even among your schoolfellows, you can do some good if you wish to do it, which I do not for a moment doubt.'"

XVII.—JOHN GRAHAM.

Another name which deserves a place in the "Annals of Ackworth," is that of John Graham. The "Leeds Mercury," of September 26th, 1889, in an obituary of him, says:—

"Yesterday the remains of this gentleman were interred in the Friends' Burial Ground, Low Ackworth. For many years prior to 1878, he was proprietor of the Temperance and School Hotel and Posting House attached to the famous Friends' School at Ackworth. He died a few days ago at the age of 76 years. He was a member of the Society of Friends, and in connection with the large educational establishment and Flounders' College at Ackworth, was well-known throughout England by members of the Society of Friends. He had resided in Ireland for about eleven years past. A few months ago he had a desire to return to his native "village of flowers" at Ackworth to end his days, and this was granted him, his death occurring at his sister's residence—Mrs. Knight's. A number of the inhabitants of Ackworth were present at the funeral, and at the grave, after a brief silence, Mr. G. Satterthwaite offered up a prayer. There were present at the graveside Mr. John Graham, Mr. Thomas Graham (sons), from Ireland; Mr. Alfred Graham and Mrs. Graham (Preston); Mr. and Mrs. Wood (Holmfirth); Mr. F. Andrews, B.A. (Ackworth School);

Mr. and Mrs. Taylor (Pontefract); Mr. G. Satterthwaite, Mr. Jonah Barratt, Mr. Ransome, Mr. J. Simpson (Ackworth); and many others. After the coffin had been lowered, the sorrowing relatives and friends adjourned to the Friends' Meeting-house, where words of consolation were given by several present.

XVIII.—WILLIAM MARCUS FALLOON, M.A.

The Rev. W. M. Falloon, M.A., was born near Belfast, in the north of Ireland, and graduated at Trinity College, Dublin, in the year 1837. He took honors in Hebrew and in Classics, and was a scholar of his college. He was ordained in April, 1838, by the then Bishop of Down and Connor, Dr. Mant; and had both Deacon's and Priest's Orders within the same year. His first Curacy was at Ballinderry, on the borders of Lough Neah, —the parish in which the distinguished Dr. Jeremy Taylor once lived and ministered. The ruins of the Church in which Dr. Taylor served may still be seen on the borders of the lake. The stumps of old pear trees, said to have been planted by the same Bishop, used also to be found in the Parish, close to a bowling green, where the saintly man was wont to play for exercise and health. Mr. Falloon remained there as Curate only for one year, long enough for him to become greatly attached to the Parish and people, and by them to be highly esteemed. Being invited, by the then well known Incumbent of St. Jude's, Liverpool, Dr. Hugh Mc.Neile, afterwards Canon of Chester, and, subsequently, Dean of Ripon, to become his Curate, he left Ballinderry, and came to Liverpool in the May of 1839. To be associated so nearly with a man so distinguished, was a serious trial to one so young, both in years, and in the ministry; and, at first, Mr. Falloon feared he had made a mistake in coming to a Church and Ministry, at that time attracting so very much attention and public interest. His early fears, however, were soon dispersed by the very affectionate treatment and sympathy he received from the Incumbent; and by the warmth of the welcome given to him and his young wife, on the part of the people. Mr. Falloon ever spoke of that time as one of the brightest and happiest in his ministerial life. He remained there, as Curate of St. Jude's, till the October of the year 1843, when, being offered by Dr. Mc.Neile the Incumbency of St. John's, Liverpool, he accepted it, and passed to a scene of earnest labour and singular success, and remained there till the Autumn of 1851, when, through over-pressure, and the ever increasing urgency of the work at St. John's, his health began to give way, and he was advised to seek a less laborious sphere. The Incumbency of St. Bride's, Liverpool, becoming vacant at the time, he was pressed by many friends to remove to it, on offering advantages of various sorts most likely to contribute to the restoration of his health. Though very reluctant to part from a people so loving and beloved as those at "dear St. John's," he was finally persuaded to accept the Incumbency of St. Bride's. There he remained and ministered for twenty-six years, carrying out a Ministry upon strict evangelical lines, and surrounded by a very large and influential congregation, who proved quite a power in the great town, by reason of the largeness of their liberality,—contributing to every good work, at home and abroad; by the spirit of unity and love existing amongst them; as well as by their unvarying loyalty to their Pastor and Friend. Many live, to whom St. Bride's is a name most dear, and the sweet memories of its services, its communion, its meetings for prayer, and its other agencies, cannot be easily forgotten. When the great Lord and Master writeth up His people, there will be this record concerning St. Bride's, "this and that man was born there."

In 1871, the late Bishop of Chester, Dr. Jacobson, appointed Mr. Falloon an Honorary Canon of Chester Cathedral, as an acknowlegment of the services rendered by him to the town and Diocese; and when he left Liverpool in 1875, amidst universal expressions of regret, not only did his brethren of the clergy present him with an Address of affection, and a case of valuable books, but his congregation and friends added another address, and a gift of one thousand guineas.

Finding increasing work in Liverpool too heavy for increasing years, and being offered by a late Chancellor of the Duchy, Colonel Taylor, the Rectory of Ackworth, Yorkshire, he left Liverpool, after a ministry there of thirty-six years, in Novr., 1875, and entered upon his work amidst strangers, in a country village and parish, where he ministered for sixteen years, true as ever to the principles of the Reformation, and to the discipline and doctrines of the Protestant Church of England. Here he preached the everlasting Gospel with burning eloquence and fervour, and with much acceptance; "ruling prudently with all his power," and administering parochial affairs with singular wisdom and tact. A handsome Chapel-of-Ease at Moor-Top, dedicated to All Saints', and consecrated by the Bishop of Beverley, on July 17th, 1891, only two days before Canon Falloon's death, will be the principal visible monument of his pastorate. He was buried at Liverpool, where his name and memory are fondly cherished.

Hessle.

The following notes respecting this hamlet, will no doubt be interesting to Ackworth readers.

The name *Hessle* is of Danish derivation, and indicates that its origin was probably due to Danish settlers,* and if so, its existence may be traced to a period or decade later than Saxon times, but sufficiently remote to entitle it to the claim of being very ancient. In 1402, we know the name was spelt "*Hesill*," which may have been derived from the Danish *Has* = water, and *ille* = a village; there is certainly an abundance of good water still in the hamlet. Or, it may have taken its name from

* Stewart, in his MS. History of Wragby, says these settlers afterwards migrated to Ackworth.

the Anglo-Saxon *hasel* = the modern hazel, a word common to all the Aryan languages. It is generally supposed that a small church existed here, in connection with Nostel Priory, but there is no trace remaining. Tradition says there used to be in one of the old houses an oblong stone trough, in which baptisms by immersion took place.

The hamlet was certainly at one time larger than it is now. The leather, or fell-mongering trade was its chief industry, but in 1740,* when the old coach-road from Wakefield to Doncaster, through Nostel, was diverted, the leather trade was principally carried on at the top of Constitution Hill. The water for tanning purposes was pumped by wind power from the valley at Hessle. In later years, nearly every farm house in the hamlet had its malt-house and kiln for brewing purposes.

An old milestone stands near Nostel Avenue, bearing the date 1722.

The old coach road appears to have entered the Nostel domain at Foulby, on thro' the Park, north of Nostel up the east avenue, crossing Brackenhill Common down to Kinsley Green, where the 'brook or watercourse was ford,' forward to Moor Top on to the main road. Although overgrown with grass, it is easily traced. About a quarter of a mile north of the said ford is a county bridge, which is the boundary between Ackworth and Wragby parishes.

---

* In this year the bridge over Nostel lake was built.

THE MEXBOROUGH ARMS.

[Argent, in a bend, sable, three owls of the field.]

Lists.

RECTORS AND CURATES.

DATE.	RECTORS.	CURATES.
1242.	Henry de Ackworth (Habuit pensionem).	No record.
1302.	Will. de Wirminstead (Sub-diac)	,,
1333.	Robt. de Creyks (Cler)	,,
1349.	Will. de Fenton (Tonsuram habeus)	,,
1352.	Johannes de Barton	,,
1359.	Alan de Waynflet	,,
1361.	Johannes de Leedes	,,
1366.	Thomas de Amcote (Cler.)	,
1367.	Johannes Amcotes (Presb.)	,
1381.	Johannes Broughton (Presb.)	
1402.	Tho. de Whiston (Cler.)	,,
1422.	Thos. Balne (Frat. Can. de Nostel)	,,
1427.	Richardus Rishton (Cler.)	,,
——	T. Gilberthorpe (Presb.)	,,
1453.	Joannes Wynton (Presb.)	,,
1498.	Jacobus Forman (Presb.)	,,
1504.	Johannes Carnabel (Cler.)	,,
1534.	Riche. Deane (Presb.)	,,
1554.	Thos. Hartyndon (Cler.)	,,
1578.	Barnab. Shepherd (Cler.)	,,
1585.	Simon Buck (Cler.)	,,
1588.	Robert Usher (Cler.)	,,
——	Johnes Wilson (Cler.)	,,
1594.	Will. Lamb (Cler.)	,,
April, 1634.	Dan Faulkner (Cler.), M.A.	,,
Sept., 1634.	Sam Carter, M.A., (Cler.)	,,
1643.	Thos. Bradley, D.D.*	,,

* Dr. Bradley was dispossessed of his house and pulpit at the usurpation by one "Anthony Burbeck, a stiff-rumped Presbyterian."

DATE.	RECTOR.	CURATE.
1673.	Jeremiah Bolton, M.A.	No record.
1694.	Jordan Tancred	,,
1695.	Benjamin Rentmore, M.A.	,,
1700.	Phil Hollings, M.A.	,,
1728.	Wil. Kay, M.A.	,,
1744.	Tim. Lee, D.D.	,,
1776.		J. Beevor.
1777.	Ashburnham Toll Newman, M.A.	Peter Heaton.
1778.	,,	
1789.	,,	Charles Butter.*
1798.	,,	George Hendrick.
1802.	Will. Robt. Hay, M.A.	,,
1813.	,,	John Morville.
1820.	W. R. Hay, M.A.	W. T. Farrington.
1821.	,,	J. Hope.
1823.	,,	R. Bassnett.
1825.	,,	J. W. Inchbald.
1828.	,,	T. F. P. Hankins.
1840.	Edmund G. Bayley, M.A.	,,
1844.	Jos. Kenworthy, M.A.	Nil.
1867.	,,	James Taylor, B.D.
1868.	,,	W. L. B. Cator.
1869.	,,	J. Magrath.
1872.	,,	C. J. Perry-Keene.
1873.	,,	Wm. H. Robinson.
1874.	,,	Arthur Mays.
1875.	Wm. Marcus Falloon, M.A.	,,
1876.	,,	H. C. Harrison.
1878.	,,	H. M. Kennedy.
1879.	,,	C. Elrington.
1880.	,,	George Dart.
1883.	,,	R. C. Atkinson.
1884.	,,	J. L. Saywell.
1887.	,,	B. L. Parkin.
1891.	Henry Howlett, M.A.	,,
1892.	,,	E. D. Cree.

* Mr. Butter died at Ackworth, January 5th, 1798, aged 74. "Old age" is inserted as the cause of death. He was buried in Ackworth Churchyard, Jan. 10.

LIST OF THE LORDS OF THE MANOR OF ACKWORTH.

DATE.	NAMES.	REMARKS.
	John Lamb, Gent.	
	Robert Hewitt, Gent...	These, it appears from the Court papers,
	Thomas Howit	were the ancient Lords of the Manor.
	John Pickering	
		They were succeeded by
	James Croft, Gent.	
	Thomas Pickering	
	William Horncastle	
	Samuel Cawood	
1681	Ralph Lowther, Esq...	
to	George Abbott, Gent.	
	William Adams, Gent.	
1692.	Hastings Pickering, Clerk	
		There is no record until 1700.
1700	Ralph Lowther, Esq...	
to	Robert Lowther, Gent.	
	Robert Mason, Gent...	
1706.	Hastings Pickering, Clerk	
		No Court holden until 1711.
1711	Ralph Lowther, Esq...	
	Robert Lowther, Gent.	
to	— Lamb	
1722.	Richard Pickering, Clerk	
		No Court holden until 1728.
1728	John Lowther, Esq.	
	Richard Mason, Gent.	
	Richard Pickering, Clerk	
		No record until 1819.
1819.	Thomas Austwick	
	Thomas Bargh	
	John Pearson	
	Peter Wilson	
	Thomas Pearson	
		No record until 1853.
1853.	John Gully, Esq.	These Lords were appointed in Sept.
	Luke Howard	1853, and the property of the Manor
	William Hepworth	conveyed to them by Indentures of
	William Nelstrop	Conveyance made the 13th day of

DATE.	NAMES.	REMARKS.
	Robert Nelstrop	August, and 10th day of September, 1853. All the deeds, books and papers were then placed in the hands of Henry J. Coleman, Solicitor, Pontefract.*
	George Fairbarn	
	John Simpson	
1860.	Same as above.	
1875.	William Nelstrop	
	Robert Nelstrop	
	Thomas Pearson	
	Thomas Tait	
1878.	Thomas Tait, Clerk	The Rector of Ackworth for the time being is an *ex-officio* Lord of the Manor.
	Henry Hill	
	Robert Nelstrop	
	I. M. Hepworth	
	Thomas Pearson	
	Joseph Nelstrop	
1881.	Henry Beetham, Clerk	These gentlemen were appointed by the Charity Commissioners in lieu of the Freeholders of Ackworth, although the appointment properly rests with the Freeholders themselves, but they are now satisfied with the privilege of recommendation. It is much to be regretted that a complete record of the Trustees has not been kept.
	Thomas Pearson	
	Thomas Tait	
	Joseph Nelstrop	
	Richard Lee	
	J. H. Cadman, Esq.	
	George Waide	
	Edward Micklethwaite	

* Vide Memorandum in Manor Minute Book.

LIST OF ACKWORTH SCHOOL TEACHERS.

Date.	Superintendents.	Assistant Masters.	Principal Governesses.
1779	Joseph Donbavand	George Lomas	Hannah Reay
1781	John Hill	Thomas Hodgkin	,,
,,	,,	Thomas Binns	,,
1790	Thomas Hodgkin Temp	,,	,,
,,	John Hipsley, senr.	,,	,,
1795	Jonathan Binns	,,	,,
1796	,,	Robert Whittaker	,,
1801	,,	,,	Mary Martin
1803	,,	,,	Isabella Harris
1805	Robert and Hannah Whittaker	Joseph Birkbeck	,,
,,	,,	John Hipsley, junr., Joseph Sams	,,
1806	,,	Joseph Donbavand, junr.	,,
1807	,,	William Singleton	,,
1809	,,	John Donbavand	,,
1811	,,	Samuel Evens	,,
1814	,,	Thomas Bradshawe Temp	,,
1817	,,	Henry Brady	,,
,,	,,	William Hayward	,,
,,	,,	Thomas Brown	,,
1823	,,	William Doeg	,,
1826	,,	,,	Lydia Palmer
1830	,,	,,	Catherine Naish Temp
,,	,,	Robert Doeg	Priscilla Kincey
1834	Thomas and Rachel Pumphrey	,,	,,
1836	,,	,,	Hannah Richardson
1839	,,	Charles Barnard	,,
1841	,,	William Sewell	,,
1844	,,	Joseph S. Sewell	,,
1846	,,	Wm. Thistlethwaite	
		John Newby	Jane Oddie
1848	,,	Henry Wilson	,,
,,	,,	Thomas Haslam Temp	,,
1850	,,	Thomas Puplett	Mary Ann Speciall
,,	,,	John W. Watson	,,
1862	George and Rachel Satterthwaite	,,	,,
1866	,,	Albert Linney	,,

Date.	Superintendents.	Assistant Masters.	Principal Governesses.
1867	George and Rachel Satterthwaite	Albert Linney	Rachel Stone
1873	Josiah & Mary Hannah Evans	,,	,,
,,	,,	Benjamin Gooch, B.A.	,,
1877	Frederick & Anna Maria Andrews, B.A.	,,	
		Albert Linney	,,
1879	,,	,,	Maria King

PAST MASTERS OF THE BADSWORTH HUNT.
Established 1730.

1730.—John Bright, of Badsworth.
Godfrey Wentworth, of Wentworth.
1780.—William Wrightson, of Cusworth.
Sir E. Smith.
Sir T. Pilkington, of Chevet.
Sir Rowland Wynn, of Nostel.
1805.—Earl of Darlington.
1811.—Sir W. Gerrard. (Mr. Scarisbrick, Deputy Master.)
1814.— — Chaworth.
1815.—Sir B. Graham.
1821.—Hon. E. Petre, of Stapleton.
Thomas B. Hodgson.
1826.—Lord Hawke, of Womersley.
1868.—J. Hope-Barton, of Stapleton.
1876.—Charles B. E. Wright, of Bolton.
1892.—Colonel W. J. F. Ramsden, of Rogerthorpe Manor, near Pontefract.

Addenda.

The following list of Luke Howard's works was recently contributed by Fred Ross, of London, to the Notes and Queries column of the "Leeds Weekly Mercury."

"Luke Howard, F.R.S., of Ackworth, originally of Plaistow, in Essex, and afterwards of Tottenham, in Middlesex, was born in 1722, the son of Robert Howard, of London, author of 'A few words on Corn and Quakers, 4th edition, 1800,' who died in 1812: and died at Bruce Grove, Tottenham, 800 years ago the residence of Waltheof, the great Earl of Northumbria, and some half century ago the school house of Rowland Hill, the Postal Reformer. He married Mariabella ——, and had issue —Joseph, who died in 1833, æt. 22; Rachael, who died in 1837, æt. 34; and John Eliot. He was a member of the Society of Friends, from whom he seceded in 1837, when resident at Ackworth, and joined a Baptist Church, in consequence of a divergence of opinion in reference to meetings for silent worship. He was a man of considerable scientific attainments, and a Fellow of the Royal Society, directing his attention chiefly to meteorology. When at Ackworth he projected and edited 'The Yorkshireman; a Religious and Literary Journal. By a Friend. Pontefract, 1832-1836,' which was published fortnightly until his secession from the Society, and consists of 5 volumes. The following is a list of his works:—

'On the Modification of Clouds, and on the Principle of their Construction, Suspension, and Destruction. London, 1804-1832.' Edited by W. D. and E. Howard, 1865. Reproduced also in several Cyclopædias.

'A Few Notes on a Letter to the Archbishops and Bishops of the Church of England . . . relative to Joseph Lancaster's Plan for the education of the Community. By Eclectus. London, 1806.' This work is attributed to him on the authority of a MS. note on the title-page of the copy in the British Museum Library.

'A Brief Apology for Quakerism. Inscribed to the Edinburgh Reviewers. Anon. London, 1808.'

'Memoir of John Woolman, etc.' No. 15. Tracts of the Tract Association, London, 1815.

'Memoir of Thomas Chalkley. No. 23. Ibid. 1817.

'The Climate of London,' deduced from meteorological observations, &c. 2 vols. London, 1818. Second and third editions, 1820. Enlarged edition, with engravings, 1833.

'An Address to Friends, on a proposal made by a member of our society to instruct some African negroes, with a view to the future translation and dispersion of the Scriptures, or some portion of them, in the languages of Africa.' Anon. London, 1820. See also " The Yorkshireman," vol. I. p. 162.

'A Companion to the Thermometer for the Climate of London.' 1820.

'Confessions of a drunkard.' Anon. 1821.

'Thoughts on Cruelty to Animals, &c.' Anon. 1821.

'On the Proper Treatment of Animals, &c.' Anon. 1821.

'A Word to the Sons of Africa.' Anon. 1822. Translated into Arabic for distribution in Eastern Africa.

'A Letter from Luke Howard, of Tottenham, to a friend in America, containing observations on a Treatise by Job Scott, entitled 'Salvation of Christ.' ' N. p. ord. (1825.)

'My Ledger; or, a Compromise with Prudence,' written in 1808. Printed for private circulation, 1856.

'The Average Barometer, showing by a scale the daily means of heights, calculated upon 18 years, from 1813 to 1830, in the climate of London.'

'The Climate of London, &c.' New and enlarged edition, continued to 1830, with engravings and addenda; 3 vols., 1830.

'A Proposal for Open Communion in the Society of Friends, rejected by the Pontefract Monthly Meeting, Ackworth, 12th month, 11th day, 1836.' Pontefract, 1836. Reprinted in 'The Yorkshireman,' vol. v., p. 287.

'Seven Lectures on Meteorology.' By Luke Howard, gent. Dedicated to John Dalton, in token of forty years' friendship. Pontefract, 1837.

'An Appeal to the Christian Public against a sentence of Disownment passed upon a member (L. H.) by the Society of Friends, for Absenting himself from their Silent Meetings and Submitting to the Ordinances of Christ.' 1838. Second edition, revised, the same year.

'A cycle of 18 years in the seasons of Britain, deduced from meteorological observations made at Ackworth, in the West Riding of Yorkshire, from 1824 to 1841, compared with others made for a like period, ending with 1823, in the vicinity of London. 1842.'

'A Barometographic: Twenty years' variation of the barometer in the climate of Britain, exhibited in autographic curves; with the attendant winds and weather. 1847.'

Papers on Meteorology, &c. 1854.

Translations.—" Liber Ecclesiasticus," &c., from the Latin vulgate. 1827. " Liber Sapientia," commonly called " The Wisdom of Solomon," from the Latin vulgate. 1827. "The Book of Tobias," &c., from the Latin vulgate. 1828. " The Apocrypha of the Book of Daniel," &c. 1829.

Edited.—John Kendall's (of the Society of Friends) " Gleaning, Moral and Religious," &c. 1826. Cowper's English version of the " Odyssey of Homer," with a Commentary, &c., 2 vols., n.d. " Memoranda of the last illness and death of Joseph Howard (his son);" by the brother of J. H. 1836.

MERIABELLE, his wife, was authoress of " Hints on the Improvement of Day Schools," 1827; 2nd edition 1828. " The Young Servant's Own Book," 4th edition 1850. "The Boy's own Book."

JOHN ELIOT HOWARD, his son, was author of " The Doctrine of Inward Light considered in relation to the Written Word," 1836. " Justification by faith." 1838.. " An Address to the Christians of Tottenham." 1839.

RACHEL HOWARD, his daughter, was authoress of " Lessons on Scripture History, &c.," 1834; 6th edition 1851. " Memoranda of Rachel Howard," edited by Luke Howard, 1839.

LIST OF LOCAL PRINTS AND ENGRAVINGS.

1. Ackworth Church. View by W. Bowman. E. Pulleyn, lith.

2. Ackworth Park Hall, large view by Chatelin.

3. Plan and elevation of Foundling Hospital, inserted in 8vo. pamphlet. London: 1778.

4. Elevation plan of Ackworth (Friends') School, in 8vo. pamphlet. London 1790. Reprinted 1795, and 1816. York, 1837.

5-11. Six illustrations from sketches by Pumphry, inserted in a History of the School, 56 pages, by G. F. Linney, published at York in 1853.

12. Map of School Estate. 1787.

13. Small view of the School, engraved by W. Darton Junr., 1803, for watch cases.

14. View taken near the Bath, by T. Stackhouse, 1813.

15. Plan of Estate. Lith. 1820.

16. View of the School, drawn by W. Doeg, engraved by W. Melville.

17-31. Fourteen wood Engravings, (vide sub datum 1879).

Additional Epitaphs.

In the North Aisle—
> Elibh., wife of Robert Hewitt. Died August, 1671.
> The above Robert Hewitt, Died 16th June, 1707,
> In the 102nd (?)* year of his age.

Under the Pulpit,—
> Thomas and John Harrison, Bros. Thos. died
> Feb. 10th, 1762, aged 69. John died
> Dec. 15th, 1769, aged 65.
> " Whosoever sees these two brothers,
> Lying here by one another ;
> Let them think that naught can save
> — his Friends from ye grave."†

In the stoke-hole, face downwards, there is a slab, the lettering upon which is really splendid workmanship :—
> Thomas Calverley, died Septr. 7, 1685.
> Ann, wife of the above, died Decr. 28, 1701.
> Thos., son of above, died Jan. 21, 1718, aged 48.
> Susannah, wife of Thos., Junr., died May 11, 1740, aged 63.
> Also Robert ——————————‡
> Ann Pearson, daughter of Thos. & Susannah Calverley,
> died Decr. 20, 1768, aged 66.
> Ann Haddon, granddaughter of above, died
> May 5th, 1770, aged 48.
> Nicholas Calverley, son of the above, died
> April 3, 1771, aged 50.

* There are three figures, but the third figure is very indistinct.
† A censor of epitaphs was sadly needed at this time.
‡ Remainder hidden beneath brick-work.

Curious Taxes.

It is notorious that in the 23rd George III. (1783), an Act was passed by which it was enacted that from the then ensuing October, '*a stamp duty of 3d. should be paid for every entry of burial, marriage, birth, or christening, under a penalty of 5l.*, and that within two years, (on petition of their own body) its operation was extended to Dissenting Chapels. This *lawful* tax to say the least was *inexpedient*; for it proved so unjust in its working, and so objectionable in its principle, that is was repealed ten years afterwards. Notwithstanding this iniquitous 'Infant Duty Act,' the people of England, like the persecuted Hebrews in Egypt 'grew and multiplied.' The pages of the parish register for baptisms and Burials at Ackworth from 1782 to 1795 are ruled with a special column for "Duty" (in some parishes "Tax"), from which we learn that upon 146 infants born between the above dates, a tax of 3d. per head was levied, but in six instances the parents, being paupers, were exempted, the words '*Pauper, excused*,' in each instance being written after the entry. During the same period 71 corpses were taxed with a similar sum, so that it will be seen that in the 'good old days' it was considered a privilege both to come into the world, and to go out of it. It appears that the Rector possessed the power of remitting the tax, and from the register we find him exercising his prerogative eleven times. It is somewhat strange that although the duty was imposed in 1783, no mention of it is found in the registers until 1789, and that although the Act was repealed in 1793, the Rector should have continued to levy the tax until 1795. No record of marriages being taxed can be found.

The following statement was printed and circulated by Mr. Kenworthy the then Vicar, and is worthy of preservation as an interesting historical document.

PARISH OF ACKWORTH, YORKSHIRE:

CHURCH OF ST. CUTHBERT.

Erected about A.D. 1242 ; contains 438 Free and, of these, 173 are unappropriated Seats. No seats are held by Faculty ; No seats are let at an Annual Rental.

Sums of ANY AMOUNT Expended in Building, Enlarging, Restoring, or Improving this Church, at various times, since January 1st, 1841, (excluding ordinary repairs.)

1850...Inside of Tower restored, £116, by private Subscriptions.

1852...Nave, North and South Aisles re-built, £1170, by private Subscriptions and special Donations ; and £120 Grant from Church Building Society.

1854-5. Chancel re-built, Chancel Aisle built, £1343, by private Subscriptions and special Donations, and £10 from Yorkshire Architectural Society.

1856-7...Stained Windows (2), Organ enlarged, £90, by special Donation and private Subscriptions.

1858...Stained Window, Heating Apparatus, £133, by special Donations and private Subscriptions.

1864...Stained Window, £15, by Special Donation.

1867...Stained Windows (2), £30, by Special Donation.

1870-2...Coronæ, Door Hangings,&c.,£76, private Subscriptions.

1872-3...Organ Chamber built, £280, by private Subscriptions.

1874...New Organ, Carved Oak Screens (2), £579, by private Subscriptions for Organ, Special Donation for Screens.

The present state of the Building is good. To complete the work,—The outside of Tower requires restoration,* Bells re-casting,* New Clock,* and New Gates to the Churchyard.*

* All these have been completed since 1875.

The Rector, in 1845, gave a small piece of ground which was added to the Churchyard. Additional Burial ground is now required.

1846.—A New School and Class Room were built at a cost of £400 by the Rector.

1842.—The present Rectory House was built, at a cost of £1000, derived from the following sources, £850 borrowed from Queen Ann's Bounty (all paid off), and old materials.

The Rector having been asked, by the Archbishop of York, to fill up a return shewing the Amount of Church Building, Restoration, and other work connected with the Church, done in the Parish since the year 1840, has taken the opportunity of having several copies of the same printed.

He thinks these particulars will be interesting to many who attend the church, shewing how the present Church has been made what it is, and also pointing out what still remains to be done.

J. KENWORTHY, Rector.

ACKWORTH,
May 1st, 1875.

PONTEFRACT : J. ATKINSON AND SON, PRINTERS.

www.ingramcontent.com/pod-product-compliance
Lightning Source LLC
Chambersburg PA
CBHW031946230426

43672CB00010B/2071